ROLE OF BANK'S IN WOMEN DEVELOPMENT

ROLE OF BANK'S IN WOMEN DEVELOPMENT

By

Dr. Basant Mehta

Associate Professor and Head
Deptt. of Banking and Business Finance
Rajasthan Vidyapeeth University
Udaipur

And

Dr. Pragya Jain

Ph.D.

DISCOVERY PUBLISHING HOUSE
NEW DELHI–110002

First Published-2003

Reprinted-2011

ISBN 81-7141-641-1

Published by

DISCOVERY PUBLISHING HOUSE
4831/24, Ansari Road, Prahlad Street,
Darya Ganj, New Delhi-110002 (India)
Phone: 3279245 • Fax: 91-11-3253475
E-mail:dphtemp@indiatimes.com

Mehra Offset Press
Delhi

Contents

Contents

Preface

Human resources being the most significant and active factor of production, become the key to optimize the utilization of all the other material resources. Developing the human resources, upgrading their skill and knowledge would lead to economic and organizational development. To take full advantage of development of men's and women's participation with increased efficiency and skill is very essential.

We can not isolate women's position as they constitute half of human resource. Women in India, are the backbone of society, they are its conscience keepers. They have kept moral and cultural values alive. They have a strong sense of responsibility and have avoided strife even at the cost of their own welfare. But the awareness of the need for change is clowning upon them. The economic development of a nation depends much on the quality of its human resources. No country can advance while large segment of its population lags behind. The women are expected to look after the home and health, be it her father's home before marriage or husband's home later. Due to growth of industrialization, urbanization and liberal education and the democratic system in the country, the tradition bound society is now undergoing a slow change. The liberal education provided since independence has created many women engineers, doctors, scientists and the like. Today women have not only safely, encodes themselves in the job situations but have also emerged as professionals and executives in many fields and found acceptance in the society.

The present investigation is an attempt to study the banking habits among the women and role of bank's in economic development of women in Udaipur and Dungarpur districts of Rajasthan.

The whole study has been divided into eight chapter. The first chapter "Introduction: Research Methodology" gives brief introduction of the study. In the second chapter, significance of women in Indian society have been discussed. The chapter third deals with Demographic profile of women. The fourth chapter analysis banking development in Udaipur and Dungarpur districts. In chapter fifth role of banking institutions in economic development of women under development programmes has been highlighted. In the chapter sixth brings out the results of analysis of the field study (Banking habits among the women). While chapter seventh brings out the results of analysis of the field study (Women working in banking sector). The last chapter gives a brief summary of the whole study and main findings of the investigation. It is also highlights the problem faced in day-to-day operation of bank and offers possible solutions. Suggestions for further improvement have also been incorporated so as to provide suitable guidelines for the successful operation of bank's in the developing economy of the country.

Basant Mehta,
Pragya Jain

1 Introduction: Research Methodology

NEED AND GENESIS OF WOMEN DEVELOPMENT IN INDIAN SOCIETY

Nobody studies separately Man's development then why scholars study Woman's Development? Is Woman not a developed one? why the government is making policies and programmes for women's development?

Lots of answers are hidden in our history as we studied. Today women's contribution in national income in quite poor. The role of women is very important not merely because it would mean efficient use of resources but women's status and opportunities are closely related to demographic variable. Women nearly contribute half of the population of India. Without the complete integration of women in development programmes, improvement in general quality of life will not be achieved.

Women's development is a human right issue. Women should be equipped with all the necessary rights, and then to make women conscious about their rights and also to the use of their rights. Development of women means 'National Development'. National Development means maximum production, full employment and attainment of economic equality and social justice apply equally to men and women.

In 1981 the first National Conference on Women's studies started a serious debate on the objectives of women's studies in India. Since 1981, a series of seminars, conferences and workshop started and diverted their full attention towards Women's studies programmes.

The planning commission has defined three major fields for women's development, i.e. Education, Health and Welfare. Education has been continued emphasis in incoming all plans.

IMPORTANCE OF WOMEN IN ECONOMIC DEVELOPMENT

There is a saying in Sanskrit which says "*Yatra naryastu pujyante, ramante tatra devta.*" (Where women are worshipped, gods themselves reside). This only indicates the importance of women in any society. God has given birth to every human being as equal individual's and women have qualities and talents of their own.

It is the women, who gives birth to the child, rears the child, creating citizens out of them. So how can she be ignored? In case, if women is ignored and not educated enough then how is our country going to progress?

Woman in the history of human development has been as important as man. The issues related to women regarding economic development and social changes have been well received in terms of research study by scholars in recent years. The international decade (1975-85) for women provided an opportunity to scholars for making conscious endeavours to understand the specific problems of women.

Women are working as an economic producer and income earner in an expanding market economy and while working in the domestic front, she is indirectly contributing to social and economic development of the nation as a whole. The census and the national sample survey, ignore the domestic front (as identified by the census survey) performed by women who are in the labour force. Thus these services/work are not included in the G.N.P. Therefore the data about the women's work and their contribution is generally insufficient and does not reflect a clear picture.

Participation of women in economic activity is common in all the developed countries but the extent of participation is different in every country. The full benefit of development can only be achieved if participation of manpower increases and women are not isolated from the total framework of development as they constitute half of his human resource. Women, besides being a home maker is also a partner in food production efforts i.e. women plays an important economic role as well.

In particularly every sphere of life the position of women is not satisfactory. Women are mostly engaged in least paid jobs, they work for long hours, bear full responsibility of the home, they fetch fuel and water, they cook in family production units, bring up children and take care of the sick and aged, without being paid for their labour. This is the stark reality of millions of women.

In Rajasthan the sex ratio, female literacy rates and women's participation in the organized sector are all very low, less access to various services and low educational level contribute in making her mere tool without any rights or claims. Enumerative data account the visibility of women in organized sector only. This can be misleading because women participation in an unorganized sector remains unaccounted.

The economic development of a nation depends much on the quality of its human resources. No country can advance while large segment of its population lags behind. Women in India by tradition and culture have for generations taken a self effacing role. They have been kept down and have always been dependent on father, brother, or husband. The women are expected to look after the home and health, be it her father's home before marriage or husband's home later. Due to the growth of industrialization, urbanisation and liberal education and the democratic system in the country, the tradition bound society is now undergoing a slow change. The liberal education provided since independence has created many women engineers, doctors, scientists and the like. The breaking up of the joint family system due to the scarce employment opportunities and the resultant migration to other places have forced women to look for jobs so as to nuclear family. Today women have not only safety encodes themselves in the job situations but have also emerged as professionals and executives in many fields and found acceptance in the society.

In spite of so many hurdles and limitations the participation of women in entrepreneurial activities are steadily increasing. A high proportion of working women in India is employed in the unorganised sector mainly in agriculture, live stock, forestry etc. working women are engaged in agricultural activities like land preparation, seed grading, sowing, dibbling, planting, irrigating, threshing, winnowing, storing crops, feeding cattle, looking after milch and poultry etc.

In urban area, women are rapidly emerging as smart and dynamic entrepreneurs. They have entered almost all areas of business activity such as textiles, engineering, goods, electronics, steel works etc. Educated urban women are making a land mark in the non-conventional fields like consultancy, advertising garment export, interior decoration, textile printing, handicrafts etc. However, the women entrepreneurs from a negligible percentage of the total entrepreneurs in the country. Due to social environment prevalent they are unable to move freely as quickly as an individual to distant places to either resources or market. This is a hindrance to their growth of business and women are not having enough accessibility to get these information's. They feel frustrated their business as well as domestic affairs.

Women labourers and their exploitation in our country is found since historical times. However, with the march of civilization, the impact of social changes and developmental efforts benefit the women much less than man. Social and religious reformers, enlightened public authorities and women's organisations waged battles against the oppressive position of women through centuries. But scourges as illiteracy, ignorance, superstition still persist in some parts of the country, resulting in unorganised low paid exploited women labourers.

Women are no more cocooned in the age old social taboos. In the midst of opposition they are brazing new path to face the challenges of life.

EMPLOYMENT PATTERN OF WOMEN IN UDAIPUR AND DUNGARPUR DISTRICTS

Udaipur District: According to 1991 census the total population of the district was 28.89 lacs of which 23.95 (82.90%) persons lived in rural areas and 4.94 lacs (17.10%) persons lived in urban area. In Udaipur district 13.02 lacs persons belongs to S.C./S.T. group. The S.C./S.T. population in the district is about 45% of the total population.

The literacy rate is 17.31% in rural areas and 20.39% in urban areas. The literacy rate in male is 40.07% and in female is 15.43%.

Employment pattern of women in Udaipur district is shown in Table No. 1.1.

Table 1.1. Employment pattern of women in Udaipur Districts (1991)

Particular	Total	Female Population	% of Female
Total Population	28.89	14.19	49.12
S.C. Population	2.4	1.17	48.75
S.T. Population	10.62	5.23	49.25
Main Worker	9.54	1.87	19.60
Cultivators	5.67	1.15	20.28
Agri. Labours	0.97	0.43	44.33
Worker—live stock, fishery and forestry	0.10	0.02	20
Worker in other activity	2.76	0.433	15.69
Marginal worker	2.97	2.83	95.31

Source: Prepare from table 3.24, 3.28 and 3.33.

Dungarpur District: According to 1991 census the total population of the district was 8.75 lacs out of them rural population was 8.11 lacs and urban population was 0.64 lacs. Thus the rural population constituted 92.7% of the total population while the urban was only 7.3% Out of the total population males were 4.39 lacs and females were 4.36 lacs in the district. The ratio of female population was 996 females per 1000 males; where the state ratio in 913. The S.C./S.T. population was about 0.40 lacs (4.6%) and 5.75 lacs (65.71%) of the total population respectively. So the district has a sizeable trible population. The density of population per sq. km. for the district is 232 persons. Working population of Dungarpur district was 2.64 lacs and marginal workers was 1.26 lacs out of them farmer 1.76 lacs, Agricultural labour 0.35 lacs, Domestic labour in household industry 0.04 lacs, Allied Agricultural activities 0.37 lacs and in other activities 0.44 lacs.

Table 1.2. Employment Pattern of Women in Dungarpur District (1991)

Particulars	Total	Female Population	% of Female
Total Population	8.75	4.36	49.83
S.C. Population	0.40	0.20	50
S.T. Population	5.75	2.87	49.91
Main Worker	2.64	0.45	17.05
Cultivators	1.76	0.20	11.36
Agri. Labours	0.35	0.19	54.29
Worker—live stock, fishery and forestry	0.012	0.002	16.67
Worker in other activity	0.508	0.048	9.45
Marginal worker	1.26	1.21	96.03

Source: Prepare from Table No. 3.35, 3.39. 3.45.

BANKING DEVELOPMENT IN UDAIPUR AND DUNGARPUR DISTRICTS

Udaipur District

The bank's of the district has a great responsibility to develop the area with wide network of branches. In 1999-2000, 183 branches of various banks was serving in the district. Out of 183 branches, 119 branches is of commercial banks. Regional Rural Bank "Mewar Aaanchlik Gramin Bank"; sponsored by the Bank of Rajasthan Ltd. was working with 41 branches in the district. There were 22 branches of co-operative banks functioning in the district, out of which 9 branches is of Udaipur Central Co-Operative Bank, 7 branches of Urban Co-Operative Bank, 2 branches of PLDB, 1 branch of Udaipur Mahila Urban Co-operative Bank and 1 of Udaipur Mahila Samridhi Urban Co-operative Bank and one branch of Madhav Urban Co-operative Bank recently start functioning in the district.

In 2000 the advances of commercial bank, Co-operative and RRB and PLDB were Rs. 66,410 Lacs, 8029.38 Lacs, 2270.73 Lacs, and 2846.68 Lacs, respectively.

Deposits of Commercial Banks, Co-operative banks and RRB were 156520 Lacs, 13999.80 Lacs, and 8379.29 Lacs respectively.

Dungarpur District

Dungarpur is an economically backward district of Rajasthan. Lacks of adequate financial facilities was one of the important factor for its backwardness. Prior to nationalisation banking development was very slow and unsatisfactory in the district. Nationalisation of banks launched a massive branch expansion in the district particularly in rural and semi urban areas. In March 2000, 71 branches of various banks were serving in the district. Out of them 41 branches of Commercial Banks, 21 branches of RRB and 9 branches of Cooperative Banks.

In 1969 (at the time of nationalisation) there were 7 bank branches in the district. In 1986, branches increased to 42 and at the end of March 2000 decreased to 41.

Regional Rural Bank's "Dungarpur Banswara Kshetriya Gramin Bank" was established in 1984, sponsored by the lead bank (BOB). In June 1985, 12 branches of DBKGB were functioning in the district, which has been increased in March 2000 to 21 branches. The Dungarpur Kendriya Sahakari Bank (DKSB) is the sole central financing agency in Dungarpur district. It had 9 branches were working in March 2000. In March 2000 deposit and advances in Dungarpur district were Rs. 35443 Lacs and Rs. 6371 Lacs respectively.

Banking system occupies an important place in nation's economy. A banking institution is indispensable in a modern society. It plays a pivotal role in the economic development of a human resource. It's role in the fields of encouragement to entrepreneurship and generation of employment opportunity needs hardly to be emphasised.

Women in Banking Service

The expansion of banks, opened new avenues of employment for young men and women and today women in sufficient numbers are working in banks along with men. The process of recruitment in banks is through competitive examination and educated girls, needing jobs for various reasons, made their way in bank services after successfully qualifying in the recruitment test.

Bank Services came to be preferred by women because most of the banks are located in cities and towns and it facilitated their taking up the job. The other reason for women taking bank jobs lies in their economic need. Many girls and women needed economic security due to various reasons. One of the main reason being their family responsibilities. In the context of the present state of society where the structure and shape of the family have undergone radical changes, economic needs have assumed great significance. Educated girls are expected to contribute to the family income so as to meet the growing economic needs of the family. Moreover, educated girls wish to make use of their education for the economic betterment of their family. Employment also contributes to the upgradation of status in the family as well as in the society. They prefer banking services because of the professional nature of the jobs in banks. Many women takeup employment in banks with a view to achieve further progress through passing banks examination held for higher posts. They consider their future prospects promising in bank services. As banks are functioning in their own city or town, they would not be required to stay away from their homes and families.

Presently banks have women working on different posts and performing their duties as efficiently as their counterparts. Women may be found holding posts of higher responsibility in the banking sector.

Thus, economic needs, wish to raise their status, supplementing of family income, shouldering family's responsibilities thrust upon them, utilization of their educational qualifications and professional nature of job are the main reasons which have induced them towards services in banks.

A banker may open a saving account, fixed deposit account, recurring account and current account in the name of an unmarried/married woman. She can enter into a contract in her name. In our country, laws does not make any distinction between the males and females. A married woman enjoys the same power and capacity as a man or a single lady. According to the Indian Contract Act, "A married woman can enter into contracts, acquire and sell property and land or borrow money". Undoubtedly a married woman has power to draw cheques and give a sufficient discharge.

Unmarried/married women can also take loan/overdraft from bank. It is clear that the husband will not be responsible for any transaction or debt account of his wife. A married woman can open joint account with her husband.

It may be worthwhile to mention here that enormous changes have taken place in the whole structural pattern of banking in the last three-four decades. Many new schemes have been planned and launched for women in last few years. Banking habits are becoming more and more popular among the women. Recently in Dec. 2000 government declared to all public sector banks they should keep 2% of net loan for women entrepreneur's and in coming five years increase it upto 5%.

It is therefore high time that a proper assessment and evaluation were made role of banking institution in the economic development of women in the light of the needs of the fast changing and growing Indian economy.

Location

This is a study of banking institution in women's development, specially in the two districts of Rajasthan viz., Udaipur and Dungarpur. The selection of Udaipur and Dungarpur districts has been made on the following bias:

Udaipur and Dungarpur district respectively represent semi-tribal and tribal districts of Rajasthan.

Udaipur district is educationally non-backward, while Dungarpur district is backward.

Udaipur district is urban while Dungarpur district is rural.

Thus these two districts of different characteristics have been selected for the study of women and the area of study has been confined to Udaipur and Dungarpur districts of Rajasthan.

Objectives of the Study

It is desirable here to spell out the broad objectives of the study in the light of the work done or already in progress in this field in the country. Taking into consideration the limited time and resources, the main objective of life study were as follows:

1. To study the genesis and the need of women development in the Indian Society;
2. To study women pattern/profile (Occupation-wise, Education-wise, Income-wise, Caste-wise and Age-wise etc.) in the Country, in the state of Rajasthan, in Udaipur and Dungarpur districts of Rajasthan;
3. To assess the banking development and their role in economic development of women in Udaipur and Dungarpur districts;
4. To assess extent of banking habits among the women;
5. To Study women pattern in Banking Institution;
6. To examine the extent of popularity of various accounts i.e. Saving bank a/c, Current bank a/c, Fixed Deposits a/c,. Recurring Deposits a/c, safe deposits locker a/c, Non-resident a/c Loan a/c etc. among the women;
7. To access the awareness of women about different bank services provide by banks such as credit card, travellers cheque, gift cheque, safe deposit etc.
8. To evaluate women participation in government sponsored scheme such as IRDP, TRYSEM, SGSY, SJSRY and PMRY launched or financed by banking institutions;

9. To assess role of banking institution in economic development of women i.e. Impact of income assets and living standard etc.;
10. To identify the reasons as to why women choose banking as profession;
11. To gain a broader idea of the problems being faced by working women in banking sector;
12. To give suitable suggestions in the light of findings of this investigation so that Banking Institutions play vital role in economic development of women.

RESEARCH METHODOLOGY

Hypothesis

1. Women of big cities have more banking habits compare to the women of small cities.
2. Women employees has been given more weightage in banking sector comparatively to the male employees.
3. Well educated women are well known and availed Credit Card, Travellers Cheque and Gift Cheque facilities provided by banks.
4. Women were not given proper weightage in government sponsored schemes i.e. I.R.D.P., TRYSEM, SGSY, SJSRY and PMRY.
5. Banking institution plays a vital role in the economic development of women.

Sources of Data Collection

Data for this investigation were collected from primary and secondary sources. The primary data were collected from the women a/c holders and the women bank employees of banks.

While secondary data were collected from Journals, Bulletins, Publications of RBI, Publication of Rajasthan Govt., District credit plan of Udaipur and Dungarpur district. Lead bank of Udaipur and Dungarpur districts, Government institutions and various libraries, Govt. departments and persons who may have any information on the subject.

Tools for Collection of Data

For collection of primary data the following two schedules were constructed and used:

1. Schedule for women a/c holders; and
2. Schedule for women bank employees.

Sample Design

For this study two districts of southern Rajasthan, Udaipur and Dungarpur has been selected for collection of primary data related to banking habits among the women. We select 100 women at random for each sample district so in all 200 women had been selected for this study.

To study women pattern in banking sector, a list of 25 women from Udaipur district was drawn at out of 50 women while in Dungarpur district only one woman was working in banking sector so in all 26 women bank employees selected for this study.

Field Work

Field work of the present study was carried out during August 2000 to December 2000.

Plan of Analysis

The data collection from primary and secondary sources were analysed by using proper mathematical techniques such as percentage and average etc.

Importance of the Study

Lack of utilisation of human potential is perhaps the most burning problem for developing countries. The Government has launched a number of programmes to cope with the problem. Some eminent economists, bankers still plead for more structural changes. So it is, therefore, high time that proper assessment and evaluation should be made of all the new institutions and schemes in the light of the needs of the fast changing and growing Indian economy and society. So these programmes can be effective only when people specially women get real benefit from it. It is found that most of the women are either unaware with various self employment programmes or unable to get advantage of it. The present investigation is an attempt to study banking habits and make a comparative assessment of the economic development of a woman in semi tribal and tribal districts of southern Rajasthan. This type of study/investigation would be helpful to the government, economic planners and banking system in preparing the future programmes for the development of women. The usefulness of such indepth studies are widely accepted because women are substance of our society. Role of banking institution in economic development of women need periodic assessment and reassessment to find out the real impact they made on the economy.

2 Significance of Women in Indian Society

The success of any organisation and institution depends on the synergy created by its human resources. An organisation's prime resources consists of men, machine, money and material. Of all the prime resources human resource is accepted as the most vital and valuable. Because other resources depreciate in value with the passage of time and use. The human resources appreciate in value through increased knowledge, experience, and efficiency.

Human resource is consisted of men and women. To take full advantage of development of men's and women's participations with increased efficiency and skill is very necessary. We can not isolate women's position as they constitute half of this human resource. The women's studies activists and academics, world over agree that women at present have a lower status than men, that socially, economically and politically women are discriminated against and this state of women is very hazardous and should be changed in future.

Women are rational creature. Women work harder. Women are managing two fronts one is domestic and the other is economic. The contribution they make as workers can not be recorded and not having any specific and quantified value. Maximum women of India are involve in domestic and non marketed activities. The census and national sample survey ignore the domestic and non-marketed activities performed by women. So these two sources of survey are not able to provide comprehensive and accurate data about the working of women. Even the census 1991 does not reflect any additional information regarding women's work.

There has been growing recognition throughout the world that for increase in national income and rural development in poorest countries, it is necessary to utilize the maximum potential of the human resources.

So far women have had less than equal access to power resources and service than men.

Women as a part of the society are inextricably connected with economic activities. Women are working as an economic produce and income earner in an expanding market economy and while working in domestic front, she is indirectly contributing to social and economic development of the nation as a whole. Women's is the builder and moulder of the nation's destiny.

HISTORICAL STATUS OF WOMEN IN INDIAN SOCIETY

To gain knowledge of the present one has to look at the past. In order to have a better understanding of the present social structure and position of women in society, it is imperative to know the operation of various historical, political, cultural and economic factors moulding the society.

We found that Indian society compared to other societies has a very long past nearly all other civilizations of the ancient world unable to stand on the slaught of time.

The development of women positions in Indian society can be studied under the following periods:

1. Women in Indus Valley civilizations (3500 B.C.)
2. Women in Vedic Period (2500 B.C. to 1500 B.C.)
3. Women is Post Vedic Period (1500 B.C. to 500 B.C.)
4. Women in Buddhist Society (567 B.C. to 480 B.C.)
5. Women is early Smiriti Period (500 B.C. to 500 A.D.)

6. Women in Post Smiriti Period and pre Mughal Period (500 A.D. to 1200 A.D.)
7. Women in Mughal India (1200 A.D. to 1800 A.D.)
8. Women in British Period (1800 A.D. to 1947 A.D.)
9. Women in Post-Independence India (1947 to 1999)
10. Women in Contemporary India.

WOMEN IN INDUS VALLEY CIVILIZATION (3500 B.C.)

Today Indian women is a part of thousand years old culture. The real history of women began when we found the pictures of Mohan Jodaro and Harrappa civilization. In the pictures of Mohan Jodaro we found their daily life and social activities.

At the time Indian sub-continent was supposedly matriarchal. Through pictures we found that they were peaceful people who lived around 3500 B.C. like the other societies and of the most important and significant was that of the mother goddess. But history means written record of past. All recorded history is post-Aryan. And the script (pictographic script) prevailing in the Indus Valley still remains undeciphered.

WOMEN IN VEDIC PERIOD (2500 B.C. TO 1500 B.C.)

Vedic period is one of the golden time period in Indian history. When India was known as "golden bird" country.

No doubt, Vedic society was patriarchate one. Father dominated in the family matter but the position of women was not neglected in the society, either of course! the society favours the birth of a son but the birth of a daughter could not be a cause of anxiety at that time. Hymn XXI of the Rig Veda extols the virtues of women as even greater than those of men. The Aryan sought co-operation of their women in almost every walk of life. Women enjoyed a high position in household affairs. Vedic society was highly civilized. Women used to visit fairs and festivals and could fight wars, take part in meetings, tournaments and in philosophical discussions.

Marriage institution was also liberal for women. In Rigveda Sanhita, there is no mention of early marriage. Marriage usually performed at the age of 16 to 17. For widows remarriage was permitted. Niyoga was in practice for progeny. Girl could remain unmarried if she so wished. Monogamy was prevalent in vedic period but people was not unknown from polygamy. Sati was not in vogue at all.

Education was easily accessible to women. It was an accepted norm during that period. Female child was educated like the boy and had to pass through a period of Brahmcharya. Daughter enjoyed as much freedom as son. In religious matters too, women enjoyed equality with men.

The main disability from which women suffered in this period was proprietary rights. Women had only control over 'Stridhan' and her personal property. An issueless widow had a share in her deceased husband's property. But a married women had no share in the property of her father or husband.

Except few disabilities, Aryan in community as a whole showed proper concern and equal status and respect to women. And they were given full freedom for their intellectual and moral development and also provided freedom of move to social and political spheres.

WOMEN IN POST-VEDIC PERIOD (1500 B.C. TO 500 B.C.)

In the later part of vedic period, decline in women status had been started. Discrimination had been started in education. But men, women both were admitted to take part in philosophical gatherings. Gargi and Matreyi were very famous philosophers of that period. And women used to study scriptures and were respected better than Greek sisters.

In this period, religious rights and privileges also curtailed of average women. Marriage pattern and property right continued to be the same as they were in vedic period. Despite this, women's positions was satisfactory in this phase of history.

WOMEN IN BUDDHIST SOCIETY (567 B.C. TO 480 B.C.)

Buddhism formed to protest against steadily rigidifying brahmanism. Increase of rituals in post-vedic period provide excessive indomitable power to brahmins, that's why, Jainism and Buddhism revolted against the brahmanical religion. Buddhism is believed in self-culture and self restraint. So, if these two qualities is achieved then one can access to 'Nirvana' (Salvation) whether a man or women. Buddhism believed in social and religious equality. Though woman can achieve highest state but she is however inferior to male. The women were assigned an honoured place in society and were admitted to the Buddhist order. Even the prostitutes were admitted in the Buddhist order. Buddhism allowed women the freedom to be educated opportunities for development.

The marriageable age of girls was between sixteen and twenty. In certain conditions divorce was permissive. The presence of widow was not regarded as inauspicious. Buddhism aroused the feeling of self-respect and self-confidence. In Buddhist literature women does not seem to be suffering from social condemnation, however, she was still in male control and dominance. The Buddhist age proved short lived.

WOMEN IN EARLY SMRITI PERIOD (500 B.C. TO 500 A.D.)

This is the age of Sutras, Epics and early Smriti period. In this phase of history, however we can not actually find a whole process of change since Manu Samhita and Mahabharata came into existence. However it was not written by one person at one time. They were actually works of a school and spread over centuries.

The birth of a daughter which was not a cause of anxiety in previous period of history, now become a source of disaster for the father.

Deterioration of women started with the advent of Manusmriti. Codes of Manu prohibited women's equality with men. Manav code provide subordinate status to women and Sudras in their basic frame work. Even in Bhagavad Gita most religious and scared book placed women Vaisyas and Shudra in the lower category and described their birth sinful.

Not only this, now the practice of Upnayana ceased for women education effected adversely. Manu's code lowering down the marriageable age for girls. Women was not entitled to hear vedas.

Remarriage, widow marriage, inter caste marriage, and even to remain unmarried was disapproved by Manu. He approved pre–puberty marriage for girls. Man could marry second time but women have no right of second marriage. And a wife has to be loyal to her husband even if he was devoid of all virtues. Man was not bounded towards loyalty. Not only this the horrible practice of sati was also more eulogised as an ideal. A middle-aged man could marry a girl aged between 8 to 12. No freedom for women in any stage of her life. First, she was under the control of her father then husband and at last under his son's domination. The women abstract did not exist.

Society is happy to quote from Manu, that a woman should be under the authority of her father, her husband, her son's but none quote the insight of Manu that divine blessings cannot come upon a land where women are unhappy.

No scripture described a position of inferiority or bondage for women, even if scriputers describe women should not be discriminated. All religious teachings should be purified of all that goes against the grain of our humanity and the bottom line of natural justice.

The traditional Indian society was patriarchal in character and hence patriarchal norms and values determined sexuality, reproduction and social productions. "These were expressed through specific cultural metaphors. Overt rules and covert practices restricted women's activities and circumscribed their rights. Through a complex of ritual symbolism, meassages of inferiority of women were clearly communicated and perpetuated."[1]

On the other hand, Kautilya represents a progressive view places the husband and wife almost on equal stand. Buddhism and Jainism also tried to deviate the pattern which was slowly evolving.

Only in property rights women were given few concessions which was really important. According to Manu, women could neither earn nor own property except stridhan. But Yajnavlkya gives her wide power over stridhan except when the husband utilizes it in the time of destitute. In case, if a wife is deprived of stridhan then she has a right to get a share equal to that of a son. Yajnavalkya and Vishnu first recognized wife as the foremost heir if person had no son which was previously the chaste widow is allowed to inherit.

Around 200 A.D., onward, pre-puberty marriages become quite popular and prevalent. This period was recorded as the starting of a dark and negligible period of women.

WOMEN IN POST-SMRITIS AND PRE-MUGAL PERIOD (500 A.D. TO 1200 A.D.)

The marriageable age of girls was lowered down still further from 12 or 14 to 10 or 8. The age of 8 was regarded as the ideal for a daughter's marriage. Pre-puberty marriage formed nothing could be compared with the most tragic and subservient condition of a high caste widow, she was not only forbidden to remarry but she was considered inauspicious, harbinger of ill luck for the family. The prohibition of widow remarriage was the question of status and respectability for both higher and lower class.

The custom of sati was practised by the ruling classes. There were no education because of lower marriageable age. Her right regarding marriage were brutally demolished. Down to about 1200 A.D., only the daughter of rich family continued to get education through special teachers but with the incoming of muslim rule this tradition was also dead.

In later smrities women's positions continued to deteriorate except the field of property rights.

WOMEN IN MUGAL PERIOD (12TH CENTURY TO 18TH CENTURY)

The women's life became insecure and worse with the muslim invasion in the country. During the Turks attacks and in Mugal period Hindu society became more rigid towards women and the outsiders attacks was responsible for encouraging and evolving bad customs regarding women through which women degraded. In this period of history, women were forcibly converted into Islam and married. So, consequent insecurity and instability further narrowed down women's social liberties.

In this environment new evils formed i.e. Purdah (seclusion), Infanticide, Dowry system, Devadasi system. Illiteracy, other evils, like shows of gold and wealth, Shaven head of widows. And the evils that got stronger were sati, polygyny, humiliating widowhood, early marriage, illiteracy, unequal marriages.

WOMEN IN BRITISH PERIOD (1800 A.D. TO 1947)

In the mid of eighteenth century, Indians came in vital contact with the British. At the dawn of British rule, the position of women was in humbling state. The golden vedic period's practices were forgotten. On the eve of British rule, Indian women not only lost her independence but she was not able to think on her own. She was drastically tied in the evil customs. At the end of eighteenth century, no change occurred and women's position had reached to the maximum degree of deterioration. And in the beginning of 19th century it was indeed in most deplorable state of womenhood. The attitude of British government not to interfere with the religious sentiments of local people stopped all social reforms for a century.

19th century, marked a "Social Reform Movement". Raja Ram Mohan Roy (1774-1833) was the first Indian who initiated Social Reform Movement first of his attention was drawn towards *'sati'*. He worked very hard and made people aware of the malpractices associated with sati custom through regular speeches and writings. With Lord William Bentincks's cooperation *'Sati'* practice was declared illegal in 1829. This was a great achievement for Ram Mohan Roy and Indian women. Raja Ram Mohan Roy was also against the social evils like early marriage, polygamy and he was supportive towards widow remarriage and women's property rights. In 1828 he founded Brahma Samaj for social reform. Devenda Nath Tagore and Keshav Chand Sen made Brahma Samaj more active, Ram Mohan Roy's revolution was in progress.

Main social reforms in British period are as follows:

1829 : Ban on Sati

1856 : Widow Remarriage Act

1873 : Civil Marriage Act

1874 : The Married Widows Property Act

1881 : The Age of Consent Act

1929 : Child Marriage Restraint Act

1937 : Hindu Women's Right to Property Act.

Ishwar Chandra Vidya Sagar (1820–91) was a great reformer, he attacked on early marriage, polygamy, illiteracy among females. With the unwearied efforts of Ishwar Chandra Vidya Sagar, Hindu Widows Remarriage Act was passed on July 26, 1856.

The age of Consent Act was passed with the efforts of B.M. Malabari, a Parsi social reformer who was against early marriage and widowhood.

The names of Raja Ram Mohan Roy, Ishwar Chand Vidya Sagar, and B.M. Malabari were ranked first and foremost in the upliftment of women in India. After this, the notable social reform made by P.C. Banerjee, M.G. Ranade, Mahatma Phulay, Lokhitwadi, Durgaram and others from all parts of the country raised their voice against the unjust practices. While, Dayananda Saraswati, Swami Vivekananda and Annie Besant was in favour to revive the old vedic society. Swami Dayananda and Vivekananda did their great efforts in the upliftment of women.

After the social reform movement, National movement/ freedom movement had been a very powerful source of change in women's position in society. In this movement, women actively participated with men in 'satyagraha' or 'go behind bars.'

Period of Great Social Reformers are as follows:

Raja Ram Mohan Roy	(1774–1833)
Devendra Nath Tagore	(1817–1905)
Keshav Chandra Sen	(1838–1884)
Ishwar Chandra Viday Sagar	(1820–1891)
Mahadev Govind Ranade	(1842–1901)
Swami Dayanand Saraswati	(1824–1883)
Swami Vivekananda	(1863–1902)
Gopal Kirshna Gokhale	(1866–1915)

Gandhiji apart from being a political leader was also a great social reformer. He was against child marriage, prohibition of widow remarriage, purdha and temple prostitution. Mahatma Gandhi insisted that women must play an equal role with men in the achievement of freedom and social justice.

The platform of women's development had been ready in the beginning of 20th century. Simon Commission observed the change regarding women status and report.

"According to the Simon Commission Report of 1930 no document discussing India's constitutional system and the directions in which it could be developed improved could omit the women of India."[2]

This statement was the indicator of the change which had taken place.

"Mr. K. Natrajan, a famous journalist aptly observer that if a person who died a hundred years ago came to life in 1937, the first and most important change that would strike him was the revolution in the position of women."[3]

"Mahatma Gandhi believed that the freedom movement to be successful, had to be a movement of the masses. He felt that *'Swaraj'* would be meaningless without the reform of the social structure and the upliftment of the weaker sections, namely, the women and the lower social strata to a position of equality with others. While lending his support to the cause of improving women's conditions through education and reform of marriage laws, he declared himself to be uncompromising in the matter of women's rights."[4]

So massive participation of women in freedom struggle make women visible in the eyes of society, that woman is not less than man.

WOMEN IN POST-INDEPENDENCE INDIA (1947 TO 1999)

Another feature of the 20th century is the independence of our country, as well as of women. Now the door of education were opened for women. Now, women were considered as an asset instead of liability.

"The women's question today is... no longer an issue confined to the position women within the family or their rights to equality with men in different aspects of social life. It is part of the total far broader question regarding the direction of change of that process."[5]

Government made a number of efforts to raise the status of women. Government enacted legislation to improve the condition of women and provide better opportunities for the development. There were the main act's passed by government.

1955 : The Hindu Code Bill

1961 : The Dowry (Prohibition) Act

1961 : The Maternity Benefits Act

1971 : M.T.P. (legalising of abortions)

1976 : Equal Remuneration Act

1986 : The Child Labour (The Prohibition and Regulations Act).

So, after independence government are regularly forming policies and plans and carry out that extensive plans. In this period women organisation's emerged to represent the needs of women. Attempts are being done to end the miseries of women.

Women started participating in various fields such as industrialization, higher education, self employment, communication, transport, medical, engineering, space technology, pilots, fashion, and in many other fields.

In the mid of 20th century changes in the country proved fruitful for Indian women. It uplited the living conditions of average women to reattain her rightful place.

WOMEN OF CONTEMPORARY INDIA

Women's issues need to be focused upon since they have been neglected for centuries. Whatever our country has achieved in whichever way it has progressed in past 50 years. We could have probably done it 10 times better if women had been given equal status in the society.

India is the country of very large segments pertaining to caste, area (rural urban) development of states. And in every segment position and role of women is different.

Ever since the freedom movement of the country, the role that women can play in every dimension of developmental activity has been recognized. The various plans strategies have also emphasised on women's participation in the social and economic activities both within the family, in the community as also civil society. This is to enable them to inculcate a sense of confidence and bring about awareness about their own potential for development, rights and privileges.

INDIAN INITIATIVE TOWARDS WOMEN'S DEVELOPMENT THROUGH NATIONAL PLANS

"Ever since the important role of women in national development was specially recognized through the declaration of the UN Decade for women—1976-85 world wide, the approach to women's role has undergone a significant change. In India too, the special initiatives towards women has been primarily one of promoting primary health and child welfare initiatives till the 4th five year plan. The fifth plan laid emphasis on the need to extend training to women in vocational trades and also the need to provide working women's hostels to mitigate the problem of working women, in large cities. In Sixth five year plan, special reservations were made for women in the target for receiving benefits, under the TRYSEM and IRDP. Further a special programme for Development of Women and Children in Rural Areas (DWCRA) was also formulated. The seventh plan emphasised the need to integrate inputs covering health, educational and capacity building inputs and also ensuring their participation through specific reservation for women in development initiatives, to make any realistic impact on the overall improvement of women in the society. Setting up of the National Commission on self-employed women and women in the informal sector, preparation of a National perspective plan for women's development, setting up of women's development corporations in various states and some other initiatives which have together institutionalized the issue of women's development as an inherent part of the working of the governments rather than treating the same as a subsidiary activity. The special programmes in the Eighth and Ninth five year plans have addressed the requirements of women in its totality towards empowering them to participate in the economic development of the country, through comprehensive programmes for access to health and educational facilities, access to credit, access to promotional inputs for self help initiatives including setting up of micro-enterprises etc. The Swarna Jayanti Shahri Rojgar Yojana (SJSRY) — The Golden Jubilee Urban Employment Programme, has a special component for Development of Women and Children in Urban Areas (DWCVA). As part of the scheme special incentive is extended to the urban poor women who decide to setup self-employment ventures in a group as opposed to individual effort. Groups of Urban poor women are encouraged to take up any economic activity suited to their skill, training, aptitude and local condition's. Besides generation of income, this group strategy strives to empower the urban poor women by making them independent as also providing a facilitating atmosphere for self-employment.

A series of legal initiatives by the government has also helped in improving the quality of life of the women to a large extent. The Equal Remuneration Act came into existence in 1976. A number of housing projects with women as the beneficiaries were also started during the International Year for Shelter for the Homeless (1987). The initiatives in the form of community mobilisation and participation particularly women, as part of the UBSP, through the formation of Resident Community Volunteers (RCVs), Neighbourhood Groups (NHGs), District Development

Societies (DDSs) and the Community Development Societies (CDSs) have been extremely successful in promoting group based community action for promotion of the collective well being of the people.

COMMITMENTS OF THE NINTH PLAN (1997–2002)

- To create an enabling environment for women to exercise their rights, both with and outside home, as equal partners along with men, through early adoption of 'National Policy for Empowerment of Women'.
- To legislate reservation of not less than 1/3 seats for women in the Lok Sabha and in the State Legislative Assemblies and thus ensure adequate representation of women in decision making.
- To adopt an integrated approach towards empowering women through effective convergence of existing services, resources, infrastructure and manpower in both women-specific and women-related sectors.
- To adopt a special strategy of 'Women's Component Plan' to ensure that not less than 30 per cent of funds/ benefits flow to women from other developmental sectors.
- To organise women into Self-Help Groups and thus mark the beginning of a major process of empowering women.
- To accord high priority to reproductive child health services and thus ensure access to maternal and child health services.
- To universalize the on-going supplementary feeding programme—Special Nutrition Programme (SNP) and Mid-Day Meals (MDM).
- To ensure easy and equal access to education for women and girls through the commitments of the Special Action Plan of 1998.
- To initiate steps to eliminate gender bias in all educational programmes.

- To institute plans for free education for girls upto college level, including professional courses.
- To equip women with necessary skills in the modern upcoming trades which could keep them gainfully engaged besides making them economically independent and self-reliant and
- To increase access to credit through setting up of a Development Bank for Women Entrepreneurs' in small and tiny sectors."[6]

ROLE OF WOMEN AS CITY MANAGERS

"Since women constitute nearly half of society, their empowerment and participation in all spheres of decision making in Government bodies, public administration, judiciary and in corporate and technical bodies is very important.

The maximum number of women at decision making levels have been in the welfare and development oriented sector or human resource development which includes education, culture, women and child development.

In other wings of Government too, there has been limited representations. For example, there are only few women Judges in the Supreme Court and the High Court.

A few eminent women have no doubt, occupied important administrative positions such as Secretaries to Departments in the National Government as well as Chief Secretaries to State Government.

It is noteworthy that within the premier civil services of the country, the representation of women is poor as shown in (Table 2.1).

Since relatively few women enter the civil services, several efforts have been made to improve the situation. The Department of Personnel and Administrative Reforms of the Government of India has also provided, whenever possible, women officers on the selection boards for posts and services.

Table 2.1. Representation of Women in Selected All India Services

			No. of Personnel in position			
S. No.	**Services**	**Year**	**Total**	**Males**	**Females**	**% of female**
1.	Indian Administrative Services	1985	4284	3973	311	(7.3)
		1992	4928	4498	430	(8.7)
		1996	5047	4546	501	(9.9)
		1997	4991	4479	512	(10.3)
2.	Indian Police Service	1985	2343	2325	18	(0.8)
		1992	2825	2773	52	(1.8)
		1996	2947	2883	64	(2.2)
		1997	2964	2868	96	(3.3)
		1998	2985	2885	100	(3.4)
		1999	3115	3007	108	(3.5)
3.	Indian Foreign Service	1985	535	485	50	(9.3)
		1992	721	658	83	(8.7)
		1995	547	481	66	(12.1)
		1996	567	501	66	(11.6)
		1997	586	519	67	(11.4)
		1998	587	520	67	(11.4)

Source: Platform for Action: Five years after—An Assessment, Department of Women and Child Development, Ministry of H.R.D., Govt. of India, June, 2000.

Women also need to be better represented in the public sector undertakings, especially at decision making levels. It is estimated that only about 1.2 per cent of the executive cadre in the private sector are women. They belong mainly to a few selected segments like advertising and hotels.

A considerable progress has been made by women, in India, particularly in the professional fields but, in politics, career backwardness is visible. However, financially sound country like

USA, has not elected a lady President upto now. The reservation of 33% seats for women in local government institutions or panchayat is cited as an another plus for women.

The government has also recognized the organised effort made by females and hence passed a resolution that incase 50% of the ladies of concerned area demand for removal of liquor shop from the locality it should be removed by the govt. authority"[7].

Truly, there is a whiff of change in the air. It may not be dramatic but a slow and steady transformation is definitely under way in the remote villages. Women, who had, so far, been different and withdrawn, are gradually shedding their earlier reticence and stepping out of the four walls of their homes to acquire an identity of their own. The wind of change is blowing all over the country, some places it is of high intensity and some places of low intensity. But change is a constant feature all over the country. Women are also bringing radical changes in the customs and traditions of their area. This traditional concept is changing with girls taking up white collar jobs.

Women in contemporary India are very strong, independent, self-sacrificing and career oriented. Indian women is moving towards an ideal balance of tradition and progressive/ modern values. Today, educated women aspire professional careers and becoming Doctors, Engineers, Managers, Scientists, Pilots, I.A.S., I.P.S., I.F.S. and Bank officers.

The work place of today and certainly tomorrow is no longer going to remain an exclusive 'man's world'. It is going to transform itself into a much fairer 'Person's world', where men and women work together as individuals.

AREA WHERE WOMEN ARE STILL STRUGGLING

The locality, educational level, and the way of thinking is changing, society is getting modernization, but the real differentiation remains. Today, women are primarily associated with home, child bearing and child rearing activities whether they are working or non-working they are expected to look after domestic chores. Today women is associated and identified with femininity not as an independent individual.

Today, a lot of women's have to cope with both house work and employment outside the home. While in urban life brings certain aids and makes house work easier by modern electric appliances and of course! urban women have not to fetch water and fuel from a distance. But today, the efficiency that is required of them in full time employment and with its consequent professional responsibilities and home responsibilities, create considerable psychological stress which make their life very difficult. In contemporary India, man may come late from work and may take time off from family responsibilities in the interest of their career, but women can not do the same. So, these emphasis of feminine roles has an inevitable effects on girls personalities and identities. Cooking, child care, tailoring can be taken up by men as profession but inside the house, these are left to women. Decision making in the community and exercise of political power is still in male preserve. Boys are not asked to share in domestic work instead develop aptitude for cooking, tailoring are ridiculed and discouraged. Previously boys use lend a hand in marketing, doing escort duty for their mother and sisters, but today girls are trained to do all shopping, so here again her responsibilities increases.

True, parity will be possible only when the implication of the constitutional equality are accepted in peoples mind.

In small towns, change is very slow. Over there, it is difficult for a women to take up unconventional work because of the society. And men still do not relish working under a female boss. Women in small towns and rural areas work very hard, they work in the fields in the day time and rest of the time do cooking, fetch water from well, collect fire-wood, take care of pets and animals.

Women of poorer section and women who are under poverty line, are extremely overworked in both fields of earning out of the house and in house work. Mostly, their children have been neglected. In the year 1977 during the month of October and November the ravages of the nature had created havoc in the lives of the poor in the low-income settlements of Chennai. This led to the poor losing their lines, homes, livelihood and all their belonging to the floods. In the year of 2001, month of January the havoc of the nature had created again in the lives of poor in the low-income group of Gujarat. Lots of poor lost their everything to the earth quake. Living in abysmal conditions of poverty and working in harsh and exploitative conditions of powerlessness women were heavily indebted and in the grips of moneylenders and middle men.

The emphasis on feminine roles has an inevitable effect on girls personalities and identities. They learn early in life the need for flexibility, adjustment and submissiveness and hesitate to develop strong opinions and commitments which they may not be allowed to pursue after marriage.

To cope with this problem society has to remove the distinction between men's work and women's work within and outside the families through the channel of home and the school. And it is necessary to provide the facilities of modern living like, creches, easy transport, labour saving devices and changes in life style to makes home making easier and less time consuming process.

The greatest obstacle towards social change is conservative women herself. She thinks women is unfortunate and supports dowry system to increase wealth and cannot see another women working outside home and spread rumours like working women are bad mothers and inefficient housewives. It is unimaginable that any civilized society will actually kill the baby girls at birth. This is the mother, who first started discriminating between boys and girls in home and outside world.

CRIME AND POSITION OF WOMEN

Since independence, government is making policies and plans for the upliftment of women still women are facing various types of crimes. According to the latest report of National Crime Records Bureau (NCRB): shows the another picture of women.

"On the ground, noting has changed. Atrocities against women are steadily mounting. Crime against women have been increasing at an alarming rate all over the country and the incidence of such offences could be more than the rate of increase in population over the next decade."

The report states that crimes against women in 1998 increased by 10,073 cases (8.3 per cent) over that of 1997. Even the regions with high literacy rate and better indices of quality of life like Kerala are not safe haven for women as state accounts for a four per cent share in the national crime account. However, rape cases showed a marginal decrease of 2 per cent as there were 15,033 cases in 1998 against 15,336 cases in 1997. The cases under indecent representation of Women Act and Importation of Girls Act increased by 163 per cent and 87.2 per cent respectively.

There had been 582 cases of abandonment of infants in 1998, including 279 in Maharashtra, 115 in Madhya Pradesh and 101 in Gujarat. Of the 107 cases of infanticide, 45 were reported from M.P., 25 from Maharashtra and 11 from Bihar.

Incidents of child rape had increased in 1998 by eight per cent, while incidence of abetment to suicide and procuration of minor girls had gone up by 115.4 per cent and 96.6 per cent, respectively. The incidence of selling girls for prostitution increased by 22.2 per cent while child rape victims (below 16 years) alone accounted for 27 per cent"[8].

For long it was believed that women were subjected to harassment and violence in the streets and at their work place. But now it is becoming increasingly clear that women are not necessarily safe in their homes. Wife beating, sexual abuse of the girl child and other forms of physical and psychological torture of women are common place in homes. It is a world-wide phenomenon and India is no exception.

"A survey, spanning seven Indian cities and covering both rural and urban populations, reveals that 45 per cent of the women surveyed had been subjected to at least one incident of physical or psychological violence in their life time. Infact the study indicates that severe physical violence is all pervasive and through slapping was not included while undertaking the survey, yet 26 per cent women said they had experienced moderate to severe form of physical violence.

This figure would go up considerably if slapping was also included in the study, "explains Geeta Rao Gupta, director of the U.S. based International Center for Research on Women (ICRW) which conducted this survey"[9].

The Convoluted procedures and the limited benefits that the criminal system offers to women are also major hurdles that prevent women from lacking action against the perpetrators of domestic violence.

Concerted efforts for enhancement of gender sensitivity, awareness generation, precautionary measures, punitive action and community support are essential in dealing with crimes against women.

MAIN FINDINGS OF BEIJING CONFERENCE REGARDING INDIAN WOMEN

It is now five years since India, along with other countries, participated in Women's World Conference in Beijing. There are considerable positive changes over the past 25 years but if we look back only five years, we can see much that is terrible and disappointing", says the report, which seeks to reflect the opinions and assessments of women across the country.

There is more violence, more discord, more disparity, more poverty, more indifference to the demands of economic justice", the report point out as it goes down the list of India's "hits and misses" on this point. Here's a brief checklist on India's performance on its promises:

- The move to appoint a national commissioner has not succeeded. The proposal has been turned down by the home ministry.
- The promise to raise the education budget has not been fulfilled to date.
- A national policy for the empowerment of women was drafted in 1996 but is yet to be approved and adopted.
- The plan to establish a national resource centre, envisaged as a nodal body to main stream gender issues in politics and programmes, has not moved.
- The emphasis in health investment is slanted towards reproductive health concerns while the government announces plans to 'privatise' many public health

> services. The cost of health care has gone up in the last five years. Drug policies have changed leading to a sharp increase in the prices of medicines while the quality of primary health care is bad.

India's poor performance in implementing Beijing's Platform Action (PFA), according to the report, is attributed to the lack of political will in addressing women's issues.

The failure to adopt the National Policy for Women's Empowerment, to get the women's reservation bill passed and to implement the major commitments made at Beijing are evidence of this", the report adds. Another indicator is the failure to control the rise in crime and violence targeting women while overall investment in social development has fallen with predictable negative fall out on women"[10].

WOMEN IN BACKWARD STATES OF INDIA

Women in India are treated as vulnerable section of the society. No doubt, changes are taking place from one corner of the country to another corner but the intensity is different in every state.

In some state of the country, condition of the women is still lagging behind in the race of development like Bihar, Rajasthan, U.P. and M.P. etc.

"Bihar today is the pathetic state of women. 'Women in Bihar have to first think of survival than think of change.' "Without cloths, without food and under the constant threat of being raped, assaulted or even killed, 'A nine or ten year old mother is common in the state. In rural Bihar, which is 80 per cent of the state, rarely do women live like human beings"[11].

According to the National Family Health Survey—II Health "sex ratio in UP. continues to fall from 885 in 1981 to 879 in 1991. Life expectation of women in U.P. is 52.8 years for women against 57.1 in the case of men while in India remains as whole in favour of women (60.6 years in case of males to 61.7 females). For men the literacy rate is said to be 55.7 per cent, for women it remains 25.3 per cent. Women's literacy is as low as nine per cent in Bundelkand region"[12].

LATEST STEPS HAS BEEN TAKEN BY GOVERNMENT TO DECREASE WOMEN BACKWARDNESS

On March 8th, 2000 (International Women's Day), "In a major ruling which may benefit all daily-wage women employees, the Supreme Court said that, "they are entitled to the maternity benefits available to regular women employees." This is a very welcome step to uplift poorer section of women. "Failure to extend these basic rights by an employer would be penal offence punishable with at least a one year jail term and fine". A bench comprising Justice S. Saghir Ahmed and Justice D.P. Wadhawa which recently held that a woman divorced by her husband for having deserted him would also be entitled to maintenance, directed the Municipal Corporation of Delhi to extent the Maternity Benefit Act 1961, to its daily wage women employees many of whom have been working for over 10 years as 'Muster Roll' employees at meagre wages in activities like digging trenches and carrying heavy loads at constructions. Not only this, on May 31, "The Central Government of India announces five 'Stari Shakti' award to promote talented hard working and struggled women. This award is to boost the moral value and determination of specific women in the country. In this award women will be entitled to get 1 lakh rupees cash and certificate"[13].

Women of contemporary India is in much better condition comparing to the women in the period of 500 B.C. to 19 century. Conventional wisdom has it that career women have to function in a man's world. Now-a-days, this conventional wisdom under threat, as more as qualified dedicated and highly motivated women take charge in offices, factories, business and other male preserve.

WOMEN OF CONTEMPORARY WORLD

Not only in India throughout the world women play a very important role in their society.

Today the world has 6 billion people. About fifty per cent of the same are women. The Human Development Report 1999 by UNDP indicates that women bear almost 13 per cent more work than men in developing countries and women spend around 65 to 70 per cent of their time in performing non-market activities, involving household work. On the other hand, men spend about 70 to 80 per cent of their time on market activities. After all, about forty billion hours are estimated to be lost each year to girls and women carrying water or collecting cooking fuel in rural areas of developing countries. And, about forty per cent of the women in the world are illiterate.

The UNCHS indicates that the female representation in the highest circles of government was less than 10 per cent in 1990 and only 3.5 per cent of the world's cabinet ministers were women. The proportionate representation of women in the national level legislature in Asian countries has been estimated to be 14.1 per cent on an average. The UNCHS also indicates that the representation of women in local governments is generally better than the national level, but is no way equal to men's representation. In Africa the percentage of women in local government is estimated to be 5% and in European countries, the average percentage of women in municipal councils is indicated as 23%.

INTERNATIONAL INITIATIVES FOR RECOGNITION OF WOMEN'S ROLE

"The historic perspective, at the organised global level of mobilising public opinion for the cause of ending discrimination towards women could be traced back to the feminist movements of the fifties. The issue of empowerment of women came to the forefront with the convention on the political rights of women (1952) and the International convenant on civil and political rights (1966), aimed at giving women equal opportunity in the public life. The declaration of 1975 as the International Women's Year was a significant turning point, followed by the convention of the Elimination of All Forms of Discrimination Against Women (1979), urging governments to ensure women's participation in formation and implementation of government policy.

The Nairobi Conference in 1985 advocated the 'forward looking strategies for the advancement of women which urged the national governments to appropriately ensure women's participation in the formulation of policies, programmes and projects for the provision of shelter and services in human settlements. The declaration advocated for increased involvement of women in the technical and managerial professions, concerning human settlement development. In addition to enabling them to participate in shelter and services initiatives as partners, it advocated for incorporation of their suggestions in the design of shelter and human settlement development efforts and also in the maintenance of services provided.

The 1992 UN Conference on Environment and Development at Rio De Janeiro called for a participatory approach with dialogue and involvement of indigenous population especially women in the human settlement development, while the Habitat (ii) Conference at Istanbul in 1996, laid emphasis on a holistic approach in partnerships for urban management, with focus on gender needs.

The grassroots women issued the first major international statement on community development at the Forth World Conference on Women in Beijing China in 1995. The Huairou Commission established as a follow-up had moved the grassroots women to the centre of international policy making. The core of the co-ordination Committee is made up of representatives from international women's network organisations. Since 1995, Huairou Commission has worked closely with its international colleagues to introduce a grassroots women's dimension to policy making.

The "World-wide Declaration of Women in Local Government" by the International Union of Local Authorities in 1998, identified the local bodies as the most accessible and best suitable launching pad for the involvement of women in governance."[14]

WOMEN IN USA

"In US, women make up about 46 per cent of management, although they are still in tiny minority at top levels, according to a UN study."

"According to the latest U.S. government estimates, there were more than 7.1 million women in full time executive, administrative, or managerial positions in 1998 — a 29% jump from 1993. Approximately 9.4 million men had the same kind of significant jobs, but that represented only 19% increase. "The glass ceiling definitely exist but the same time, there are an increasing number of women who are breaking through it, "said Debra Meyerson, a professor of management, science and engineering at Stanford University, "It's proof that more women are entering the work force."

Here's more proof: in 1998, there were 514000 more women in executive positions than in 1997, compared to 392000 more males in such top-level posts during that same time-frame.

The broad category of executive administrative and managerial positions covers job from CEOs to mid-level and lower-level management positions, to women who own their own businesses.

While the median income level for men and women in executive positions both rose at the same 20 per cent clip in 1998, men made nearly $ 17000 more-women $ 51351, the statistics show.

There is a huge gap in term of finding, salaries and compensation. But what we do have is recognition; women are recognised now that they can contribute equally at the boardroom as men"[15].

WOMEN IN U.K.

In Britain, "Recent data covering the employer intake of graduates show that 55 per cent are now female—whereas 10 years ago the figure was 45 per cent."

"And in a study of Britain's most powerful women the magazine Management Today identified 60 women in top roles. Not surprisingly, 45 per cent were aged 45 or younger. But more significantly, only 28 per cent were over 50 [16]".

WOMEN IN JAPAN

Tokyo: "A labour ministry study released in August showed that "the proportion of women in management hardly changed between 1995 and 1998. The study looked at about 6000 companies employing 30 or more people."

A major Japanese Bank said that "It plans to promote more women to management to take advantage of their experience and because it costs less than men."

Tsyoshi, Yamashita, the spokesman of Tokai Bank said that: Tokai Bank Ltd., a national wide tender based in Nagoya, Central Japan, wants women to occupy 800 of its 4000 management positions over the next few years.

Tokai Bank employees 11162 people, about 4000 are women. Like many other Japanese companies, the bank has hired women mostly as clerical workers, giving them fewer responsibilities and fewer chances for promotion than its male-dominated staff of "career-track" employees.

The bank wants to promote more women to make more efficient use of its resources; "This initiative will also help save money, since its costs more to hire career-track employees than to promote clerical staff"[17].

WOMEN IN INDIA

According to U.N. Report on India

"After the Human Development Report, the Progress of the World's Women Report and like the UNDP document, which lauded India for significant improvements in the human development index, the UN Fund for Development of Women (UNIFEM) score card has given India credit for efforts at gender equality but underlined that the country still had a long way to go.

"The advances toward gender equality have been uneven and there is still a long way to go to make the promises made at Beijing is reality", was the verdict of the report summarised by UNIFEM regional programme director Chandni Joshi.

The report notes India has improved its score in education, employment and per capita income of women, but has not been improved women's representation in Parliament, removed their unequal wages or lessened their debt burden. These, in fact, have deteriorated, the report says.

Stressing the need to give women a place in decision-making structures, the report says greater equality in the number of women holding political office is important as it gives women a greater say in determining laws and policies which regulate women's progress. While governments have endorsed 30 per cent representation to women in political positions, the report says, only few countries—Sweden, Denmark, Germany, Finland, Norway, Iceland, the Netherlands and South Africa—have met this target. In India, there are only a dismal 8.9 per cent women MPs.

The report says that the share of women in paid employment in India has improved though it is still a mere 15 per cent. However, women's share of national income has not improved because women tend to be paid less than men. In fact, the report says the women's average wages are less than men's in all 63 countries for which data was available.

According to Diane Elson, the report's author, the data does not take into account the women working in the informal sector. She says though the number of employed women might have risen, the quality of their work is not taken into account. "Women from less well of families are often pressured to take poor quality, low paying jobs in industry and services to make up for falling family income, rather than through their own choice," the report adds.

Among obstacles to women enjoying the gains of greater share in the job market: violence against women, the burden of HIV/AIDS and the unequal sharing of unpaid caring work. Data shows that in India, 40 per cent women have experienced violence by an intimate partner"[18].

WOMEN IN PAKISTAN

Women in Pakistan raise their voice that itself is a change.

One effot has been done by UNESCO, "to make March 8, International Women's Day, In this concern UNESCO has appealed to the media world wide to give editorial charge of news on this day to women.

Gender equality and gender justice should be the hall marks of the new emerging world of the 21st Century. Equal participation by women in decision-making will also accord a value-added perspective, an essential imperative for good governance. One effort has been done by UNESCO for the women living world wide.

THE ROLE AND DISTRIBUTION OF WOMEN IN THE ECONOMY

The role and contribution of women in the economy is of vital significance. Economist hardly pay attention to assess women's contribution to the economy.

EARLY THEORIES OF WOMEN EMPLOYMENT

The main stream economics has long ignored differences in economic behaviour and reward between man and woman.

Karl Marx, the first and foremost advocate of the working class had only a blurred vision of the women at work. He did refer to the women workers but neither attempted to expose the exploitation of women within each class structure nor condemned the inadequate opportunities to women workers that was so very apparent in the working of factories.

Engles argued for emancipation of women following their full entry into social production. Experience, however proves that Engels was over optimistic since women workers are still at the tail of the labour market.

The long sustained vaccum on gender based differences in individuals was for the first time realized by the founder of institutionalism. Thorstein Veblen. His endeavour to establish a theory of economic behaviour in which the identification of the different role of women as opposed to that of men is noteworthly as the starting point of theoretical comprehension of women's behaviour. However he could focus only on partial facts of life of the 'leisure class', to whom work of any kind is 'infra dig'.

Neither classical or neo-classical economic thought has much to contribute by way of treatment of women's place in the economy. In the valuation of the Gross National Product (G.N.P), household activities are ignored as unproductive work"[19].

A study by NIUA on women in urban informal sector (1988) identifies that women suffer from two sets of discrimination in the labour market, namely the pre-market discrimination, that refers to the lack of access to factors such as education, training, experience, and so on which increase human capital and enhances the marginal product of labour, and secondly the post-market discrimination covering the differential wages for a similar quantum of human capital. It further indicates that gender determined segmentation within the informal sector compels women to take up activities which are symbolically 'women's work' such as laundry, domestic service, embroidery and so forth. Although there has been increasing feminisation of certain occupations such as nursing, teaching, domestic service and petty trade, women continue to be engaged largely in low skill and low wage occupations, and participate at low ranges of occupational hierarchy. While the majority continues to be on this pattern, the study has also identified an interesting feature of the gradual increase in the concentration of females in jobs which were hitherto primarily male preserves. There is an increasing number of women working now as mathematicians, public health physicians, teleprinter operators, ministerial and office assistants and bookkeepers and calculating machine operators.

Contrary to the general perception that women do not get full employment and remain under-employed particularly in the informal sector, the NIUA study which analysed the employment pattern in six large cities of India based on an extensive sample survey, found that three-fourths of the workers in the informal sector get work throughout the year and less than 10 per cent are engaged in seasonal work while about 15 per cent work for most of the year. Less than 10 per cent of the women reported irregular work of less than 20 days a month. The informal sector is therefore able to provide most of the women with work and income, almost throughout the year.

Notwithstanding the substantial improvement in the recent past in the extent of participation of women in economic endeavours, the increasing emphasis on larger mechanised production processes has indeed marginalised the involvement of women from active participation, delegating them to perform only supportive 'low skill and low paid' jobs. Even though, there has been an emergence of increasing number of self help initiatives by women, the income receipt by the women as compared to the labour put-in, has not been commensurate.

While the need of upgradation of production technologies and processes is an unavoidable necessity in the changing era of globalisation, the activities such as building industry, in which the participation of women has been substantial, need to innovate and promote technologies which are gender positive and gender adaptive.

Rastriya Mahila Kosh is a Central Government loan fund, which makes loan assistance available to the poor women and children. It makes loan fund available to poor women, through NGOs and community savings. The Mahila Milan savings groups have tapped this credit since 1993, through an efficient, decentralised system, where the individual savings groups manage the processing of loans and repayments. This partnership helps everyone, the women economic position improves, the savings groups which are strengthened by the additional lending capital, and the government that furthers its commitment to women's economic upliftment"[20].

Economy wise, women's work still remains invisible and under-estimated. All of those who believe in this myth that female participation in work is relatively low becomes false when we consider the overall work profile of rural women. In rural areas, women perform a extensive part of agricultural operations like, breaking of clods of earth, manuring, wedding, transplanting, harvesting, threshing and winnowing etc. Rural women also take care of dairy animals and marketing of their products. They also involve in small scale industries like jute making, rope and basket making, pottery, match stick, bidi udyog, handloom weaving, food processing etc.

Not only they are economically active but performing the part of household duties without any helping hand. Household duties demand extra energy to fetch fuel, water, and food. They are actually overburdened because of multifarious duties.

Women working in home-production units are significantly and economically contributing to family income as well as national income.

In non-household industry/units women commanding high participation in water supply, sanitary services, educational, scientific services, medical and health services.

The role of poor women is not quite happy situation. They are working hard. In many families they are the sole earning members. Most of the women in this strata of our society is working under economic pressure. And take care of sick in-laws, unemployed husband. These women are employed in unskilled and semi-skilled jobs. Women who are working as agricultural labour, with new agricultural strategy unskilled female labour are unable to adjust technological change. In that way female participation in economy reduces.

One new fact is also emerging i.e. increase of female child labour and decrease of male child labour in rural areas. Female girls are working on fields and men and boy's getting opportunities out and trained for better skills.

The urban educated women engaged in professional and high status job. Education play a significant role in urban economy. With the spread of education middle class urban women is also emerging as working women and supporting their family economically.

In India, this is misfortune of those women who are economically active but not recognized as worker. Working as housewives and mothers, when they perform productive-non-domestic work.

Female participation rate is different in every state, However, it increases as we move from north to south and east to west in India.

Since 1911, female participation rate start declining from 33.7% to 23% in 1951 and after 1951 it rose to 28% in 1961 and again drop down to 12% in 1971, and 14 per cent in 1981.

This overall decline in the percentage of women workers is visible in all states for both rural and urban areas but is sharper in urban areas.

The forces which have most affected the role of women in the Indian economy are:

- the general decline of handicrafts
- increase in population on agriculture
- increasing technological advances

- increase of poverty in rural areas and resulting migration to urban areas
- Increasing cost of living i.e. in urban areas
- Education and social change in urban areas.

Transition from traditional agricultural and household sector to modern organised industry and sector, destroys the traditional division of labour. And technological changes in production methods call for new skills. Women, handicapped by lack of opportunities to acquire these new skills, find themselves unwanted by the new economy.

To cope with this problem, Indian women have to be equipped with modern education, technological aspects. And due to neglect of female education and development in the past, today women are lagging behind in employment and salaried jobs.

And women who are enjoying high status and economic independence as such but no doubt leading subordinate status and discharging duties of household.

Obstacles in Women's Employment

1. Dual role of duties
2. Dominate over her husband
3. Inconvenient timings
4. Transfer of the husband seriously affects a women's career
5. When husband and in-laws are not supportive
6. Transfer and promotion in her own job
7. Not able to provide wholesome food and failure to become a good cook
8. Unable to maintain an orderly home
9. Possible chances for husband and wife conflict
10. Working in irregular shifts
11. Night duties in Nursing

Women employment differs from that of men and is identified by discontinue due to marriage, child bearing, home conflicts and post-natal demands on her time at home.

In the last 100 years, very little changes has taken place regarding female employment. Industrialization of India not able to drawn women, the last three decades are slightest better.

In other avenues of employment, women's share in total employment had increased significantly in household and non-household manufacturing units. In non-household manufacturing, their number had increased fast though not as fast as that of men. Excluding domestic work of women from National income underestimates National Income in developing countries like India.

Globalisation/liberalisation present new opportunities involving structural readjustments. The Strategy to integrate women more effectively into the economy includes training in non-trade areas, access to institutional credit, access to education, increased wage employment opportunities and support services eg., day care for children. Within the urban areas, women are involved in a range of income generating activities albeit in the informal sector- incense makers, bidi makers, food processing, fish processing, textiles, zari work, pottery etc. Estimates show that there are 10 to 12 million women employed as home based workers.

ROLE OF WOMEN IN UNORGANISED AND ORGANISED SECTOR

Unorganised Sector

In India, large part of women are engaged in this sector of economy.

The National Commission on labour, specifying its difficulties in identifying unorganised labour by any exact definition took resource to describe some of their characteristics and constraints, namely:

(a) Casual nature of employment;

(b) Ignorance and illiteracy;

(c) Small size of establishment with low capital investment per person employed;

(d) Scattered nature of establishment;

(e) Superior strength of the employers operating singly and in combination.

"The National Commission on Self Employed women estimates that 94% of the total female work force is to be found in this sector (GOI, 1988)"[21].

Women have noticeable presence in several segments of this sector of economy. As it is stated that 94% is the total female work force engaged in this sector of the economy, 81% engaged in agriculture.

So, Agriculture holds an extensive part of unorganised sector. Other segment of this sector where female workforce engaged are animal husbandry, dairying, social and agro-forestry, handloom weaving, small village industries, khadi, handicrafts, fishery and working as housemaids.

In unorganised sector women are spending longer hours of work and doing least skilled jobs. The earnings are low because of wage discrimination and seasonal work. However, low wages is an extensive problem from which most of the women worker are suffering, as well as insecurity regarding job and sexual harassment.

Where women perform work as part of family labour and home based producer her work is not recognised. Female work force in unorganised sector is unaffected by the protection of labour laws regarding equal wages for equal work. The gradual commercialisation and modernization of the economy and the efforts made by Govt. to replace traditional by modern institution of credit and marketing, to stabilise ownership of land to maintain minimum wages, but not succeeded in organising the production relations to control the degree of exploitation of the weaker sections, and problem of low productivity, poverty unemployment and under employment.

This is very unmanageable for women to perform household chores then do hard efforts to get extra pay. Majority of women of this sector are in rural areas, they carry out tedious, arduous and low skilled job and earning low while men are doing skilled and less onerous task and getting fine pay-packet. However, majority of women are playing a vital part in this sector, so, it is very necessary to uplift the position of women.

Women in Organized Sector

According to National Committee on status of women in India, the percentage of women working in organised sector is only 6 per cent.

The organised sector offers women the best opportunity of employment it draw women out of the family and household world. It provides a scale of freedom to women to contribute house economy.

Urban educated women with new skills, engaged in professional careers which are better paid and are highly prestigious. Thoroughly study shows the fact that during planning period women's status and position improved.

Rapid changes in technology, automation and growth of modern organised industries, such as petro chemicals, fertilisers and engineering offers reduced job opportunities for women in the sector.

In our country, women are engaged in unskilled, semi-skilled and low grade office jobs i.e. typing, computer operator, receptionist etc.

Women position is better in service sector such as bank, media, insurance, tourism, transportation and public financial institutions. But this segment is open for only educated women. Development of advanced technology is very rapid women are trying to cope for work opportunities.

"The report of the committee on the status of women in India shows that out of about 200 operations in the textile industry, women are employed in no more that four or five (GOI, 1974)"[22].

Women have to struggle hard with the present demand of the organised sector. The future of women would be very bright only if she adopt high education as a weapon, Otherwise, the future appears uncertain.

ROLE OF WORKING AND NON-WORKING WOMEN

Non-working Women

Non-working women are women who are not going out to work and are not financially independent. Women who are not financially independent leading alter-life. Non-working women do not have her own identity, her identity is because of her Father/Husband/and Son. These women have to depend on their Husband's and fathers earning.

Non-working women means not they are not working. They are actively involve in household chores but this sort of contribution is not recognised in the country. No body, can deny from this fact that, when women are working in the domestic front, she is indirectly contributing to social and economic development of a nation as a whole. Class of housewives is the largest in our country but the only unremunerative work force in the world.

Household work include massive procedure of cooking, washing, cleaning, ironing, purchasing, watering to plants, child care, care of elders etc. So, sometimes, she even does not get time for herself.

Rural women engage themselves in fetching fuel, fodder, water for cattle household, animal care, managing kitchen, cleaning, food processing such as threshing grain, grinding, storing etc. All this work is marked as non-income producing and gives women a low economic status.

The situation becomes more vulnerable when women are working hard in family business, working in our field, managing massive household chores but they are not financially independent.

Working Women

In a tradition bond society women had been confine to the kitchen and the four walls of house. There is one thing which is constant i.e. change after independence lots of efforts has been made for the improvement of the society, resulted with the spread of education. Women emerged as high professionals, officials, entrepreneurs were playing an independent role in the society. Working women is the part of busy world.

Presently, working women's position is very challenging. Because they are performing dual role, working out as well as managing full household duties. No doubt, today lots of modern appliances are in every home even then it is not an easy task to manage both activities. Another problem in working field they have to face some major difficulties such as long working hours, transfers, night duty, irregular working hours etc.

"The lower the income level, the greater is the pressure on women to seek work to sustain themselves and their families. The relationship between earning income or being employed by itself is not an indicator of status. The kind of work done, the terms under which it is done, the reason for which it is done are really matter. Women also have unequal control and access to cash."[23]

Women of lower class/working as an agricultural labour getting wages of hard work done by them. But wages for agricultural work even when paid to women are taken over by men. In some regions where husband wife teams or family labour is employed, the cash is handed over to the male.

"In some cases the wife feels that she is obliging her husband by making financial contribution and she becomes compliance of her economic independence. This attitude makes her intolerant and disregardful towards her husband or in-laws. In India, generally the tradition husband and in-laws are prejudiced against working wife"[24].

Today, working women are facing heavy physical and strains in their life. The people at home should try to help working women as much as possible. A woman found herself in tension when her husband and in-laws do not co-operate with her.

This is common phenomena found in working that they are unable to do full justice to either to work or domestic front and both spheres of her activities suffer. Those women are struggling hard who are doing work under economic pressure.

Jain Shashi, "select a sample of 200 working women and 200 non-working women.

Studies found that majority of working women belong to higher age group (26-40). If we look at the educational level of the working and non-working women it has been noticed that the educational level of the working women is higher than the non-working housewives.

Amongst the working women, the two large caste groups Brahmins and the Intermediary castes—Kayastha and Khatris. High percentage of Brahmins found in teaching"[25].

ROLE OF UNMARRIED WOMEN AND MARRIED WOMEN

Unmarried Women

Unmarried woman after completing education seek out if she is career oriented. Otherwise, wait for her fortune to get married. Women who are career oriented choose the career with the permission of elders/parents. With the consent of permission they work outside otherwise, vice versa. When unmarried women do work outside she does magnificently because no tension and no burden of responsibility she carries with her.

In our country, unmarried females are not independent enough. They have to work according to their parent's wish. Employment of an unmarried women is not looked upon with favour in our Indian society.

Married Women

In case of married women the influence of husband and other members of family is very great in determining their choice of career. Women choose a career as per according to the wish of her in-laws husband and relatives.

Married women who are working in administrative services and political leadership have actually no time for household duties and families. Larger responsibilities of services leaves no time to look after their family and when husband is also working long hour duty then the child is brought up by the servants and relatives. Some married working women are facing dual burden to life.

Some women who are working hard at home depend on husband's earning, and face conflict when husband says "I work full day and you spend time in leisure".

However, the position of married women is not calm and quite. She is struggling in her life. She tries her best to make other happy.

ROLE OF WOMEN IN NUCLEAR AND JOINT FAMILY

Women in Nuclear Family

Nuclear families are the result of migration of rural people to urban areas. People of rural areas are going out to seek job opportunities and education. And then start living over there.

Women working as a housewives in nuclear family enjoying liberty in their lives, specially in urban areas, because in rural areas we hardly find nuclear families. If we find then they are mostly in service class.

Today the market is full of modern appliances and readymades. Modern housewives complete their household work in just half time comparatively to the tradition housewives. Housewives feel isolated in day time because most of things they are getting readymade, kitchen is full of modern appliances so even, after doing all household responsibilities women find time in spare, then they spent their time watching T.V., gossiping, etc. Role of working women in nuclear family is quite tedious. Specially for those women who are doing job under economic pressure, and whose husband are not co-operating in work.

Working women's day start early in the morning and they work till late at night. Working women do all household duties like cooking, washing, cleaning, get there kids ready for school, check their books, pen, pencil etc. while returning home do all purchasing as per the requirement and then again evening cooking, spent time with children, and help them in their homework, fulfill the demand of husband etc.

In nuclear family, only husband can co-operate with women if he is not co-operating then that leaves the women frustrated mentally and physically. Few husbands do not co-operate because they are doing hours of duty (more than 8 hours) and few don't because they are male of tradition bound society, who are not ready to accept change regarding work.

Marriage is a fifty per cent partnership for husband and wife. When both are earning equally both are doing hard work then they should understand each other and help in reducing the burden of each other. After all the women is helping the family financially. In such cases her contribution is more than her husband.

Women in Joint Family

Adjustment and understanding is the key in joint family. In urban areas where women is working out and in-laws are co-operating, women can lead a happy life. Because when she is out, there is someone at home who can take care of her child.

A sample survey (400) conducted by Jain Shashi found that more than half of the working respondents came from nuclear families whereas more than one third were from joint families. It is clear, that women of nuclear families have better opportunities and more freedom of work.

Now, the time is changing because of economic reasons and change in social values. Now educated mother-in-law wants an intelligent and working daughter-in-law. The increasing demand of a working girl amongst the educated services class families is also encouraging many parents of joint families to send their daughters for a job. Still a large majority of joint families do not prefer to send their daughter for a career.

ROLE OF WOMEN IN HIGH, MIDDLE AND LOWER CLASS

High Class Women

High-class women are liberated women. In developed areas, females of higher classes are enjoying more status, freedom than a middle class man. Mostly high class women get high education. In this class women are found to be ambitious and in order to gain social prestige and recognition, they work. They also work because they are having household extra facilities and have spare time, they face loneliness in the isolation of the home.

Some high class women do work to maintain high standards and easy-going life. Some to get extra pay-packet. Women who do not go out to work usually don't find highly prestigious job.

Middle Class Women

Middle class women are more conscious about work compared to high-class women. Present demand, make women conscious and concerned with personal advancement.

Middle class women try to imitate the living standard of high class society. That's why, the standard of living is rising day by day and the cost of maintenance too, is also rapidly increasing.

Some household wife find themselves bored with the monotony of household duties.

Some middle class women go outside to work because of family conflicts. And some are doing to meet the daily needs of their families. In middle class economic need is the fundamental reason for female employment. Majority of women is this segment keep themselves busy in teaching profession.

Lower Class Women

Lower class women are struggling hard. Doing long hours of work, getting low wages. Employment options available to the lower class women are severely limited and as the opportunities for skill acquisition and job mobility are more limited, work for them becomes an endless drudgery, humiliation and misfortune in the sense that they have to do with too little or no male earning.

ROLE OF WOMEN IN METRO AREAS, URBAN AREAS AND RURAL AREAS

Women in Metro City

"Educated, talented, career oriented. Yet vulnerable. This, in essence, seems to be the situation of the modern women in the metros. Despite her independence, she does seem to be a victim of eve-teasing, sexual harassment and lewd behaviour, both at work place and on the streets. Home again, often becomes a battle ground where she is forced to valiantly juggle her multifarious roles of wife, mother, daughter-in-law, etc. While womenfolk may be breaking out of the shackles that have impeded their growth for long, it seems the gender equation still needs to find its new equilibrium. It's time too for the urban male to break free of a mind-set which views a women as an object alone. For things to improve, a beginning has to be made within the family itself. Good parenting can go a long way in fostering the right attitude in daughters and, more important, in sons. Society—and this include schools, work places—too need to constantly reinforce the concept of gender equality. Most importantly, women have to empower themselves in the true sense of the term. Nobody can do it for them"[26].

The liberated Indian women lives mostly in big cities. Be it the civil services, medicine, politics, or any other field women have made their mark in every field. This is also one of the emerging fact that women is not respected in big cities.

Metro cities are actually cruel places where the battle for survival is fierce. Norms like, humanity, courtesy, concern for the under privileged respect for elders, women are forgotten. Situation can improve only with education and economic opportunities for women. Gender bias is very deep rooted, women is still perceived as a 'body' rather than a person. So, to change this phenomenon both should follow a strict code of conduct.

Women in Urban Areas

"Pauperization of farming families in the rural areas and their journey to the urban areas in search of employment opportunities is one among the important reasons for swelling of families in the urban areas.

Millions of people living in slums. Most of women even today live in abysmal and slushy surroundings in highly congested areas as against the resource rich who enjoy lavish life style in the same city. Also the lives of the resourceless poor are characterized by severe deprivation, malnutrition, lack of shelter, lack of access to resources, vulnerability to diseases and lack of education towards upward mobility."[27]

Women of urban areas are far away from the evil effects of metros, women are living a quite life here, and urban women are not as much liberated as of metros. Percentage of working women is low comparatively to Metro areas. Women of urban areas are not conscious about their career. Few females who belongs to educated mass are coming forward to explore economic opportunities.

Women in Rural Areas

It is a agreed fact that position of women all over the world has been low, of course, India is no exception. Government are doing hard efforts to uplift women's position, but even then position of rural women is continued to be low.

It is embarrassing in the extreme that the naive religiosity of rural people continues to be exploited by the heartless custodians of the orthodoxy. When we are preparing ourselves to enter in 21st century, on Nov. 11 1999, women named 'Charan Shah' committed sati in Satpura village in U.P. Glorification of sati is crime under the Sati (Prevention) Act 1988. Child marriages are still prevalent in rural areas specially of Rajasthan. Early marriages are common phenomenon in rural areas. She is given no time for the development of her personality. Once she get married no freedom remains. She gets a subordinate position. Looking at the position of women's education in rural areas, the efforts for the progress seem to be going waste.

"The overall violation was more in the affluent families who though pretended to be progressive when expressing opinions, were conservative in action. Their affluence had rather helped them in performing early marriages of their children. An early marriage is still a value. It begets prestige to the family in the community. They do not wait for completion of the education of a girl even upto primary level if they have arranged her marriage. In their perception education has no purpose in women's life. It comes very low in their priority"[28].

Rural women have not witnessed any radical change in their life styles over the years. They live in the condition which is exploitative and traditional. Now-a-days, rural men migrate to the cities, leaving the women behind to carry the burden of agricultural and other tasks.

If, child marriage, sati, early marriage is to be a norm of society then definitely these cases rise in horrifying state, which

Raja Ram Mohan Roy fought so hard in the 19th century to eliminate.

THE ROLE OF WOMEN AND SIGNIFICANCE OF EDUCATION

Education is, quite simply, an investment that yield a higher profit than any other. It is what makes possible the development of entire communities, countries and continents. It is the most effective form of defence spending there is.

In many societies, women are systematically marginalized; and yet, when catastrophe strikes—whether it be in the form of illness, conflict or hardship—they bear the biggest burden. Noting illustrates this more amply than the impact of HIV/AIDS. Girls are most likely to care for a sick family member and help manage the household. Prevented from going to school, they are denied information about how to protect themselves against this deadly virus. Deprived of an education they risk being forced into early sexual relations with older men or earning a living as a prostitute, and thereby becoming infected. They pay many times over the deadly price of not going to school. The first step is for societies to recognize that educating girls is not an option; it is a necessity.

Education is one of the most significant factor in the over all development of women.

In ancient times, education regarding script and so on has been given in madarsas, path shalas and at toils.

At the time of colonial rulers, the position of female literacy was in worst condition. With the advent of British rule, East India company made efforts for education but did not make any serious and significant efforts for women's education, they of course! support 'Zenana' system.

The contribution which really matter actually given by the pioneering work of foreigners and of missionaries. Among the Indians we can mention the names of Raja Ram Mohan Roy and Pandit Ishwar Chandra Vidyasagar.

Indian women influenced with the western education. Even the British education system made considerable impact on Indian

Muslims specially under the leadership of Sir Syed Ahmed Khan and his associates.

However, the noticeable improvement and expansion of girls education has been steadily and phenomenal since independence. After independence rate of growth in women's education is high comparatively to men's education. But with rapid increase in population gap of education between men and women continued to be widen.

Independence India realized the need to uplift women's position and status in society. Not only in India, but the position of women was not good enough all over the world. So, all over the world education is regarded as one of the most significant weapon to improve the status of women. India as a member of UNESCO, introduced a long term massive "Five year plans for women's education. Change through formalised education is a long term process. We can not get results immediately as we had 150 million adult women scattered throughout India. In 1901, the female literacy rate was 0.69 per cent and in 1971, the rate increased to 18.4 per cent. The number of illiterate women has also increased from 161.9 million in 1950–51 to 215.3 million in 1970-71.

A National committee on women's education (1958–59) was set up by the Government of India in the ministry of education. This committee was appointed to examine the role of education in women's development whether working successfully or not. And then a number of committees were formed to keep eagle's eye watch on women's education. The committee on differentiation of curricula between boys and girls (1962), Bhaktavatsalam Committee (1963). In 1964–66 Kothari education commission also came towards eqalization of education, and higher education enrolment.

The National Education Policy (1967-68) emphasised women's education. The year of 1976, declared as "Women's Education Year" because of development.

The National Education Policy steadily contributing towards women education. A nation's welfare depend upon its educational system. Educated men and women make their world better.

"It is the educated nations that are the civilised nations, and it is the civilised nations that rule the world"[29].

Though there is a tremendous increase in school and college going number of girls, there is a great lag between boys and girls.

Education is the only key which open the door of life for women and men in the society, and education appears to be an equally powerful factor in making women modern in attitudes and create a happier society with a higher standard of life.

Today, the role of women is not confined to the kitchen and house keeping. But today, the term. "Role of women, is much broader...." Women have entered the various professions. Education has more effect on women's employment in urban areas than in rurals. Educated women had a significant effect on their attitude family size and marriage age. Women who are educated bring up their children better. Thus, women's status has changed, but not fully, it is still changing.

Women are still largely brought up in a tradition of subordination and inferiority of course! Women are aware about the given rights but still the society is unable to accept and recognise the double role of women. The problem of illiteracy among the rural women, and S.C., S.T. women is quite high. Variety of factors are responsible for female illiteracy, such as, cultural, economic, sociological, anthropological, geographical etc. First, is the reluctance to give girls and women freedom and keep them in economic subjection. Second, early marriage not given the chance of education. Girls are considered as a burden on their parents until they were married. The custom of marriage is deeply rooted in that way, that first the question of education is hardly thought of, and where few consider education as a marriage qualification. Like, graduation is, now-a-days, necessary for marriage. Some women students came to college without definite aim.

Thirdly, parents do not want to spend money on daughters education. Some prefer to give less education to the girls and this attitude is very common among parents of both rural and urban areas. Very few who mostly belong to high and educated family get the opportunity of high education.

When we study Education Pattern of women we found that lots of imbalances inequalities are in our country. Like, illiteracy among rural is high and urban is low. In advanced and high class rate of literacy is high where among backward class literacy is low. Christians are marked by high literacy rates while Muslims or S.C., S.T have low.

Statewise education in disparities exist. State such as Maharashtra, Karnataka, Andhra Pradesh, U.P., Himachal Pradesh, Assam have achieved higher rate and Rajasthan, Bihar, Madhya Pradesh marked low literacy rate.

Now, at last instead of eliminate total illiteracy, new inequality formed, i.e. literate, illiterate, high literate. And one more inequality which formed i.e. boys school and girls school.

Separate institution for education according gender is not desirable as per according to psychological and financial view point. Instead of open separate educational institution for boys and girls, one should provide integrated facilities in one building. And when women will go out to work we would not be able to provide separate working places as per according to gender.

"The University Education Commission (1949) has rightly remarked:

"There can not be any educated people without educated women. If general education had to be limited to men and women, that opportunity should be given to women, for them it would more surely be passed on to the next generations"[30].

This is education, which make us aware about our rights, duties, morals, and courage to do something and to attain some goal in our life. All else is half education.

"Lacordaire spoke wisdom when he said:" you have written upon the monuments of your city the words, Liberty, Equality, Fraternity. Above Liberty write Humanity, above Equality write Service. Above the immemorial creeds of your rights inscribe the divine creed of your duties"[31].

There are welcome examples. But they are not nearly enough. We need all those with the power to change things to come together in an alliance for girl education: governments, voluntary progressive groups and above all, local communities schools and families. That is why this spring, the United Nations is launching a new global initiative to educate girls.

"India fails in its endeavours to provide universal primary education despite half-a century of elected governments, says the UNDP and quotes the findings of a survey that 30 per cent of all children aged 6 to 14 years about 59 million boys and girls are out of school. It reveals the all round failure of parents and teachers, politicians and the media, none of whom has fulfilled its role. The survey, it adds, shows that 12 per cent of primary schools had only one teacher, 58 per cent schools had two rooms, 60 per cent had a leaking roof and only 25 per cent teachers were found teaching while the remaining were either absent or engaged in other activities. The country's constitution, it points out, has failed to make mandatory primary education a right for all citizens. The report also says that resources are not a critical constraint since countries with similar constraints, such as China, have legal guarantees for this right"[32].

CONSTITUTIONAL PROVISIONS REGARDING WOMEN

Women's status in the Indian society is the typical example of this gap between the position and roles given to them by the constitution and the laws and those imposed on them by social traditions.

British Government did not interfere much with Hindu and Muslim law, this policy of non-intervention in social and religious matter perpetuated multiple system in socio-economic society, led to stagnation and hardening differences between the various religious communities and even within the sub-sections of the communities.

The process of social reform has been started in the nineteenth century, the most vital achievement being the law against the practice of sati.

The revolution started with the strengthening of the national movement and the untiring efforts of Mahatma Gandhi; a demand for major changes in law and for removing the legal inferiority of women and abolishing the discrimination against them in matters like marriage, divorce, inheritance or guardianship of children which affected their life and personality.

Reform of law has been initiated even before independence although, conservative society was not ready to accept laws. But, of course, serve some useful purpose. Forming of legislation alone can not change the society, specially when educated people contribute unashamedly towards social evil. Making of laws is not enough, practising of law is very important.

There is no doubt that constitution contemplates a social revolution, brought about through the use of law as an instrument of directed social change. The attainment of equality of status for women was one of the specific objectives, which is implicit in the Preamble, Fundamental Rights and the Directive Principles of State Policy.

Marriage Legislation

In traditional India, polygamy was prevalent in the country, has been declining in the last few decades. Monogamy has been accepted in the laws for Christians, Hindus, Parsees and Jews, Muslims remained unaffected by this changing trend towards monogamy, and are still practising polygamy. Full equality of the sexes is hardly possible in legal system which permits polygamy as a social system which tolerates it.

And enforcement of provision against bigamy under the Hindu Marriage Act, bigamy has been an offence for the Hindu and the second marriage is void in law.

Registration of marriages is compulsory among Parsees and Christians and for all marriages performed under the Special Marriage Act, 1954. Section 16 of this act permits registration of marriages celebrated under other laws. This is the most effective way to check out child and bigamous marriage, and on the bias of reliable proof ensure legitimacy and inheritance right of children.

Age of Marriage

'Age of marriage' is one of the most important factor which affects women development. The disastrous effects of child marriages persuaded social reformers to restrain them by legislation. The Civil Marriage Act, 1872, fixed the minimum age of marriage at 14. The Child Marriage Restraint Act, 1929 fixed the minimum age for marriage for males at 18 and for females at 14 (which was later amended to 15). One of the Special Marriage Act 1954, fixes the minimum age at 21 and 18 for males and females respectively.

Remarriage and Widow Marriage

Hindu Widow Remarriage Act guaranteeing the right to remarriage Hindu women.

Dowry: The Dowry Prohibition Act, 1961 (Sec–6) requires that dowry amount should be referred to the bride within the period of 1 year from the celebration of marriage.

MTP Act and Maternity Benefit Act, 1961

The termination of pregnancy act, the maternity benefit acts some of the measures of relief to all women. Under the Criminal Law Act, 1983 women can not be punished for the offence of adultery committed by her.

Inter-caste marriage is permissible under the Hindu Marriage Validating Act, 1949 and in the Hindu Marriage Act, 1955.

In 1984, Government grant permission on the demand of women to establish family court to solve quickly matrimonial disputes.

Divorce: Monogamous marriage without the right of divorce causes great hardship to both parties. Divorce usually occur by mutual consent, by the husband, and by the deeds. Under customary law there is no waiting period after divorce for remarriage.

The Hindu Marriage Act, 1955, permits divorce to both parties for (a) living in adultery; (b) conversion; (c) insanity; (d) communicable leprosy; (e) venereal disease; (f) renunciation; (g) disappearance for seven years and more; (h) failure to resume co-habitation for two years after a decree of judicial separation; and (i) failure to comply with a decree for restitution of conjugal rights. A wife has two additional grounds (1) if the husband has another living life; and (2) If he has been guilty of rape, sodomy, or bestiality.

In Muslim, Law, husband has absolute and unlimited right to repudiate the marriage at his will, but Muslim wife has no such right. This is very unilateral right of divorce by husband. By, Maliki and Shafi schools the dissolution of Muslim Marriages Act 1939, recognizes the wife's right to divorce on the following bias:

1. Husbands disappearance for four year;
2. Neglect and failure to provide maintenance for two years;
3. Husband's imprisonment for seven years or more;
4. Failure to perform marital obligations for 3 years;
5. Impotency;
6. Insanity, leprosy, venereal disease;
7. Option of puberty;
8. Cruelty or any other ground recognized as valid for divorce under Muslim law.

Because of husband's unilateral right to divorce, life of Muslim women is full of insecurity, fear and inferiority.

The Parsee Marriage and Divorce Act, 1936 adds special right of wife to obtain divorce, in case if she has been compelled by her husband into prostitution.

Special Marriage Act, 1954, under this act, special feature of divorce by mutual consent.

Maintenance: The new criminal procedure code, 1974 continues to reflect the old attitude to women and give the right to demand maintenance to divorced wife. This obligation has been only for men.

Under Hindu Marriage Act, 1955, wife can claim maintenance from her husband is not living with her and also after divorce as per the orders of the court. The right is absolute but lost if the wife becomes unchaste.

In Muslim law, no right to maintenance beyond three months for divorced women.

The Indian Divorce Act 1869, which governs christians, concede the right only to women. The same right of maintenance for Parsees.

Inheritance: In pre-independence India women had only some rights, specially relate to life interest and not full ownership.

The Hindu Succession Act 1956, made some radical changes, given the right of succession equal to that of male heirs. Actually now women is entitled to more property benefits than men because now women take share in her husband's property and as a daughter in her father's property. And women is not bound to discharge the debts of her father as the son is bound under Hindu law.

Muslim law, while recognizing the rights of women to inherit, discriminates between male and female heirs of the same degree. The share of latter being half that of the former.

IMPACT OF CONSTITUTIONAL LAWS

Where educated mass is living they are aware and utilizing their rights. On the other hand, some educated mass are aware but they are reluctant to change their traditions. In traditional families still major goal for girls in marriage not their career.

There are large numbers of women who were ignorant about their rights of inheritance and so conditioned that they opposed the ideas of sisters depriving brothers of the property.

Dowry is still in practice. Of course! Now-a-days bride's are not burnt alive for dowry. In Rajasthan, people of villages like, Railmagra violating Child Marriage Restraint Act.

Where people are not educated and are not able to use their rights, That's o.k. but, thoroughly study shows that women, who are educated graduates are not aware of the laws related to their own position.

However, large mass of Indian women still uneducated so they are unconscious of all those laws made for them and living destitute and neglected life.

It is very necessary that people should be well acquainted with these laws, only in this way they may be benefited by them. Education has some connection with awareness of laws. So, only proper and fruitful education can play vital role and make women understand and aware about those rights which especially formed for them.

WOMEN PARTICIPATION IN POLITICS

Democratic and secular India endeavours to provide the necessary conditions for greater participation of women in all spheres of life. Equality of opportunity is guaranteed, and discrimination on grounds of sex, language, region, class or creed is prohibited. Yet, in reality, women's participation in decision-making (politics) at all levels—national to local is low.

There is now, however, an acceptance that women's participation in decision-making in large enough number at every level is needed. The election manifestos of the polities' parties accept that women constitute a backward segment of the society to whom special privileges have to be granted to bring them at par with men.

"The early twentieth century saw the birth of women's organisations and the beginning of the demand for political rights. In 1917, a deputation of Indian women led by Shrimati Sarojini Naidu presented to the British parliament a demand for the enfranchisement of women on the basis of equality with men. The Reforms Act of 1921 extended the franchise only to wives who had property and education. The foreign rulers could not believe that Indian society would ever regard women as equal partners of men. Nor did they regard women as a separate political force.

In 1930, a meeting of representative women's organisations demanded immediate acceptance of adult franchise without sex discrimination. Though rejected by the government, the Karachi session of the Indian National Congress in 1931 accepted the demand and committed itself to women's political equality, regardless of their status and qualifications"[33].

Participation of women is an integral part of democratic process and strengthening the quality of civic life. As they are half the population, women must be in decision making in all socio-economic and political organisations.

Passing of legislations and given political equality was not quite enough. The women involved in politics mostly come from the economic and political elite of states and enter the representative process, more because of support within a party rather than through work among the people. Inspite of increase in political participation, women's ability to produce impact on the political decision-making process has been negligible.

Obstacles which do not let women participate fully need to be identified and removed. Often structures and social norms are barriers, and stem from social conditions which inhibits women from aspiring to decision making positions. Government and Non-Governmental interventions should facilitate and promote women's participation in decision-making. Emancipation of women and their increased participation in governance would continue to remain a dream if the two crucial issues of literacy and economic independence are not adequately addressed.

Effective participation of women in local as well as national government will not only improve the quality and alter the style of governance, keeping it in tune with the ground realities but will also be reflective of the needs of both women and men.

REASONS FOR LOW PARTICIPATION

"Down the ages women have always been treated as subordinate to men in every aspect of life. Her identify was always attached to that of her father, husband or son, i.e. she was given a status in accordance with that of her male partner.

With the passage of time and reform movements and the growth of literacy, people came to realize that the development of society ultimately lies in the development and empowerment of women. Hence, many economic and social changes were introduced for women's upliftment, however, the domain of politics was kept out of their reach. It is not that women in the past have not contribute substantially in politics, but because of their secondary status and low esteem, most of them were denied entry in political decision-making and at higher level of party.

After independence, women alongwith men were given the right to vote. The idea behind this was to accord equal status to women vis-a-vis men and make them politically more aware and active, however, the status of women still remains low.

Although more women are entering politics, particularly in villages, the middle class urban women are still negatively inclined to enter politics. Majority of women is not prepared to participate in politics beyond voting. Family responsibility, women's pre-occupation in the struggle to survive and the prevalence of violence and the role of money power in elections and women's lack of control or access over monetary resources are reported to be the main constraints.

In order to ensure their participation in politics, most women make use of their upper caste lineage and political connection, as widow's daughters, wives or daughters-in-law of well-known politicians. This has been possible because of the view that women are mostly silent and ineffective as participants. Further, these women take a stand in favour of women only, if and when it would not conflict with their party's stand on the issue and be branded as only women's leaders. However, we do see some exceptions to this rule among those who always uphold women's cause and/or take a stand according to their personal convictions. For women elected members to be constantly informed about women's needs it is essential for them to have frequent dialogue with women leaders"[34].

"Since Independence, due to exercise of their franchise, Indian women have been exposed to the political processes and are showing increasing awareness about not only lack of rights but also their utility. A majority of illiterate rural women are also politically sensitive and aware of the various issues confronting them. Women get easily mobilised in the political processes by the political parties who approach women very often for party issues and for short-term goals of winning elections, but not for long-term goals of bringing about social changes and gender equality in political power-sharing.

In all the elections held since independence, women had the voting rights and the pattern of participation by women in the national elections is given in table 2.2.

Table 2.2. Pattern of Participation by Women in National Elections

Election Year	Voting % of men	Voting % of women	Total seats contested by women	Seats won by women	% Seats won of contested seats	Total seats	% of women members
1952	53.00	37.10	51	23	45.09	499	4.40
1957	56.00	38.77	70	27	38.57	500	5.40
1962	62.10	46.63	68	35	51.47	503	6.70
1967	66.70	55.48	66	31	48.43	523	5.90
1971	69.70	49.15	86	22	27.50	521	4.20
1977	65.62	54.96	70	19	25.70	544	3.40
1980	57.69	51.22	142	28	19.70	544	5.14

The percentage of seats won against the seats contested is showing a declining trend only because the number of women contesting elections has increased sharply. However, it may be seen that voting for women in all tiers of government has always been a feature of the Indian polity since 1947. Due to the paternalistic family and male dominated political structures which do not provide space for women in decision-making bodies women constituted 3.1% of the total contestants in 1996 election and did not occupy more than 6-10% of the total seats in the State Legislative Assemblies and Parliament"[35].

WOMEN PARTICIPATION IN RAJYA SABHA AND LOK SABHA (NATIONAL ASSEMBLY)

Article 79 of Indian Constitution Defines

"There shall be a Parliament for the Union, which shall consist of the President and two houses, the Council of States (Rajya Sabha) and the House of People (Lok Sabha)."

Article 80 of Indian Constitution Defines

The Council of States shall consist of not more than 238 elected representatives of States and Union Territories and 12 members to be nominated by the President."

Article 81 of Indian Constitution Defines

The House of People shall consist of not more than 500 members chosen by direct election from territorial constituencies in States and not more than 25 members to represent Union Territories."

Later amendment in 1973 increased the upper limit of elective seats in the Lok Sabha from 525 to 545 and in Rajya Sabha seat increased from 240 to 244.

The number of women contestants in parliamentary elections has not increased significantly over the years. Political parties are still reluctant to field women candidates.

WOMEN PARTICIPATION IN RAJYA SABHA

The Constitution of India came into effect on 26th January 1950. In India first general election held in 1952. As women's membership in the Rajya Sabha is very low against the male membership is concerned.

Even in the Rajay Sabha, where there is indirect election and nomination there has been a low representation of women (table 2.3).

The number of women members of Rajya Sabha were 15 (6.9%) in 1952 which has been reached upto 18 (7.3%) in 1998.

Table 2.3. Women's Representation in the Rajya Sabha (Upper House)

Year	Total seats	No. of women	% of women
1952	216	15	6.9
1954	219	17	7.8
1956	232	20	8.6
1958	232	22	9.5
1960	236	24	10.2
1964	238	21	8.8
1966	240	23	9.6
1968	240	22	9.2
1970	240	14	5.8
1972	243	18	7.4
1974	243	17	7.0
1976	244	24	9.8
1977	244	24	10.2
1978	244	23	9.6
1982	244	24	10.2
1986	244	28	11.4
1990	245	24	9.7
1991	245	38	15.5
1992	245	17	6.9
1994	245	20	8.1
1996	245	18	7.3
1997	245	18	7.3
1998	245	18	7.3

Source: 1. Bhatt, Shanta, Women, Parliamentarians of India, Shiva Publishers, Udaipur, p 55.

2. Statistical Abstracts, 1998.

WOMEN PARTICIPATION IN LOK SABHA

Before first General Election there were only seven women members in the House and there were 225 men i the provisional parliament of 1950.

The table 2.4 shows the number of women members and the percentage of women members elected to Lok Sabha. The number of women member of Lok Sabha were 14 (2.8%) in 1952, which has been increased up to 49 (9.02%) in 1999.

Table 2.4. Women's Representation in Lok Sabha (Lower House)

Term of Lok Sabha	Total seats	No. of women member	% of women
1952-57	489	14	2.8
1957-62	494	18	3.6
1962-67	494	30	6.0
1967-71	520	31	6.0
1971-77	520	20	3.8
.1977-80	542	19	3.5
1980-84*	529	28	5.3
1984-89	542	42	7.7
1989-91**	523	23	4.4
1991**	536	39	7.2
1996	542	40	7.3
1998	543	43	7.9
1999	543	49	9.02

Source: Election Commission of India.

* Elections were not held in 12 constituencies in Assam and in Meghalaya.

** Elections were not held in J & K and Punjab. Figures include women elected from Punjab during the by-elections in 1992.

ROLE OF WOMEN IN STATE LEGISLATURE

The table 2.5 shows women's representation in state legislature. The situation it appears has not improved much since the 1950's.

Table 2.5. Representation of Women in State Legislatures

State	Year	Total	Women
Assam	1996	122	6
Haryana	1999	90	4
J & K	1996	87	2
Himachal Pradesh	1998	68	6
Gujarat	1998	182	4
Kerala	1996	140	13
Meghalaya	1998	60	3
Punjab	1997	117	7
Pondicherry	1996	30	1
NCT Delhi	1998	70	9
Nagaland	1998	60	0
Madhya Pradesh	1998	320	26
Tamil Nadu	1996	234	9
Tripura	1998	60	2
Uttar Pradesh	1996	424	20
West Bengal	1996	294	20
Bihar	1999	324	19
Maharashtra	1995	288	11
Arunachal Pradesh	1995	60	1
Manipur	1999	60	1
Orissa	1999	147	13
Rajasthan	1998	200	14

Source: Election Commission of India.

ROLE OF WOMEN IN RAJASTHAN STATE ASSEMBLY

Area wise, Rajasthan is the largest state having area 3,42,239, Sq. km. The legislature is unicameral the legislative assembly. The state is divided into 30 districts, 90 sub-districts and 211 tehsils. At present total Vidhan Sabha seats are 200.

Table 2.6 depicts the number of women members in the Rajasthan State Assembly.

Table 2.6. Number of Women Members in the Rajasthan State Assembly (1952-1999)

Year	Elected women
1952	0
1957	9
1962	8
1967	6
1972	13
1977	8
1980	10
1985	17
1990	11
1993	9
1999	14

Source: Rajasthan Patrika, 8th Dec. 1999. p. 3 of "Patrika Parivar" by Prof. Asopa, Sheel K.

In 1952, 4 women contestants stand in the general election but not a single woman won, because society was not ready to elect women contestants. In 1985, 17 women members were elected in Vidhan Sabha. That was the record achievement for women during 1952 to 1999.

In 1999, only 14 (7%) women members were elected in 200 member State Assembly. It is very low when government are passing 33% reservation of women in Parliament and State Assembly.

73RD AND 74TH AMENDMENT TO CONSTITUTION OF INDIA—NEW ERA IN THE DEMOCRATIC PROCESS

"Since 1959, the representation of women at grassroots level institutions of governance has been through several ups and downs and strategies such as nominations and limited quotas have been tried by states.

After the 73rd Constitutional Amendment Act of 1993 all State Legislatures have amended their respective legislation's to conform to the Constitutional Amendment and introduced a three-tier system of local governance from the village to the district level. Each Panchayat now has a uniform five year term and elections are expected to be held regularly to constitute new bodies before the term expires. In the event of dissolution, elections are to be held within six months. In all, panchayats, seats are to be reserved for Scheduled Castes and Scheduled Tribes in proportion to their numbers in the populations. One-third of chair-persons of panchayat at all levels are to be women.

The 74th Constitutional Amendment Act extends similar provisions as the 73rd Amendment to the urban Local Bodies, which are now categorised as Municipal Corporations, Municipal Councils and Nagar Panchayats. It is equally significant in the political empowerment process of women of the country as are third of the seats of elected representatives are reserved in the local bodies.

Women are governing after being elected through a democratic process of universal adult franchise, multiparty system and mandatory elections as regular intervals. They are a part of the local Government in their area, at the village, town, city or a larger District level".[36]

Table 2.7 shows state-wise participation of women in Panchayati Raj institution.

In states where elections have been held the results have been extremely encouraging. In the States of West Bengal and Karnataka women have gained more than the number of seats reserved for them. In other states, the reserved quota has been filled. The overwhelming response has been unprecedented in the history of the country.

Table 2.7. Women in Panchayati Raj Institution

State	Year	Gram Panchayat (Village)			Panchayat Samities (Block)			Zilla Parishad (District)		
		No. of Gram Panchayat (GP)	Total No. of Members	No. of Women Members	No. of Panchayat Samitis	Total No. of Members	No. of Women Members	No. of Zilla Parishad (ZP)	Total No. of Members	No. of Women Members
Gujarat	1995	13256	60052	19936* (31.1)	182	3765	1275 (33.84)	19	761	254 (33.38)
Haryana	1994	5958	54159	17928 (33.10)	110	2418	807 (33.37)	16	303	101 (33.33)
Karnataka	1993	5641	80627	37689 (46.74)	175	3340	1343 (40.2)	20	919	335 (36.4)
Kerala**	1995	990	10700	3878 (36.2)	152	1543	565 (36.6)	14	300	104 (34.6)
Madhya Pradesh	1994	30922	443429	147809 (33.33)	459	9097	2991 (32.88)	45	942	315 (33.44)
Punjab	1993	11596	60584	8776 (14.49)	136	24024	8222 (34.22)	14	273	89 (32.60)
Rajasthan	1995	9189	103712	36722 (35.4)	237	5231	1738 (33.23)	31	997	331 (33.20)
Tripura	1994	525	5427	1809 (33.33)	16	196	67 (34.18)	3	70	24 (34.29)
West Bengal	1993	3223	61011	21489 (35.22)	328	9543	3182 (33.66)	16	656	224 (34.15)

Figures in brackets are percentages.

Source: Institute of Social Science, PRIs Data Centre, New Delhi.
The Constitutional Amendment (73rd and 74th) is applicable only for 21 States. Four States are exempted.
There are about one million elected women members in Panchayats and Municipalities in India.

"I am convinced that women in their way of working in politics always seek alternative solutions rather than struggle for power."[37]

ROLE OF NATIONAL COMMISSION FOR WOMEN FOR EMPOWERMENT OF WOMEN

"The National Commission for Women (NCW) was set up as a statutory body in January 1992 under the National Commission for Women Act, 1990 (Act no. 20 of 1990 of Government of India) to review the constitutional and legal safeguards for women; recommend remedial legislative measures, facilitate redress grievances and advice the Government on all policy matter affecting women.

1. **The Mandate of the Commission:** Section 10 of the Act:

(a) Investigate and examine all matters relating to the safeguards provided for women under the Constitution and other laws;

(b) Present to the Central Government, annually and at such other times as the Commission may deem fit, reports upon the working of those safeguards;

(c) Make recommendation for the effective implementation of safeguards for improving the conditions of women by the Union or any State;

(d) Review, from time to time, the existing provisions for Constitution and other laws affecting women and recommend amendments, (thereto) so as to suggest remedial legislative measures to meet any lacunae, inadequacies or shortcomings in such legislation;

(e) Take up cases of violation of the provision of the constitution and other laws relating to women with the appropriate authorities;

(f) Look into complaints and take *suo moto* notice of matters relating to:

I. Deprivation of women's right;

II. Non-implementation of laws enacted to provide protection to women and also to achieve the objective of equality and development;

III. Non-compliance of policy decision, guidelines or instructions aimed at mitigating hardship and ensuring welfare and providing relief to women, and take up the issues arising out of such matters with appropriate authorities;

(g) Call for special studies or investigation into specific problems or situation arising out of discrimination and atrocities against women and identify the constraints so as to recommend strategies for their removal;

(h) Undertake promotional and educational research so as to suggest ways of ensuring due representation of women in all spheres and identify factors responsible or impeding their advancement, such as, lack of access to housing and basic services, inadequate support services and technologies for reducing drudgery and occupational health hazards and for increasing their productivity.

(i) Participate and advice on the planing process of socio-economic development of women.

(j) Evaluate the progress of the development of women under the Union and any State.

(k) Inspect or cause to be inspected a jail, remand home, women's institution or other place of custody where women are kept as prisoners or otherwise, and take up with the concerned authorities for remedial action, if found necessary.

(l) Fund litigation involving issues affecting a large body of women.

(m) Make periodical reports to the government on any matter pertaining to women and in particular various difficulties in which women toil.

(*n*) Any other matter, which may be referred to it by the Central Government.

2. The Central Government shall cause all the reports referred to in clause (b) to be laid before each House of Parliament along with a memorandum explaining the action taken or proposed to be taken on recommendations relating to the Union and the reasons for the non-acceptance, if any, of any of such recommendation.

3. Where any such report or any part thereof relates to any matter with which any State Government is concerned, the Commission shall forward a copy of such report or part of such State Government who shall cause it to be laid before the Legislature of the State along with a memorandum explaining the action taken or proposed to be taken on the recommendations relating to the State and the reasons for the non acceptance, if any, of any of such recommendations.

4. The Commission shall, while investigating any matter referred in clause (a) or sub-clause (i) of clause (f) of sub-section (I), have all the powers of a civil court trying a suit, and in particular in respect of the following matters, namely;

   (*a*) Summoning and enforcing the attendance of any person from any part of India and examining him under oath;

   (*b*) Requiring the discovery and production of any document;

   (*c*) Receiving evidence on affidavits;

   (d) Requisitioning any public record or copy thereof from any court or office;

   (*e*) Issuing commissions for the examination of witnesses and documents;

   (*f*) Any other matters which may be prescribed.

STATE COMMISSIONS FOR WOMEN

The State Commission for Women have been setup in Andhra Pradesh, Assam, Delhi, Goa, Haryana, Himachal Pradesh, Karnataka, Kerala, Madhya Pradesh, Mizoram, Maharashtra, Orissa, Punjab, Rajasthan, Tamil Nadu, Tripura, West Bengal and Jammu and Kashmir and networking with them in an important methodology adopted by the NCW.

The Commission found many legal provisions contrary to the concept of women's empowerment and suggested following legal amendments to:

- Criminal Procedure Code, 1973
- Indian Penal Code, 1860
- Indian Evidence Act, 1872
- Dowry Prohibition Act, 1961
- Commission of Sati (Prevention) Act, 1987
- Hindu Marriage Act, 1955
- Child Marriage Restraint Act, 1929
- Indecent Representation of Women (Prohibition) Act, 1986
- Immoral Traffic (Prevention) Act, 1956 (for elimination of child prostitution and devising a comprehensive package for rehabilitation)
- Medical Termination of Pregnancy Act, 1971
- Family Courts Act, 1984
- Foreign Marriage Act, 1969
- Guardians and Wards Act, 1890
- Indian Succession Act, 1925
- Representation of the People Act, 1951

Bills

- The Marriage Bill, 1994
- The Domestic Violence to Women (Prevention) Bill, 1994

- The Orphan and Destitute Children (Adoption) Bill, 1994
- The Criminal Laws (Amendments) Bill, 1994, (with reference to child rape)
- The Criminal Laws (Amendments) Ordinance, 1996
- The Prevention of Barbarous and Beastly Cruelty against Women Bill, 1995
- The Constitution (Eighty-first amendment) Bill, 1996.

Other than these suggested amendments, the Commission has intervened in some important court matters, like Bhateri Gang Rape Case (Rajasthan), Capital Punishment/Death Penalty (Ramshree's Case), Obscenity Cases against Outdated Customs and Traditions: Maimon Baskari's Nuh (Haryana) Case and Divorced Muslim Women's Entitlement to Maintenance beyond the Iddat Period etc.

The Commission has committed itself for the realisation of the empowerment of women and has tirelessly worked for the purpose through the above-mentioned infrastructure and activities. The Commission always appreciated positive efforts made by various agencies of the civil society to make Indian women's movement successful and invites experts on various issue related to the empowerment of the women. The importance of the efforts of the NGOs in this process is greatly acknowledged by the NCW in its Report on the "Partnership in Action: National Consultation with Voluntary Organisations" (1999). It says, "Women's movement in India is essentially a voluntary effort initiated, organised and directed by NGOs. The NCW is, in fact, the result of sustained campaign over a period by NGOs or a national level organisation to protect and promote the interests of women. This partnership in action can be traced to many positive development in the realm of women's development and gender equality and gender justice". The commission also welcomes and encourages the efforts made by the individuals, social activists, academicians and many more in the process of women's empowerment.

Whereas the role of women in the changed domestic and global perspective has been considered most important to the political life of our society it is the area of socio-economic equality, liberty and decision making where they have to carve out a meaningful space for themselves. Though constitutional safeguards and progressive legal enactment have endowed jurisdictional equality but right to equal status and opportunities in education, law and political participation influencing the key decisions having serious imprints on socio-economic structures have been still a distant dream which needs urgent attention. We find that majority of the womenfolk, particularly in the rural India, are operating in a closed social system where they are subordinate to their male counterparts in almost every sphere of their lives and are left with no tasks other than the kitchen affairs to display their skills.

It is now widely accepted that assertion for by women for their rights and their admissions by the civil society is of utmost importance for the overall development of democratic fabric of our society. In fact political equality is meaningless where the mass of the population from poverty, continuous threats of starvation, lack of health and inequality of class, status and power. It is more so in the case of women who suffer from another dimension of inequality, namely, the weight of traditional attitudes that regard them as physically and socially inferior to men.

Women's participation in the political process is central to their struggle against oppression. Different aspects of women liberation depend on their articulation to express their demands and aspirations, politically associating themselves with the larger mass movements of liberation, equality, liberty and justice. There is almost every field where issues relating to women emancipation have to be addressed and it only through consistent organised political behaviour and action that they can achieve their objectives in the social, cultural, religious and economic fields; whether it is health, employment, education and training or demands for their rights, it is through collective endeavour that they can achieve their particular objectives.

Political participation, in India particularly by women, has been considered in the narrow sense with participating in the elections and casting their votes. Party politics is not the only expression of political participation. People's organisations and movements both at the grass-root level and macro level for transformation of society and women's liberation are to be amply recognised.

Associated with the above issues is the major concern for a dignified human life. Every individual must enjoy a dignified life not a subjugated or a subordinated nor a life that is appropriated by the male dominated social order. We must thrive for a society that should work for the dignity of the individual and every one should be so nurtured that he/she should have a respect for the human life and should cherish the christened goals of equity, liberty and fraternity in his/her life approach. This can be an ideal but does not seem unachievable if the entire society works collectively and consciously for the attainment of the same for years. This objective needs a serious introspection on the part of each individual and the entire structure of the social system to impart training towards that direction. This also demands certain commitments and more so in shedding down one's prejudices and inhibitions regarding gender, caste, colour, creed and religion etc.

The NCW is consistently endeavouring to develop a comprehensive methodological framework where Indian women's movement find itself associated with the larger mass movement for the social development that envision an empowered society with an empowered women as its inherent ingredient. It is urgently required from the actors of the civil society that women power should not be underestimated as a weaker section. Women are the vanguard of civilisation and its future. Mahatma Gandhi correctly pointed out that "to call women the weaker section is a libel; it is man's injustice to women. If by strength is meant brute strength, then indeed in women less brute than man. If by strength is meant moral power than a woman is immeasurably superior to man. Has she not greater intuition, is she not more self-sacrificing, has she not greater power of endurance, has she not greater courage? Without her, man could not be. If non-violence is the law of our being, the future is with women." (In Young India, 30th April 1930)[38].

References

1. Desai, N. and Krishnaraj M., *Women and Society in India,* Ajanta Publications Delhi, (1987).
2. *Simon Commission Report, Vol. 1*, p. 49.
3. Quoted O'Malley, L.S.S., Ed., *Modern India and the West*, p. 696.
4. Young India (17th October 1929), quoted in M.K. Gandhi, *The Role of Women* (Bombay, 1964), p. 71.
5. Muzumdar, Veena, *Emergence of Women's Question and Role of Women's Studies,* New Delhi, Centre for Women's Development Studies, 1985, p. 6.
6. *Shelter, Women in Urbal Governance,* World Habital Day Special Issue, A hudco-hsmi publication, October 2000. Vol. III, No. 4 pp. 4, 5.
7. *Ibid* pp. 17, 18, 67 and 68.
8. *Spurt in Crimes Against Women, Warns Report.* Times of India, New Delhi 24th Feb., 2000, p. 1.
9. *"Physical Abuse of Indian Women in Homes is Rampant: Survey"* Times of India, Friday, Feb. 25, 2000, p. 7.
10. *"India Yet to Honour Commitments to Women"* Times of India, New Delhi, Tuesday, March 14th, 2000 p. 10.
11. *Bihar Women are the Worst Sufferers,* The Sunday Times of India, New Delhi, July 16, 2000.
12. Times of India, Saturday, March 11, 2000, p. 9.
13. Rajasthan Patrika, 1 June, p. 14.
14. *Shelter, Op Cit,* pp 3-4.
15. *Woman Care Taking More Top Jobs but Income Gap Still Wide,* Times of India, June 23, 2000.
16. *"More Women will Get to the Top on the Glass Escalator"* The Sunday Times, 5 Feb. 2000.
17. *"Promote Women to Save Costs"* The Sunday Times of India, New Delhi, July 8, 2000. p. 5.
18. *Women in India Better Off, But Not Quite: U.N. Report,* Times of India, New Delhi, July 8, 2000, p. 5.

19. *Women's Contribution to Economic and Social Development* (1989), Mahajan V.S., Deep and Deep Publications p. 44.

20. *Shelter, Op. Cit*, pp 6-7.

21. *Women and Work, Changing Scenario in India* (1993), Sharma Alakh N. Singh, Seema B.R. Publishing Co., Delhi.

22. *Ibid.*

23. Chakravarty, A.K. *et al., Health Status of Rural Population, Sinur* as quoted by Bina Agarwal p, 46.

24. Jain Shashi, *Status and Role Perception of Middle Class Women* (1998), Puja Publishers.

25. *Ibid.*

26. Editor, The Sunday Times of India, New Delhi, Nov. 21, 1999, p. 6.

27. *Shelter, Op. Cit*, p. 51.

28. Mathur, I., *Change in Agrarian Society*, Print Well Publishers, 1987.

29. Wardia, A.R., *The Ethics of Feminism*, Asian Publications Service, 1977.

30. Siddiqui, Mujibul Hasan, 1993. *Women Education*.

31. Mrs. Colquhoun's, *The Vocation of Women*, p. 266.

32. *"UNDP's Kudos for India on Good Growth Records"*, The Times of India, New Delhi, June 30, 2000 p.1.

33. *Status of Women in India* (1975) ICSSR, Published by, Indian Council of Social Science Research, p. 103-104.

34. *Shelter, Op. Cit.*, p. 42, 48.

35. *Shelter Op. Cit.*, p. 42.

36. *Shelter Op. Cit.*, pp. 69 and 72.

37. Trautmann, Catherine, Mayor of Stasbourg, interviewed by Veronique Degraef, 1994.

38. *Shelter Op. Cit.*, pp. 32-38.

3 Demographic Profile of Women

DEMOGRAPHIC PROFILE OF WOMEN IN INDIA

Population explosion is a problem that has baffled the politicians, scientists, researchers ad the common men all over the world. The world population, which was at 5,800 millions in 1991, is estimated to rise to the level of 6,220 millions in 2000 and further to 8302 in 2025 A.D., were both China and India will continue to be the world's most populous countries. Population explosion has created a crisis which can spell social, ecological and economic disaster. Unless population growth is put under control, it will be impossible to provide basic amenities of life like food, clothing, shelter and health care facilities to the future generations.

India is in the continent of Asia. It is located in the southern part of the continent. To the western, eastern and southern part of our country lies a huge body of water.

India lies to the north of the equator between 8°4′ and 37°6′ north latitude and 68°7′ and 97°25′ east longitude. It is bounded on the south west by the Arabian sea and on the south east by the Bay of Bengal. On the north, Himalayan ranges kept India apart from the rest of Asia. The southern tip, Kanya Kumari is washed by the Indian ocean.

India is the seventh largest country in the world. India measures 3,214 km. From north to south and 2933 km. from east to west with a total land area of 3,287263 sq km. It has a land frontier of 15,200 km and a coast line of 7516.5 km. Andaman and Nicobar islands in the Bay of Bengal and Lakshadweep in the Arabian Sea are parts of India.

India shares its political borders with Pakistan and Afghanistan on the west and Bangladesh and Burma on the east. The northern boundary is made up of the Sinkiang province of China, Tibet, Nepal and Bhutan.

India consist of 28 States. 6 Union Territories and 1 National Capital Territory.

POPULATION GROWTH IN INDIA

India has 16.7 per cent of the world's population on 2.4 per cent of the land area. Thus every sixth person now in the world is an Indian and above all, at the rate we are growing, by the year 2011 we will have the questionable privilege of being the most populous nation on the planet having at last overtaken our neighbour China. According to an estimate, 17 million people every year added to Indian population, which is equal to the population of Australia.

The population growth of scenario can be visualised from table 3.1. The first all India census, though not synchronously taken, was completed in 1872. Since 1881 the census in India has been taken regularly after every 10 year. The latest in 1991 marked the completion of 120 years of decennial census in the country.

According to the 2001 census, the total population of India was 127015247, i.e. 10270 crores consisting of 53.12 crores males and 49.57 crore females.

Population growth of India, prior to 1921 was not only slow but also sporadic. In 1891, population of India was only 236 millions. The population increased by 15 million during 1891 to 1921. Since the year 1921 the population grew at an accelerated as well as progressive rate. The year 1921 is regarded as the year of 'great divide' in the demographic history of India.

Table 3.1. **Population Growth in India**

(In lacs)

Year	Population	Increase over the decade	
		Pure	Percentage
1901	2384	—	—
1911	2521	+137	+5.75
1921	2513	–008	–0.32
1931	2790	+277	+11.21
1941	3187	+397	+14.23
1951	3611	+424	+13.30
1961	4392	+781	+21.63
1971	5473	+1082	+24.64
1981	6852	+1378	+25.11
1991	8463	+1611	+23.51
2001	10270	+1807	+21.35

Source: Census of India, 1991.

The rate of population explosion has slightly fallen from the last one decade. Growth rate for the decade 1971–81 was 25.17% which came down to 23.51 per cent. This slight fall in the growth rate was the result of increasing adoption of family planning measures by the married couples since last two decades. Table shows that Indian population has risen to more than two and a half time the population of 1901. According to the Census of India 1991, total Indian population was 8463.03 lacs, out of 6287 lacs lived in rural areas and 2176 lacs lived in urban areas. These figures reveal that nearly three fourth of the Indian population still lives in villages i.e. rural areas, where population growth rate is very high as compared to urban areas.

According to 1991 census (Table 3.2), in the country, the rural sector has 3043.70 lacs females, whereas 1027.02 lacs females have been recorded in the urban areas. In other words,

Table 3.2. Gender-wise and Area-wise Distribution of Population in India

(Figures in lacs)

Census year	Rural			Urban			Total		
	Males	Females	Total	Males	Females	Total	Males	Females	Total
1901			2125.44			258.52	1207.91 (50.72%)	1173.59 (49.28%)	2381.50 (100%)
1911			2261.52			259.41	1283.85 (50.93%)	1237.08 (49.07%)	2520.93 (100%)
1921			2232.35			280.86	1285.46 (51.15%)	1227.75 (48.85%)	2513.21 (100%)
1931			2455.21			-334.56	1429.30 (51.28%	1357.89 (48.72%)	2787.19 (100%)
1941			2745.07			-441.53	1636.85 (51.41%)	1546.90 (48.59%)	3183.75 (100%)
1951			2986.44			624.44	1855.28 (51.38%)	1755.60 (48.62%)	3610.88 (100%)

(Contd...)

(Figures in lacs)

Census year	Rural			Urban			Total		
	Males	Females	Total	Males	Females	Total	Males	Females	Total
1961	1835.04	1767.94	3602.98	427.89	361.47	789.36	2262.93	2129.42	4392.35
	(50.93%)	(49.07%)	(100%)	(54.21%)	(45.79%)	(100%)	(51.52%)	(48.48%)	(100%)
1971	2247.29	2138.51	4385.80	585.23	502.64	1087.87	2832.52	2641.15	5473.67
	(51.24%)	(48.76%)	(100%)	(53.80%)	(46.20%)	(100%)	(51.75%)	(48.25%)	(100%)
1981	2693.64	2560.93	5254.57	850.34	746.93	1597.27	3543.98	3307.86	6851.85
	(51.26%)	(48.74%)	(100%)	(53.24%)	(46.76%)	(100%)	(51.72%)	(48.28%)	(100%)
1991	3243.22	3043.70	6286.92	1149.09	1027.02	2176.11	4392.31	4070.72	8463.03
	(51.59%)	(48.41%)	(100%)	(52.80%)	(47.20%)	(100%)	(51.90%)	(48.10%)	(100%)
2001							5312.77	4957.38	10270.15
							(51.73%)	(48.27%)	(100%)

Source:

1. Census of India 1961, General Population Tables, pp. 71, 181.
2. Census of India 1971, Paper I of 1971 – Supplement India p. 76.
3. Census of India 1981, Series–1 India, p. 4.
4. Census of India 1991, (PCA) NIC Udaipur.

74.77 per cent of the total female population lives in rural areas. During 1961 to 1991, in the country female population increased from 2129.42 lacs to 4070.72 lacs (91.16%) and female population in urban areas increased from 361.47 lacs to 1027.02 lacs i.e. increase by (184.12%) while in rural areas female population increased from 1767.94 lacs to 3043.70 (72.16%).

DECADAL VARIATION OF FEMALE IN INDIA

The decadal female population growth rate in the country (Table 3.3) during 1901–11 was 5.41% while during 1981–91 it was only 23.06%. The decadal female population growth rate was negative (-0.75%) during 1911–21 and growth rate was highest (25.24%) during 1971–1981.

Both man and woman are responsible for growth in population. Women have special significance because of their child bearing and child rearing capability. Lack of awareness and empowerment have made them instrument of child birth in male dominated society.

Table 3.3. Decadal Variation of Female in India

(Figures in lacs)

Census year	Total females	Decade variation
1901	1173.59	—
1911	1237.08	+5.41%
1921	1227.75	-0.75%
1931	1357.89	+10.60%
1941	1546.90	+13.92%
1951	1755.60	+13.49%
1961	2129.42	+21.29%
1971	2641.15	+24.03%
1981	3307.86	+25.24%
1991	4070.72	+23.06%

Source: Census of India, 1991.

SEX COMPOSITION OF POPULATION IN INDIA

The sex-ratio in India has always been in favour of males (Table 3.4). In 1901 it was 972 females for 1000 males and this trend has since prevailed. In 1991 it was 929 females for 1000 males. The sex ratio in the country varies from 894 in urban area to 939 in rural area. The lower sex ratio in urban area is largely attributed to migration of males to urban centres for educational, employment purpose. It is also dis-concerning to note that the sex ratio has declined considerably from 972 in 1901 to 929 in 1991. The main reasons for the sex imbalance seem to be relatively low status of women, preference for son etc.

Kerela is the only state in the country where sex-ratio is always favourable for women. In 1991 the relative figure was 1040 females for 1000 males. In 1981, 1032 females for 1000 males. In fact, right from 1901 till to date, the trend in Kerela has been favourable to females.

Table 3.4. Sex Composition of Population in India

(Female per thousand male)

Census year	Rural	Urban	Total
1901	979	910	972
1911	975	872	964
1921	970	846	955
1931	966	832	950
1941	965	831	945
1951	965	860	946
1961	963	845	941
1971	949	858	930
1981	951	878	933
1991	939	894	929
2001	—	—	933

Sources: Census of India, 1991

Rajasthan (Ecology, Culture and Society) 1999, Bhasin, M.K. and Bhasin Veena. Published by Kamla –Raj Enterprises, Delhi, p. 25

Statistical Analysis of Women. p. 6.

An analysis of the male/female ratio in various states revealed that in Bihar from 1901, to 1921 females were more than males, in Goa, Manipur, Mizoram and Orissa from 1901 to 1961 female/male ratio was favourable to females. In Meghalaya in 1901 and 1911, and in Tamil Nadu from 1901 to 1951 there were more females than males. Among Union territories in Daman and Diu from 1911 to 1981 and in Lakshadweep from 1901 to 1961 there were more females than males.

CASTEWISE DISTRIBUTION OF POPULATION IN INDIA

The table 3.5 shows caste-wise and gender-wise population of India. The 1991 census shows that there were 4033.68 females against of 4352.16 male population.

Table 3.5. Gender-wise and Caste-wise Distribution of Population in India

(Figures in lacs)

Religion	1971	1981	1991		
			Males	Females	Total
Hindus			3572.53 (82.1%)	3303.93 (81.9%)	6876.46 (82%)
Muslims			526.31	489.64 (12.1%)	1015.95 (12.1%)
Sikhs			86.1	76.49 (1.9%)	162.59 (1.9%)
Jain			17.22	16.3 (0.40%)	33.52 (0.40%)
Christians			98.49	97.91 (2.4%)	196.4 (2.3%)
Buddhist			32.72	31.15 (0.8%)	63.87 (0.76%)
Others not stated			16.49	16.2 (0.4%)	32.69 (0.39%)
Religion not stated			2.2	1.95 (0.05%)	4.15 (0.05%)
Total			4352.16	4033.68 (100%)	8385.84 (100%)

Source: Census of India, 1991, Series 21 Rajasthan, Part IV-B (ii) Religion Table C-9, pp. 12 to 15.

Note: In bracket percentage has been shown to total population of the country.

According 1991 census gender disparity existed in each and every caste. According to 1991 census, 81.9%, 12.1 per cent women belonged Hindu and Muslim community respectively.

According 1991 census (Table 3.6, *See page 96*), total female population has been 4070.72 lacs of the country, out of them 662.94 lacs (16.29%) and 333.95 lacs (8.20%) females belong to S.C. and S.T. respectively.

Scheduled caste female population increased from 314.99 to 662.94 (110.46%) lacs during the period of 1961 to 1991. While female population of Scheduled Tribe increased from 148.41 lacs to 333.95 (125.02%) lacs during 1961 to 1991.

Table 3.7 *(See page 97)* displays percentage of S.C. and S.T. females to total population. In 1961, 14.79% female belong to S.C. and 6.97% belongs to S.T. however, the percentage increased in 1991 census year upto 16.29% and 8.20% respectively.

LITERACY AMONG FEMALES IN INDIA

In the country only 65.38% of the population have been found literate in the census 2001 (Table 3.8 *See page 98*). However, some progress may have been made over the years, as the per cent literate in 1961, was only 24.02%. There also seems to be a wide gender gap in literacy, with only 54.16% as against 75.85% of males being literate. In last five decades (1961-01) percentage of literate females increased from 12.95% to 54.16%. Among states, Kerala topped the list with 90.92% literacy.

Table 3.9 *(See page 99)* focus attention towards area-wise literacy of male and female in the country.

In 1961, out of 2129.42 lacs females only 275.79 lacs (12.95%) female were literate (Table 3.10, *See page 100*). While in 1991 out of 4070.72 lacs female 1297.47 (31.87%) lacs females were literate.

In rural area 151.04 lacs (8.54%) female were literate in 1961 which increased upto 749.22 (24.62%) lacs in 1991. In urban area, they were 124.75 (34.51%) lacs females were literate in 1961 and increased upto 548.25 (53.40%) lacs in 1991.

Table 3.6. Gender-wise and Caste-wise Population of Scheduled Castes and Scheduled Tribes in the Country

(Figures in Lacs)

Census year	S/C Population									S/T Population								
	Rural			Urban			Total			Rural			Urban			Total		
	Males	Females	Total	Males	Females	Total	Males	Females	Population	Males	Females	Total	Males	Females	Total	Males	Females	Population
1961	292.70 (50.9%)	282.77 (49.1%)	575.48 (100%)	36.47 (53.1%)	32.22 (46.9%)	68.69 (100%)	329.17 (51.1%)	314.99 (48.9%)	644.16 (100%)	146.31 (50.3%)	144.76 (49.7%)	291.07 (100%)	4.07 (52.7%)	3.65 (47.3)	7.72 (100%)	150.38 (50.3%)	148.41 (49.7%)	298.79 (100%)
1971	362.66 (51.5%)	341.83 (48.5%)	704.49 (100%)	50.77 (53.1%)	44.79 (46.9%)	95.56 (100%)	413.43 (51.7%)	386.62 (48.3%)	800.05 (100%)	184.99 (50.4%)	182.22 (49.6%)	367.21 (100%)	6.82 (52.7%)	6.12 (47.3%)	12.94 (100%)	191.81 (50.5%)	188.34 (49.5%)	380.15 (100%)
1981	453.55 (51.5%)	426.42 (48.5%)	879.97 (100%)	88.56 (52.8%)	79.02 (47.2%)	167.58 (100%)	542.11 (51.8%)	505.44 (48.2%)	1047.55 (100%)	243.64 (50.3%)	240.63 (49.7%)	484.28 (100%)	16.74 (52.3%)	15.27 (47.7%)	32.01 (100%)	260.38 (50.4%)	255.9 (49.6%)	516.28 (100%)
1991	583.42 (51.9%)	540.01 (48.1%)	1123.44 (100%)	135.86 (52.5%)	122.93 (47.5%)	258.79 (100%)	719.28 (52%)	662.94 (48%)	1382.22 (100%)	317.56 (50.6%)	309.95 (49.4%)	627.51 (100%)	26.07 (52.1%)	24.00 (47.9%)	50.07 (100%)	343.63 (50.7%)	333.95 (49.3%)	677.58 (100%)

Source:

1. Census of India 1961, TRI, Library, Udaipur
2. Census of India 1971, TRI, Library, Udaipur
3. Census of India 1981, Series 1 India, S.C. Part II (B) & (iii) (P.C.A.) pp. 4 and 18
4. Census of India 1991, (PCA) NIC Udaipur.

Table 3.7. Female Population of Scheduled Castes and Scheduled Tribes in India

(Figures in lacs)

Census year	Rural					Urban					Total				
	Total female population	S.C. female population	% of S.C. female population to total population	S.T. female population	% of S.T female population to total population	Total female population	S.C female population	% of S.C. female population to total population	S.T. female population	% of S.T. female population to total population	Total female population	S.C. female population	% of S.C female population to total population	S.T. female population	% of S.T. female population to total population
1961	1767.94	282.77	15.99%	144.76	8.19%	361.47	32.22	8.91%	3.65	1.01%	2129.42	314.99	14.79%	148.41	6.97%
1971	2138.51	341.83	15.98%	182.22	8.52%	502.64	44.79	8.91%	6.12	1.22%	2641.15	386.62	14.64%	188.34	7.13%
1981	2560.93	426.42	16.65%	240.63	9.40%	746.93	79.02	10.58%	15.27	2.04%	3307.86	505.44	15.28%	255.90	7.74%
1991	3043.70	540.01	17.74%	309.95	10.18%	1027.02	122.93	11.97%	24.00	2.34	4070.72	662.94	16.29%	333.95	8.20%

Source:

1. Census of India 1961, TRI, Library, Udaipur
2. Census of India 1971, TRI, Library, Udaipur
3. Census of India 1971, Paper I of 1971, Supplement India p. 76.
4. Census of India 1981, Series I India, S.C. Part II B (ii) & (iii) (PCA) pp. 4 and 18.
5. Census of India 1991, (PCA) NIC Udaipur.

Table 3.8. Percentage Distribution of Literates in India

Census year	Male	Female	Total
1961	34.44%	12.95%	24.02%
1971	39.51%	18.69%	29.34%
1981	45.51%	24.11%	35.18%
1991	52.26%	31.87%	42.45%
2001	75.85%	54.16%	65.38%

Source: Prepared from table 3.2 and 3.39

In the year 1961, 12.95% females were literate out of the total population and increased upto 31.87% in 1991.

The death rate for children below 5 years for India according to SRS, 1992 in 26.4 while death rates for the age groups 50 + is 33.4. The death rate for females below 5 years, 5–14, 15–34 groups are more than males (Table 3.11 *See page 101*).

GENDER-WISE AND OCCUPATION-WISE DISTRIBUTION OF POPULATION IN INDIA

The percentage of female main workers in the country in 1991, stood at 15.93 per cent, whereas the percentage of non-workers was quite high at 77.75% about 6.32 of the total population were marginal workers. There is a wide gender difference in the work force participation too, as the percentage of female main works was only 15.3% as against 50.93% of male main workers. Table also shows that most of the female workers are engaged in cultivation (34.57%) and agricultural labour (44.24%).

However, variation is evident when the place of residence is taken into consideration. That is, whereas in rural areas of country the majority are engaged in cultivation (33.93%) and Agricultural labour (48.49%), in urban areas the single largest section of workers seems to be engaged in other services (40.36%) followed by agricultural labours (15.49%).

Table 3.12 *(See page 102)* focus our attention towards working population in rural areas of the country.

Female main workers were 311.12 lac recorded in the year of 1971, which grown upto 559.96 lacs against 1662.94 lacs males in 1991.

Table 3.9. Gender-wise and Area-wise Literacy in India

(Figures in Lacs)

Census year	Rural			Urban			Total		
	Males	Females	Total	Males	Females	Total	Males	Females	Total
1961	533.38 (77.93%)	151.04 (22.07%)	684.42 (100%)	246.01 (66.35%)	124.75 (33.65%)	370.76 (100%)	779.40 (73.86%)	275.79 (26.14%)	1055.19 (100%)
1971	760.58 (72.99%)	281.40 (27.01%)	1041.98 (100%)	359.86 (62.89%)	212.32 (37.11%)	572.18 (100%)	1120.43 (69.41%)	493.71 (30.59%)	1614.15 (100%)
1981	1060.66 (70.46%)	444.51 (29.53%)	1505.17 (100%)	552.19 (61.01%)	352.96 (38.99%)	905.15 (100%)	1612.85 (66.91%)	797.47 (33.09%)	2410.32 (100%)
1991	1512.17 (66.87%)	749.22 (33.13%)	2261.39 (100%)	783.15 (58.82%)	548.25 (41.18%)	1331.4 (100%)	2295.32 (63.88%)	1297.47 (36.11%)	3592.79 (100%)

Source:

1. Census of India 1981, Series 1 India Part II B (i) p. 5
2. Census of India 1991, (PCA) NIC Udaipur.

Table 3.10. Female Population and Literacy in India

(Figures in Lacs)

Census year	Rural			Urban			Total		
	Female	Literate female	% of literate female to total rural female Population	Female	Literate female	% of literate female to total urban female Population	Total female	Literate female	% of literate to total female Population
1961	1767.94	151.04	8.54	361.47	124.75	34.51	2129.42	275.79	12.95
1971	2138.51	281.40	13.16	502.64	212.32	42.24	2641.15	493.72	18.69
1981	2560.93	444.51	17.4	746.93	352.96	47.3	3307.86	797.47	24.11
1991	3043.70	749.22	24.62	1027.02	548.25	53.4	4070.72	1297.47	31.87

Source:

1. Census of India 1971, paper I of 1971, Supplement India p. 76.
2. Census of India 1981, Series I India II B (i) pp. 4 & 5.
3. Census of India 1991, (PCA) NIC Udaipur.

Table 3.11. Age-specific Death Rate in India, by Sex (1992)

Age specific death rate	Male	Female	Person
0–4	24.9	28.2	26.4
5–14	1.9	2.5	2.2
15–34	2.4	3.0	2.7
34–49	6.0	4.5	5.3
50+	35.5	31.4	33.4

Source: 'Rajasthan' (Ecology, culture and society) 1999. Bhasin, M.K. and Bhasin Veena, Published by Kamla Raj Enterprises, p. 29.

Female marginal workers is also increase in the year of 1991 recorded 244.34 lacs. In 1981 there were only 177.85 lacs female marginal workers. Male marginal workers recorded low against of the females.

Female non-workers are high in numbers in comparison to males. In 1971, there has been 1827.39 lacs female non workers and increased in the year of 1991 upto 2210.95 lac females.

The figures show that females participation in occupation is remarked low in compare to males. To make progress on the front of economic development, full participation of females is very necessary.

Table 3.12 analysis is coverage of working population in urban areas of the country.

In 1971, 37.03 la female main workers has been on the economic front and increased in the year of 1991 upto 87.78 lacs females.

Females marginal–workers registered 7.67 lacs in 1981 and increased in the year of 1991 upto 10.59 la.

With the increase of population female non-workers are also increasing every census year. In 1971, there were only 465.61 lacs female non-workers. In 1991, recorded 924.97 la females.

Table 3.12. Gender-wise and Occupation-wise Population in India

(Figures in Lacs)

	Classification	1961				1971			
		Rural		Urban		Rural		Urban	
		Males	Females	Males	Females	Males	Females	Males	Females
	1	2	3	4	5	6	7	8	9
1.	Main workers	1111.32	557.61	141.02	31.01	1203.36	311.12	284.54	37.03
1.1	Cultivators	640.74	322.56	12.60	6.22	674.53	96.00	15.12	1.41
1.2	Agricultural labours	166.58	137.11	4.44	4.03	299.84	154.16	13.29	5.76
1.3	Livestock, forestry, fishing, hunting and plantations, orchards and allied services	35.25	10.95	3.77	0.67	–	–	–	–
1.4	Mining and quarrying					–	–	–	–
1.5a	Manufacturing, processing servicing and repairs in household industries	61.69	39.51	10.67	6.36	–	–	–	–
1.5b	Manufacturing, processing servicing and repairs in other than household industries	37.90	5.40	28.97	2.27	–	–	–	–

(Contd...)

	1	2	3	4	5	6	7	8	9
1.6	Constructions	11.89	1.95	5.33	0.45	–	–	–	–
1.7	Trade and Commerce	36.77	6.13	24.79	1.92	–	–	–	–
1.8	Transport storage and communication	15.47	0.36	11.58	0.25	–	–	–	–
1.9	Other services	105.03	33.64	38.87	8.84	–	–	–	–
1.10	Other workers (Total of 1.3 + 1.4 + 1.5(b) + 1.6 + 1.7 + 1.8 + 1.9)	–	–	–	–	228.99	60.96	256.12	29.86
2.0	Marginal workers	–	–	–	–	–	–	–	–
3.0	Non-workers	781.29	1243.22	172.69	247.34	1043.93	1827.39	300.69	465.61
	Total	1892.61	1800.83	313.71	278.35				

(Contd...)

(Table 3.12 Contd...)

(Figures in Lacs)

Classification	1981				1991						
	Rural		Urban		Rural		Urban		Total		
	Males	Females	Males	Females	Males	Females	Males	Females	Males	Females	Total population
1	2	3	4	5	6	7	8	9	10	11	12
1. Main workers	1368.31	396.03	407.12	53.70	1662.94 (51.8%)	559.96 (18.6%)	553.65 (48.6%)	82.78 (8.1%)	2216.59 (77.5%)	642.74 (22.5%)	2859.33 (100%)
1.1 Cultivators	754.76	146.82	21.15	2.50	857.71	217.97	27.10	4.24	884.81 (79.9%)	222.21 (20.1%)	1107.02 (100%)
1.2 Agricultural labours	328.35	198.78	18.97	8.89	431.87	271.51	29.77	12.82	461.64 (61.9%)	284.33 (38.1%)	745.97 (100%)
1.3 Livestock, forestry, fishing, hunting and plantations, orchards and allied services	–	–	–	–	37.44	11.96	9.71	1.28	47.15 (78.1%)	13.24 (21.9%)	60.39 (100%)
1.4 Mining & quarrying	–	–	–	–	8.81	1.58	6.56	0.56	15.37 (87.8%)	2.14 (12.2%)	17.51 (100%)
1.5a Manufacturing, processing servicing and repairs in household industries	39.31	15.01	17.15	5.63	31.83	16.27	13.72	6.22	45.55 (66.9%)	22.49 (33.1%)	68.04 (100%)
1.5b Manufacturing, processing servicing & repairs in other than household industries	–	–	–	–	66.14	12.89	128.00	11.64	194.14 (88.8%)	24.53 (11.2%)	218.67 (100%)

(Contd...)

1	2	3	4	5	6	7	8	9	10	11	12
1.6 Constructions	–	–	–	–	21.70	1.49	29.53	2.72	51.23 (92.4%)	4.21 (7.6%)	55.44 (100%)
1.7 Trade & Commerce	–	–	–	–	66.94	6.07	131.68	8.27	198.62 (93.3%)	14.34 (6.7%)	212.96 (100%)
1.8 Transport storage & communication	–	–	–	–	27.01	0.46	51.09	1.61	78.1 (97.4%)	2.07 (2.6%)	80.17 (100%)
1.9 Other services	–	–	–	–	113.47	19.75	126.48	33.41	239.95 (81.9%)	53.16 (18.1%)	293.11 (100%)
1.10 Other workers (Total of 1.3 + 1.4 + 1.5(b) + 1.6 + 1.7 + 1.8 + 1.9)	245.89	35.42	349.85	36.67	–	–	–	–	–	–	281.98 (100%)
2.0 Marginal workers	30.89	177.85	4.47	7.67	23.05 (0.72%)	244.34 (8.1%)	4.00 (0.04%)	10.59 (1%)	27.05 (9.6%)	254.93 (90.4%)	
3.0 Non-workers	1201.33	1901.66	427.17	676.67	1526.72 (47.5%)	2210.95 (73.3%)	581.72 (51.0%)	924.97 (90.9%)	2108.44 (40.2%)	3135.92 (59.8%)	5244.36 (100%)
Total					3212.71	3015.25	1139.37	1018.34	4352.08	4033.59	8385.67

Source:

1. Census of India 1971, Paper I of 1971-Supplement India, p. 7.7.
2. Census of India 1981, Series 1, India, Part II B (i) pp. 6–9.
3. Census of India, 1991 (PCA) NIC Udaipur.

DEMOGRAPHIC PROFILE OF WOMEN IN THE STATE OF RAJASTHAN

Rajasthan is the land of legends, colourful costumes, magnificent forts and it is the land of lofty hills sand shifting and dunes of scorching heat and freezing cold of fertile plains, rugged ravines and dense forests.

Rajasthan is situated at 23°4′10″ to 30°15′5″ north latitude and 69°30′5″ to 78° 16′50″ east longitude, tropic of cancer touches its southern boundary. Rajasthan has a rhombus shape. It is 826 kms long from north to south 869 kms wide from west to east. And the area of the state is 342,239 sq. kms, which is equal to the area of 10.74% of the country. Rajasthan is the second largest state in the country. Land territorial boundary of the state is 5,920 kms and its International boundary is 1070 kms separating Indian Union with Pakistan. State shares its territorial boundary with Punjab bounds its on the north, Haryana and Uttar Pradesh on the north-east and east, Madhya Pradesh on the south and south east and Gujarat on the south-west.

However, the state may be divided into 6 regions. (1) Western arid region, (2) Semi arid region, (3) South eastern region, (4) Chambal ravines, (5) Aravali region and (6) Eastern region.

The Western arid region covers the whole of Jaisalmer district, north-western part of Barmer and Jodhpur, south east Bikaner, South western Churu and Western part of Nagaur. This region is identified by typical desert conditions and forms the largest region in the state.

The semi arid region lying west of the Aravalli ranges covers the districts of Jalore, Pali, South-eastern Jodhpur and Nagaur, Sikar, Jhunjhunu and north eastern part of Churu. The Southern part of this area is watered by the Luni river while the northern part is an area of inferior drainage.

The Rajasthan Canal (named as Indira Gandhi Canal) passes through the north west portion of this region irrigating at present Ganganagar district and Bikaner district.

The Aravalli region covers almost the whole of Udaipur, South-eastern part of Pali and Sirohi and the Western part of Dungarpur districts. The area is dominated by the mountains of the Aravalli range and outlying hills.

The eastern region comprises the districts of Jaipur, Ajmer, Sawai, Madhopur, Bhilwara, Bundi, Alwar, Bharatpur and north-western part of Kota. It is mainly drained by the Banas river and its tributaries. The region has the largest number of industries, located mainly at Jaipur, Ajmer, Kota, Bhilwara and Shahpura.

The south-eastern region embraces the districts of Banswara, Chittorgarh, Jhalawar and Kota. The Kota–Jhalawar area consist of stony uplands but the Chambal river and its tributaries have formed an alluvial basin in Kota.

The Chambal ravine region lies along the river Chambal, where it forms the boundary between Rajasthan and Madhya Pradesh. Administrative structure of Rajasthan consist of 32 Districts, 100 Subdivisions, 229 Tehsils, 237 Panchayat Samities, 222 Towns and Cities, 39810 villages.

The civilization and culture met from the Harrappan times upto the late Maurya and Gupta periods. Rajasthan is the home of Rajputs. The history of Rajasthan is replete with the rise, recession and repeated resurgence of Rajput power.

Rajasthan handicrafts are famous all over the world. Important handicrafts are marble work, woollen carpets, jewellery, embroidery, articles of leather, pottery and brass embossing.

The economy of the state is largely depended on agriculture. Total cultivable area is 274. 71 lakh hectare and irrigated area 53.50 lakh hectare. Agriculture contribute nearly 50% of the state income.

Rajasthan is rich not only in the land resources but in mineral resources too. Over 30 important minerals both metallic and industrial and a large variety of building stones are found.

Rajasthan has several sights to offer tourist. Tourism was given Industry status in 1992. About 47.94 lakh tourists visited the state in 1991.

Rajasthan is well connected by air, rail and road with all the big cities of the country.

POPULATION GROWTH IN THE STATE OF RAJASTHAN

The population of Rajasthan was 1.50 crores prior to independence (1947) and it increased to 1.60 crores in 1951 (Table 3.13). According to the 1951 census the population of Rajasthan increased at the rate of 15.2% during the decade 1941-51. It was higher than the rate of all India increase in population which was only 13.3%.

Table 3.13. Population Growth in Rajasthan

(Figures in lacs of Rs.)

Year	Population	Decennial growth rate %
1911	110	+6.70
1921	103	–6.29
1931	118	+14.14
1941	139	+18.01
1951	160	+15.20
1961	202	+26.20
1971	258	+27.83
1981	343	+32.97
1991	440	+28.44
2001	565	+28.33

Source: Mathur N.D. and Sharma S.N., Book: India Economic Environment, p. 445.

Seventy seven per cent of the population of Rajasthan lives in rural areas as compared to 74 per cent in India. The state is ranked ninth among the major Indian states in terms of its population size. The decennial growth is high in Rajasthan (28.44%) as compared to the country (23.51%).

GENDER-WISE AND AREA-WISE DISTRIBUTION OF POPULATION IN THE STATE OF RAJASTHAN

Population of Rajasthan was 103 lacs in 1901 (Table 3.14, *See page 110*). It grew to 565 lacs in 2001. In a century span of time it has increased more than five times. Table 3.14 depicts that in first fifty years, population of Rajasthan increased only 57 lacs whereas in later 40 years it has increased to 261 lacs. Hence, there have been rapid growth of population in Rajasthan after independence. The total female population of the State has increased form 52 lacs in 1911 to 96 lacs in 1961 and 210 lacs in 1991.

According to census 1991, 77.53 per cent of female population in Rajasthan lies in rural area and the rest 22.47 per cent in urban areas. The urban female population increase from 1961 to 1991 (16.04 to 22.47 per cent) resulting in a consequent decrease of rural population which was 83.96 per cent in 1961 and came down to 77.53 per cent in 1991. This shows the migration of rural female to urban areas.

In urban area, in 1961, there were 15.38 lacs females, which grown upto 47.10 lacs (205.24%) in 1991. The percentage of urban female to total population is constant between 46.5 to 47 per cent against of 53 to 53.3 per cent of males.

In the rural area, female recorded 80.53 lacs in the year of 1961 and raised to 162.52 lacs (101.81%) in 1991. The percentage of rural female to total rural population is constant between 47.5 to 48.5 where males where 51.5 to 52.5 per cent.

The amazing fact is that in urban area, gender gap is wider, which shows that women are neglected in urban areas.

DECADAL VARIATION OF FEMALE IN THE STATE OF RAJASTHAN

The table 3.15 (*See page 111*) displays females decadal variation in the State. The only period when population of females actually fell was the decade of 1911-21 wen negative

Table 3.14. Gender–wise and Area–wise Population in the State of Rajasthan

(Figure in lacs)

Census year	Rural			Urban			Total		
	Males	Females	Total	Males	Females	Total	Males	Females	Total
1901			87.43			15.51	–	–	103
1911			95.07			14.76	58 (52.7%)	52 (47.3%)	110 (100%)
1921			88.17			14.76	54 (52.4%)	49 (47.6%)	103 (100%)
1931			100.19			17.29	62 (52.5%)	56 (47.5%)	118 (100%)
1941			117.47			21.17	73 (52.5%)	66 (47.5%)	139 (100%)
1951			130.15			29.55	83 (51.9%)	77 (48.1%)	160 (100%)
1961	88.21 (52.3%)	80.53 (47.7%)	168.74 (100%)	17.43 (53.1%)	15.38 46.9%)	32.81 (100%)	106 (52.5%)	96 (47.5%)	202 (100%)
1971	110.61 (52.1%)	101.61 (47.9%)	212.22 (100%)	24.23 (53.3%)	21.20 (46.7%)	45.43 (100%)	135 (52.3%)	123 (47.7%)	258 (100%)
1981	140.13 (51.8%)	130.38 (48.2%)	270.51 (100%)	38.4 (53.3%)	33.7 (46.7%)	72.11 (100%)	179 (52.2%)	164 (47.8%)	343 (100%)
1991	176.86 (52.1%)	162.52 (47.9%)	339.38 (100%)	53.56 (53.2%)	47.10 (46.8%)	100.66 (100%)	230 (52.3%)	210 (47.7%)	440 (100%)
2001	–	–	–	–	–	–	294 (52.01%)	271 47.96)	565 (100%)

Source:
1. Census of India 1961, Volume XIV Rajasthan Part II-A, General Population Tables, p. 166.
2. Census of India 1971, Series-18, Rajasthan Part II.A, General Population Tables, p. 2.
3. Census of India 1981, Series-1 India. Part II B (i) p. 390.
4. Census of India 1981, Series-18, Rajasthan Part II-A "General Population Tables", pp. 85 and 90.
5. Basic Statistics, Rajasthan, 1998, pp. 37 and 43.
6. Census of India (PCA) NIC Udaipur.

growth rate of 5.77 per cent over the past decade. Since the year 1921, the rate of growth has become alarming. The rate of female has slightly fallen in the last decade 1971-81 was 33.33 per cent which came down to 28.05 per cent for the decade 1981-91. The fall in the growth rate was the result of the untiring efforts of the government to spread education make people aware about the benefits of small and happy family.

Table 3.15. Decadal Variation of Female in the State of Rajasthan

(Figures in lacs)

Census year	Total females	Decade variation
1901		
1911	52	—
1921	49	–5.77%
1931	56	14.29%
1941	66	17.86%
1951	77	16.67%
1961	96	24.68%
1971	123	28.13%
1981	164	33.33%
1991	210	28.05%

Source: Basic Statistics, 1998, Rajasthan p. 37.

SEX-COMPOSITION OF POPULATION IN THE STATE OF RAJASTHAN

Table 3.16 shows number of females per thousand males in the state. In the beginning of 20th century there were 905 females for 1000 males. After independence, sex-ratio increased recorded to 921 in the year of 1951. Again fall in the sex-ratio from the next census year 1961 makes crystal clear. "That society can not accept better change immediately." Bad customs and evils had been accepted very quickly by the society. The sex ratio increased from 911 in 1971 to 919 in 1981, but declined to 910 in 1999.

Table 3.16. Sex Composition in the State of Rajasthan

(Female per thousand male)

Census year	Rural	Urban	Total
1901	898	947	905
1911	904	936	908
1921	896	897	896
1931	908	903	907
1941	907	897	906
1951	919	928	921
1961	913	882	908
1971	919	875	911
1981	930	877	919
1991*	919	879	910
2001	—	—	922

Source: Census of India 1981, Series 18 Rajasthan, Part II-A, General Population Table, p. 162.

Rajasthan (Ecology, Culture and Society), 1999, Bhasin, M.K and Bhasin Veena Published by Kamal Raj Enterprise p. 25.

The reason for sex imbalance given in census 1911 were omission of females, infanticide, neglect of girl child, early marriage, early child birth, hard work and bad treatment. These reasons were given about 90 years back and some of these reasons may not be valid today but provide a basis for new, revised hypothesis. Whatever may be the case, the social scene and situation is not improving for females in Rajasthan. Sex ratio is invariably lower in urban areas because of migration of single males from rural areas to urban centres for educational economic or other related purposes. In Rajasthan the number of females is lower than males in all districts, the lowest being in Jaisalmer (810) and the highest in Dungarpur (997).

Table 3.17 shows that 89% of the state female population comprises of Hindus. Scheduled Castes and Scheduled Tribes were 17.17 per cent and 12.58 per cent respectively, of the total population of Rajasthan. About 8.06% of Rajasthan's population is Muslim, most of whom are Sunnis. There is a small affluent community of Shia muslims in south eastern Rajasthan, known as Bohras. In 1991, Sikhs and Jain comprised 1.45% and 1.33% of the female population of Rajasthan.

Table 3.17. Gender-wise and Caste-wise Distribution of Population in the State of Rajasthan

(Figures in lacs)

Religion	1971	1981	1991		
			Males	Females	Total
Hindus	230.94	306.04	205.43	186.58 (89.0%)	392.01 (89.1%)
Muslims	17.78	24.92	18.35	16.9 (8.06%)	35.25 (8.0%)
Sikhs	3.41	4.93	3.43	3.05 (1.45%)	6.48 (1.5%)
Jain	5.13	6.24	2.84	2.79 (1.33%)	5.63 (1.3%)
Christians	0.30	0.39	0.24	0.24 (0.1%)	0.48 (0.1%)
Buddhist	0.09	0.04	0.02	0.016 (0.01%)	0.036 (0.01%)
Others not stated		0.03	0.006	0.005 (0.002%)	0.011 (0.002%)
Religion not stated		0.01	0.08	0.05 (0.02%)	0.13 (0.03%)
Total	257.65	342.6	230.40	209.63 (100%)	440.03 (100%)

Source:

1. Basic Statistics, 1981
2. Basic Statistics, 1998, Rajasthan pp. 41 and 42.
3. Census of India, 1991, Series 21, Rajasthan, Part IV-B(ii), Religion Table C-9, pp. 16 to 19.

Table 3.18 and 3.19 *(See pages 115, 116)* shows that, total S.C. and S.T. females were 16.12 lacs and 11.10 lacs respectively in 1961 and increased upto 36 (123.33%) and 26.38 lacs (137.66%) in 1991. Gender inequality exist in the table 3.18 and make crystal clear that female population is less than the male population.

In Urban area there were 1.97 and 0.21 lacs S.C. and S.T. females respectively in 1961 which increased upto 7.08 (259.39%) lacs and 1.14 lacs respectively in 1991.

Whereas in rural areas S.C. and S.T. females population was recorded 14.15 lacs and 10.89 lacs respectively in 1961 which grown upto 28.92 (104.38%) and 25.24 lacs respectively in the year of 1991.

LITERACY AMONG FEMALES IN THE STATE OF RAJASTHAN

At the time of formation of Rajasthan, educational facilities were meagre. The first university of the state was set up in 1947. The scene has changed considerably. Educational institutions which were limited to major towns, have now reached many villages. Continuous efforts are going on for the development of education in Rajasthan, Universalisation of primary education, expansion of educational facilities with great stress on girls and adult education are given priority. Free education upto college level is being provided to girls in the state.

In spite of the government's efforts of opening educational institutions and providing other factors for educating people, Rajasthan is still the most backward in terms of the percentage of literacy, (38.55%) which is far behind the state of Kerala (i.e. 90.59) and the National average of 42.45%. Female literacy rate is woefully low; it is only 20.44 against the Indian average of 31.90.

Table 3.20 *(See page 117)* visualize that the State of Rajasthan is educationally one of the most backward states in the country. Only 61.03% of the population have been found literate in the census 2001. However, some progress may have made over the

Table 3.18. Gender–wise and Caste-wise Population of Scheduled Castes and Scheduled Tribes in the State of Rajasthan

(Figures in lacs)

Census	S/C Population									S/T Population								
Year	Rural			Urban			Total			Rural			Urban			Total		
	Males	Females	Total	Males	Females	Total	Males	Females	Population	Males	Females	Total	Males	Females	Total	Males	Females	Population
1961	15.32 (52.0%)	14.15 (48%)	29.47 (100%)	2.16 (52.3%)	1.97 (47.7%)	4.13 (100%)	17.48 (52%)	16.12 (48%)	33.6 (100%)	11.73 (51.9%)	10.89 (48.1%)	22.62 (100%)	0.26 (55.3%)	0.21 (44.7%)	0.47 (100%)	11.99 (51.9%)	11.10 (48.1%)	23.09 (100%)
1971	18.21 (52.1%)	16.72 (47.9%)	34.93 (100%)	3.08 (52.9%)	2.74 (47.1%)	5.82 (100%)	21.29 (52.2%)	19.46 (47.8%)	40.75 (100%)	15.81 (51.7%)	14.77 (48.3%)	30.58 (100%)	0.38 (55.9%)	0.30 (44.1%)	0.68 (100%)	16.19 (51.8%)	15.07 (48.2%)	31.26 (100%)
1981	24.98 (52.2%)	22.92 (47.8%)	47.90 (100%)	5.54 (52.9%)	4.94 (47.1%)	10.48 (100%)	30.52 (52.3%)	27.86 (47.7%)	58.38 (100%)	20.63 (51.2%)	19.64 (48.8%)	40.27 (100%)	0.88 (56.4%)	0.68 (43.6%)	1.56 (100%)	21.51 (51.4%)	20.32 (48.6%)	41.83 (100%)
1991	32.10 (52.6%)	28.92 (47.4%)	61.02 (100%)	7.97 (53%)	7.08 (47%)	15.05 (100%)	40.07 (52.7%)	36.00 (47.3%)	76.07 (100%)	26.96 (51.6%)	25.24 (48.4%)	52.20 (100%)	1.40 (55.1%)	1.14 (44.9%)	2.54 (100%)	28.36 (51.8%)	26.38 (48.2%)	54.74 (100%)

Source:

1. Census of India 1961, Volume XIV Rajasthan Part II-A, General Population Tables, pp. 166-167.
2. Census of India 1971, Series-18, Rajasthan Part-IIA, General Population Tables, p. 3.
3. Census of India 1981, Series-18, Rajasthan, Part-IIA, General Population Tables p. 31.
4. Census of India, 1991 (PCA), NIC Udaipur.

Table 3.19. Female Population of Scheduled Castes and Scheduled Tribes in the State of Rajasthan

(Figures in lacs)

Census year	Rural					Urban					Total				
	Total female population	S.C. female population	% of S.C. female population to total population	S.T. female population	% of S.T. female population to total population	Total female population	S.C female population	% of S.C. female population to total population	S.T. female population	% of S.T. female population to total population	Total female population	S.C. female population	% of S.C female population to total population	S.T. female population	% of S.T. female population to total population
1961	80.53	14.51	17.57%	10.89	13.52%	15.38	1.97	12.81%	0.21	1.37%	95.91	16.12	16.81%	11.10	11.57%
1971	101.61	16.72	16.46%	14.77	14.54%	21.20	2.74	12.92%	0.30	1.42%	122.81	19.46	15.85%	15.07	12.27%
1981	130.38	22.92	17.58%	19.64	15.06%	33.70	4.94	14.66%	0.68	2.02%	164.08	27.86	16.98%	20.32	12.38%
1991	162.52	28.92	17.79%	25.24	15.53%	47.10	7.08	15.03%	1.14	2.42%	209.62	36.00	17.17%	26.38	12.58%

Source: Prepared from Table 3.14 and 3.18.

years, as the per cent literate in 1921, was only 4.22% and in 1961, 15.21%. These also seems to be a wide gender gap in literacy, with only 44.34% of females as against 76.46% of males being literate. In fact, the state occupied the last position according the ranking of major states of India with respect to 1991 female literacy. In almost all the districts of Rajasthan, the literacy rate is below 40 per cent, except Ajmer where it is 42.7%.

Table 3.20. Per Cent Distribution of Literates in the State of Rajasthan

Year	Male	Female	Total
1921	7.33%	0.59%	4.22%
1931	8.15%	0.72%	4.65%
1941	9.36%	1.14%	5.51%
1951	14.44%	3.00%	8.95%
1961	23.71%	5.84%	15.21%
1971	28.74%	8.40%	19.07%
1981	36.30%	11.42%	24.38%
1991*	54.99%	20.44%	38.55%
2001	76.46%	44.34%	61.03%

* Age 7 and above.

Source: Basic Statistics, 1998, Rajasthan Directorate of Economics and Statistics Raj., Jaipur (Printed at Co-operative Press Ltd., Jaipur).

Table 3.21 *(See page 118)* depicts gender-wise and area-wise literacy scenario in the state. It is evident that in the year of 1961 when 25.05 (71.7%) lacs males were literate only 5.61 lacs (18.3%) females were literate. While in the year of 1991, 34.19 lacs (25.24%) female were literate against 101.29 lacs (74.76%) males.

In Urban area, there were 3.47 lacs (28.1%) females were literate against of 8.87 lacs (71.9%) males in the year of 1961. In 1991 there were 19.25 lacs (35.8%) females were literate against of 34.45 (64.2%) lacs males.

Educational access is very poor in rural areas, specially regarding women education. In 1961, 2.14 lacs (11.68%) females were literate against (88.32%) male literate.

Table 3.21. Gender-wise and Area-wise Literacy in the State of Rajasthan

(Figures in lacs)

Census Year	Rural			Urban			Total		
	Males	Females	Total	Males	Females	Total	Males	Females	Total
1961	16.18	2.14	18.32	8.87	3.47	12.34	25.05	5.61	30.66
1971	25.30	4.09	29.39	13.45	6.29	19.74	38.75	10.38	49.13
1981	41.55	7.12	48.67	23.26	11.61	34.87	64.81	18.73	83.54
1991	66.84	14.94	81.78	34.45	19.25	53.7	101.29	34.19	135.48

Source:

1. Census of India 1961, Volume XIV Rajasthan Part-IIA, General Population Tables, p. 167.
2. Census of India 1971, Series-18, Rajasthan Part -IIA, General Population Tables, p. 3.
3. Census of India 1981, Series-1 India. Part-II B (i) p. 391.
4. Census of India, 1991 (PCA) NIC Udaipur.

In 1991, 14.94 lacs (18.3%) females were literate against 66.84 lacs (81.7%) literate males as shown in table 3.22 *(See page 119).*

In 1961, out of 95.91 lacs females only 5.61 lacs (5.85%) females were literate. While in 1991, out of 209.62 lacs females 34.19 lacs (16.31%) females were literate. In rural area only 2.14 (2.7%) lacs females were literate in 1961 which increased upto 14.94 lacs (9.2%) females in 1991. In urban area situation is slightly different 15.38 (3.47%) lacs and 47.10 (19.25%) lacs females were literate in 1961 and 1991 respectively.

The table 3.23 *(See page 120)* is showing the difference of gender inequality. Why women were not equipped with education because there were very lesser institutions for girls. When there were 46,363 total educational institution for boys only 4392 institution for girls.

In the year 1996-97, 63.41 lacs boys enrolled but females were only 34.35 lacs. This table reveals the fact that women are right now being suppressed by the society. And a large part of females are keeping away from the access of education.

In 1996-97, 5 lacs S.C. girls were enrolled in educational institutions against of 10.6 lacs boys and 2.99 lacs S.T. girls were

Table 3.22. Female Population and Literacy in the State of Rajasthan

(Figures in lacs)

Census year	Rural			Urban			Total		
	Total female	Literate Females	% of literate female to total rural female population	Total female	Literate females	% of literate female to total urban female population	Total female	Literate females	% of literate female to total female population
1961	80.53	2.14	2.7%	15.38	3.47	22.6%	95.91	5.61	5.85%
1971	101.61	4.09	4.0%	21.20	6.29	29.7%	122.81	10.38	8.45%
1981	130.38	7.12	5.5%	33.70	11.61	34.5%	164.04	18.73	11.42%
1991	162.52	14.94	9.2%	47.10	19.25	40.9%	209.62	34.19	16.31%

Source:

1. Census of India 1961, Volume XIV Rajasthan Part-IIA, General Population Tables, pp. 166-167.
2. Census of India 1971, Series-18, Rajasthan Part-IIA, General Population Tables, pp. 2 & 3.
3. Census of India 1981, Series-1 India. Part-II B (i) pp. 390-391.
4. Census of India, 1991 (PCA) NIC Udaipur.

Table 3.23. Educational Institutions, No. of Students, and Teachers in the State of Rajasthan (1996-97)

(Figures in lacs)

Classification of educational institutions	Number of institutions (1995–96)			No. of total students			No. of teachers		
	Boys	Girls	Total	Boys	Girls	Total	Boys	Girls	Total
Primary	31479	2279	33758	24.30	15.02	39.32	0.68	0.28	0.96
Upper Primary	10891	1385	12276	21.82	11.68	33.5	0.73	0.25	0.98
Secondary	2937	439	3376	15.58*	6.47*	22.05*	0.61*	0.24*	0.85*
Senior Hr. Secondary	1056	289	1345						
Colleges	–	–	196	1.71	1.18	2.89	0.03	0.2	0.05
University & Deemed University	–	–	8	–	–	–	–	–	–
Total	**46363**	**4392**	**50959**	**63.41**	**34.35**	**97.76**	**2.05**	**0.79**	**2.84**

Source: Basic Statistics, Rajasthan 1998. pp. 183, 185.

* It is the total value of Secondary and Sr. Higher Secondary.

enrolled against of 7.1 lacs boys. Table also displays in 1996-97, there were 2.05 lacs male and 0.79 lacs females were working in educational institutions as teacher.

GENDER-WISE AND OCCUPATION-WISE DISTRIBUTION OF POPULATION IN THE STATE OF RAJASTHAN

Table 3.24 *(See pages 122 to 125)* is focusing, on the working population of the state. In 1961, 32.88 lacs female rural main workers were working, which were unexpectedly decreased to 9.43 lacs in 1971. In 1991 female main workers were 24.80 lacs against of 86.91 lac males. This fact make us aware that women are not equally supportive in the economy of the state of Rajasthan. Rural female marginal workers were recorded 29.24 lacs in 1991 against of 1.65 lac males. And female non-workers were 108.49 lac. against of 88.22 males in 1991.

In urban area, female main workers were recorded at 2.53 lacs. In the year of 1991 as against 1.54 la in 1961 according to 1991 census there were 0.87 lacs female marginal workers against of 0.13 lacs male marginal workers. Female non-workers recorded 43.78 la against of 28.60 la males.

DEMOGRAPHIC PROFILE OF WOMAN IN UDAIPUR DISTRICT

Udaipur was funded by Maharana Udai Singh in 1559 AD and was made the capital of Mewar in 1568 AD. After independence it became the capital of former Rajasthan and later on, after the formation of United State of Rajasthan, it became the district headquarter. Udaipur district is situated in southern part of Rajasthan. Udaipur is located between the latitude 23.46 to 26.2 North and longitude 73.0 to 74.35 east. Girdealed by green lofty and minerally rich Aravali hills. It is bounded on the north by Rajsamand district on the south by Dungarpur and Banswara districts, on the east by Chittorgarh district on the west Pali and Sirohi districts of Rajasthan and Sabarkanta district of Gujarat state. The district covers an area of 17.279 sq. km. and density of population in 1961 was marked by 83 persons per sq. km. In the year of 1991 density of population increased to 167 persons per sq. km.

Table 3.24. Occupation-wise and Gender-wise Population in the State of Rajasthan

(Figures in Lacs)

Classification	Census year							
	1961				1971			
	Rural		Urban		Rural		Urban	
	Males	Females	Males	Females	Males	Females	Males	Females
1	2	3	4	5	6	7	8	9
1. Main workers	53.04	32.88	8.37	1.54	59.32	9.43	10.92	0.82
1.1 Cultivators	41.24	28.01	0.81	0.49	44.61	6.43	1.10	0.12
1.2 Agricultural labours	2.22	1.58	0.08	0.05	5.05	2.06	0.31	0.07
1.3 Livestock, forestry, fishing, hunting and plantations orchards and allied services	1.08*	0.45*	0.14*	0.03*	1.64*	0.33*	0.08*	0.01*
1.4 Mining and quarrying								
1.5a Manufacturing, processing service and repairs in household industries	3.43	1.72	0.54	0.28	1.77	0.20	0.68	0.11
1.5b Manufacturing, processing servicing and repairs in other than household industries	0.40	0.08	1.11	0.12	1.00	0.08	1.78	0.08

(Contd...)

1		2	3	4	5	6	7	8	9
1.6	Constructions	0.42	0.08	0.55	0.04	0.45	0.04	0.49	0.02
1.7	Trade and Commerce	1.24	0.06	1.50	0.07	1.33	0.03	2.17	0.05
1.8	Transport storage and communication	0.27	0.003	0.90	0.007	0.45	0.01	1.13	0.01
1.9	Other services	2.73	0.89	2.74	0.43	3.02	0.25	3.18	0.35
1.10	Other worker (Total of 1.3 + 1.4 + 1.5(b) + 1.6 + 1.7 + 1.8 + 1.9)								
2.0	Marginal workers								
3.0	Non-workers	35.17	47.65	9.06	13.84	51.29	92.18	13.31	20.39

(Contd...)

(Table 3.24 Contd...)

(Figures in Lacs)

Classification	Census year										
	1981				1991						
	Rural		Urban		Rural		Urban		Total		
	Males	Females	Males	Females	Males	Females	Males	Females	Males	Females	Total population
1	2	3	4	5	6	7	8	9	10	11	12
1. Main workers	71.48	13.8	17.64	1.5	86.91 (49.2%)	24.80 (15.3%)	24.83 (46.4%)	2.53 (5.4%)	111.74 (80.3%)	27.33 (19.7%)	139.07 (100%)
1.1 Cultivators	52.41	9.95	1.68	0.26	60.91	18.48	1.96	0.47	62.87 (76.8%)	18.95 (23.2%)	81.82 (100%)
1.2 Agricultural labours	4.84	2.29	0.41	0.10	8.12	4.78	0.81	0.21	8.93 (64.2%)	4.99 (35.8%)	13.92 (100%)
1.3 Livestock, forestry, fishing, hunting and plantations orchards and allied services					1.77	0.34	0.38	0.03	2.15 (85.3%)	0.37 (14.7%)	2.52 (100%)
1.4 Mining & quarrying					0.94	0.12	0.34	0.03	1.28 (89.5%)	0.15 (10.5%)	1.43 (100%)
1.5a Manufacturing, processing service and repairs in household industries	2.06	0.28	0.91	0.15	1.54	0.29	0.78	0.18	2.32 (83.2%)	0.47 (16.8%)	2.79 (100%)
1.5b Manufacturing, processing servicing & repairs in other than household industries					2.46	0.16	4.67	0.30	7.13 (93.9%)	0.46 (6.1%)	7.59 (100%)

(Contd...)

1		2	3	4	5	6	7	8	9	10	11	12
1.6	Constructions					1.41	0.07	1.80	0.09	3.21 (95.3%)	0.16 (4.7%)	3.37 (100%)
1.7	Trade & Commerce					2.95	0.08	5.75	0.15	8.7 (97.4%)	0.23 (2.6%)	8.93 (100%)
1.8	Transport storage & communication					1.21	0.01	2.07	0.03	3.28 (98.8%)	0.04 (1.2%)	3.32 (100%)
1.9	Other services					5.69	0.47	6.27	1.06	11.96 (88.7%)	1.53 (11.3%)	13.49 (100%)
1.10	Other worker (Total of 1.3 + 1.4 + 1.5(b) + 1.6 + 1.7 + 1.8 + 1.9)	12.17	1.27	14.63	0.98	–	–	–	–	–	–	–
2.0	Marginal workers	1.63	18.78	0.11	0.48	1.65 (0.9%)	29.24 (18.0%)	0.13 (0.2%)	0.87 (1.8%)	1.78 (5.6%)	30.11 (94.4%)	31.89 (100%)
3.0	Non-workers	67.02	97.80	20.65	31.71	88.22 (49.9%)	108.49 (66.7%)	28.60 (53.4%)	43.78 (92.8%)	116.82 (43.44%)	152.27 (56.6%)	269.09 (100%)

Source:

1. Census of India, 1961, Volume XIV Rajasthan Part II-A "General Population Tables", pp. 167 to 169.
2. Basic Statistics, Rajasthan 1981, pp. 41 and 42.
3. Census of India, 1981, Series 1, India Part IIB (i), pp. 392 to 395.
4. Basic Statistics Rajasthan, 1998, pp. 44 and 45.

Note:* It is the total of 1.3 and 1.4.

The northern part of the district is generally of elevated plateaus while the eastern part has vast stretches of fertile plain. The south is covered with rocks, hills and dense forests. Whereas western portion known as the hilly tracts of Mewar is composed of Arawalli range. The district is well known for its possession of artificial lakes and beautiful gardens. The average rainfall of the district is 67.76 cm.

Administration-wise, the district is divided into four subdivisions and 10 tehsils and 11 blocks. The collector is the administrative head of the district and is vested with the power of district magistrate. Each sub-division is under the charge of a sub divisional officer and each Tehsil is under a Tehsildar. From the point of view of development the district is divided in 11 Vikash Khands (Panchayat Samities). The panchayat samities and guided by Zila Parishad under the chairmanship of Zila Pramukh but supervised by the collector of the district, who is also the ex-officio district development officer. The Panchayat Samities have been entrusted with the implementation of development activities at the block level. The list of subdivisions and blocks are as under:

Subdivisions

1. Udaipur
2. Jhadol
3. Salumbar
4. Vallabhnagar

Blocks

1. Girwa
2. Kotra
3. Dhariawad
4. Badgaon
5. Mavali
6. Gogunda
7. Bhinder

8. Jhadol
9. Kherwara
10. Sarada
11. Salumber

GENDER-WISE AND AREA-WISE DISTRIBUTION OF POPULATION IN UDAIPUR DISTRICT

The table 3.25 *(See page 128)* revealed that the female population of Udaipur district was 2.64 lacs in 1901 which increased upto 14.19 lacs in 1991. During 1901 to 1991 percentage of males to total population was between 50% to 52% while percentage of females to total population was only 47.8% to 49.4%.

The percentage of females to total population is increasing in every census year except in the year of 1961 and 1991. On the other side the percentage of males to total population is decreasing.

During 1961 to 1991 female population in Udaipur district increased from 7.09 lacs to 14.19 lacs (117.61%) while female rural population increased from 6.35 lacs to 11.86 lacs (86.77%) and female urban population increased from 0.74 lacs to 2.33 lacs (214.86%).

According to 1991 census 83.58% females in Udaipur district lives in rural area and the rest 16.42 per cent in urban area. The urban female population increased from 1961 to 1991 (10.44% to 16.42%), resulting in a consequent decrease of rural females population which 89.56% in 1961 and came down to 83.58% in 1991.

DECADAL VARIATION OF FEMALE IN UDAIPUR DISTRICT

Table 3.26 *(See page 129)* shows decadal variation of female in Udaipur district. Lowest decadal variation of female 6.49% was noted during 1911-1921 while highest decadal variation of female 32.09% was noted during 1971-1981. In 1991 variation dropped upto 21.80%.

Table 3.25. Gender-wise and Area-wise Distribution of Population in Udaipur District

(Figures in lacs)

Census year	Rural			Urban			Total		
	Males	Females	Total	Males	Females	Total	Males	Females	Population
1901			4.79			0.73	2.87 (52.2%)	2.64 (47.8%)	5.52 (100%)
1911			6.27			0.56	3.53 (51.8%)	3.29 (48.2%)	6.82 (100%)
1921			6.65			0.60	3.73 (51.6%)	3.51 (48.4%)	7.25 (100%)
1931			7.59			0.70	4.27 (51.5%)	4.02 (48.5%)	8.29 (100%)
1941			9.00			0.89	5.09 (51.5%)	4.80 (48.5%)	9.89 (100%)
1951			10.15			1.48	5.93 (51.1%)	5.69 (48.9%)	11.63 (100%)
1961	6.69 (52.8%)	6.35 (47.2%)	12.66 (100%)	0.86 (53.7%)	0.74 (46.3%)	1.60 (100%)	7.55 (51.6%)	7.09 (48.4%)	14.64 (100%)
1971	8.03 (50.7%)	7.79 (49.3%)	15.81 (100%)	1.19 (53.6%)	1.03 (46.4%)	2.22 (100%)	9.22 (51.1%)	8.82 (48.9%)	18.03 (100%)
1981	10.03 (50.1%)	9.98 (49.9%)	20.01 (100%)	1.88 (53.0%)	1.67 (47%)	3.55 (100%)	11.92 (50.6%)	11.65 (49.4%)	23.57 (100%)
1991	12.09 (50.5%)	11.86 (49.5%)	23.95 (100%)	2.61 (52.8%)	2.33 (47.2%)	4.94 (100%)	14.70 (50.9%)	14.19 (49.1%)	28.89 (100%)

Source:
1. Census of India, Series-18 Rajasthan Part IIA "General Population Tables pp. 85,90,114 and 169.
2. Census of India 1961, Volume XIV Rajasthan, Part II-A, "General Population Tables" p. 206.
3. Census of India, 1971, Series 18 Rajasthan Part II-A, "General Population Tables" p. 110.
4. Census of India, Series-1, India Part II-B (i) p. 402.
5. Census of India, Series-21 Rajasthan Part XII A & B District Udaipur p. 574.
6. Basic Statistics Rajasthan pp. 40 and 43.
7. Basic Statistics Rajasthan 1981 p. 38.

Note: Percentage has been given in brackets.

Table 3.26. Decadal Variation of Female in Udaipur District

(Figures in Lacs)

Census year	Total females	Decade variation
1901	2.64	
1911	3.29	24.62%
1921	3.51	6.69%
1931	4.02	14.53%
1941	4.80	19.40%
1951	5.69	18.54%
1961	6.91	21.44%
1971	8.82	27.64%
1981	11.65	32.09%
1991	14.19	21.80%

Source:

1. Census of India 1981 Series 18, Rajasthan, Part II A "General Population Tables p. 169.
2. Basic Statistics, Rajasthan 1998, p. 40.

SEX COMPOSITION OF POPULATION IN UDAIPUR DISTRICT

The sex-ratio (Table 3.27, *See page 130*) of Udaipur district is increasing every census year except in the year of 1961 and 1991 when ratio had been slightly decreased. In 1901, the lowest sex-ratio 920 had been recorded and in 1981, the highest sex-ratio 977 had been recorded.

The urban sex-ratio display amazing facts, which is declining from 1901 to 1941. But after independence sex-ratio (932) increased in 1951. In 1991, there were 891 females for 1000 males.

In rural area, the picture is quite different. The sex-ratio is increasing every census year except in the year of 1961 and 1991. The highest sex-ratio recorded in 1981, when 995 females for 1000 males.

Table 3.27. Sex Composition in Udaipur District

(Female per thousand Male)

Census year	Rural	Urban	Sex-ratio
1901	916	944	920
1911	933	915	932
1921	943	909	940
1931	948	883	943
1941	950	878	943
1951	965	932	960
1961	949	865	940
1971	970	871	957
1981	995	886	977
1991*	982	891	965

Source:

1. Census of India, 1981, Series-18, Rajasthan, Part 11-A, "General Population Tables" p. 164.
2*. Basic Statistics, 1998, Rajasthan p. 40, Rajasthan (Ecology Culture and Society) 1999. Bhasin M.K. and Bhasin Veena, p. 25.

GENDER-WISE DISTRIBUTION OF POPULATION IN UDAIPUR DISTRICT

Table 3.28 *(See page 131)* shows that Hindu accounted for the largest community, in the year of 1991, Hindus recorded 26.99 la i.e. 93.4 per cent in strength to total population, however, S.C./S.T. is the part of Hindu community other largest community of women belongs to Muslims 0.45 lacs (3.17%) and Jain 0.44 La (3.10%).

The major religious communities of our Country are Hindus, Muslims, Christians, Sikhs, Buddhists, Jains and Parsis. Of these last three caste numerically insignificant but they are important in other ways.

In 1991, there were only 14.18 lacs females for 14.70 lacs males. Gender disparity is visible in Hindus, Muslim and Sikh community while in Jain, Christian and Buddhist society, women population is equal to male population.

Table 3.28. Gender-wise and Caste-wise Distribution of Population in Udaipur District

(Figure in lacs)

Religion	*1971	+1981	#1991		
			Males	Females	Total
Hindus	11.47	21.90	13.73	13.26 (90.20%)	26.99 (93.42%)
Muslims	0.44	0.70	0.49	0.45 (3.17%)	0.94 (3.25%)
Sikhs	0.009	0.02	0.02	0.01	0.03
Jain	0.53	0.92	0.44	0.44 (3.10%)	0.88 (3.05%)
Christians	0.02	0.03	0.02	0.02	0.04
Buddhist	0.0003	0.0006	0.0004	0.0004	0.0008
Other not stated	0.0028	0.002	0.0004	0.0002	0.0006
Religion not stated	–	0.0007	0.003	0.002	0.005
Total	**12.47**	**23.57**	**14.70**	**14.18 (100%)**	**28.89 (100%)**

Source:

(1)* Gila Sankhayaki Ruprekha, 1994, Gila, Udaipur, p. 40.

(2)+ Basic Statistics, Rajasthan, 1998, pp. 41, 42.

(3)# Census of India, 1991, Series-21 Rajasthan, Part IV-B (ii), Religion Table C-9 pp. 62, 63.

Gender-wise and caste-wise population of S/C and S/T is given in table 3.29 and 3.30 *(See pages 132 and 133)*. The district has a sizeable tribal population it constitutes about 37.76% of the total population of the district. The total SC/ST population in the district is about 45.06%. According to 1991 census the total female population of the district was 14.19 lacs out of which 1.17 (8.25%) females were of S.C. and 5.23 (36.86%) females were S.T.

In Udaipur district S/C and S/T female population was 0.62 lacs and 2.16 lacs respectively in 1961 and increased upto 1.17 lacs and 5.23 lacs respectively in 1991. Table 3.29 reveals that gender equality in S/C and S/T is more visualizing in rural area compare to urban area.

Table 3.29. Gender-wise and Caste-wise Population of Scheduled Castes and Scheduled Tribes in Udaipur District

(Figures in lacs)

Census year	S/C Population									S/T Population								
	Rural			Urban			Total			Rural			Urban			Total		
	Males	Females	Total	Males	Females	Total	Males	Females	Population	Males	Females	Total	Males	Females	Total	Males	Females	Population
1961	0.58 (51.3%)	0.55 (48.7%)	1.13 (100%)	0.07 (50%)	0.07 (50%)	0.14 (100%)	0.65 (51.2%)	0.62 (48.8%)	1.27 (100%)	2.22 (50.9%)	2.14 (49.1%)	4.36 (100%)	0.03 (60%)	0.02 (40%)	0.05 (100%)	2.25 (51%)	2.16 (49%)	4.41 (100%)
1971	0.63 (51.2%)	0.60 (48.8%)	1.23 (100%)	0.09 (52.9%)	0.08 (47.1%)	0.17 (100%)	0.72 (51.4%)	0.68 (48.6%)	1.4 (100%)	3.05 (50.7%)	2.96 (49.3%)	6.01 (100%)	0.03 (60%)	0.02 (40%)	0.05 (100%)	3.08 (50.8%)	2.98 (49.2%)	6.06 (100%)
1981	0.80 (50.6%)	0.78 (49.4%)	1.58 (100%)	0.18 (51.4%)	0.17 (48.6%)	0.35 (100%)	0.98 (50.8%)	0.95 (49.2%)	1.93 (100%)	3.98 (50.2%)	3.95 (49.8%)	7.93 (100%)	0.09 (56.2%)	0.07 (43.8%)	0.16 (100%)	4.07 (50.3%)	4.02 (49.7%)	8.09 (100%)
1991	0.96 (51.1%)	0.92 (48.9%)	1.88 (100%)	0.27 (51.9%)	0.25 (48.1%)	0.52 (100%)	1.23 (51.2%)	1.17 (48.8%)	2.4 (100%)	5.24 (50.6%)	5.11 (49.4%)	10.35 (100%)	0.15 (55.6%)	0.12 (44.4%)	0.27 (100%)	5.39 (50.8%)	5.23 (49.2%)	10.62 (100%)

Source:

1. Census of India 1961, Volume XIV Rajasthan Part-IIA, General Population Tables, pp. 206, 207.
2. Census of India 1971, Series-18, Rajasthan Part-IIA, General Population Tables, p. 111.
3. Basic Statistics, Rajasthan, 1981, p. 43.
4. Census of India 1981, Series-18, Rajasthan, Part-IIB, p. 35.
5. Census of India, 1991, Series-21, Rajasthan Part XII A & B, Distt, Udaipur, pp. 1056 and 1068.

Table 3.30. Female Population of Scheduled Castes and Scheduled Tribes in Udaipur District

(Figures in lacs)

Census year	Rural					Urban					Total				
	Total female population	S.C. female population	% of S.C. female population to total population	S.T. female population	% of S.T. female popula tion to total population	Total female population	S.C female population	% of S.C. female population to total population	S.T. female population	% of S.T. female population to total population	Total female population	S.C. female population	% of S.C female population to total population	S.T. female population	% of S.T. female population to total population
1961	6.35	0.55	8.66%	2.14	33.70%	0.74	0.07	9.46%	0.02	2.70%	6.91	0.62	8.97%	2.16	31.26%
1971	7.79	0.60	7.70%	2.96	38.00%	1.03	0.08	7.77%	0.02	1.94%	8.82	0.68	7.71%	2.98	33.79
1981	9.98	0.78	7.82%	3.95	39.58%	1.67	0.17	10.18%	0.07	4.19%	11.65	0.95	8.15%	4.02	34.51%
1991	11.86	0.92	7.76%	5.11	43.09%	2.33	0.25	10.73%	0.12	5.15%	14.19	1.17	8.25%	5.23	36.86%

Source: Prepared from Table 3.29.

LITERACY AMONG FEMALES IN UDAIPUR DISTRICT

Education is the only weapon instrument which, develops the faculties and powers of human being by teaching. It is a continuous flow, human being can acquire education at any age, at any time (Table 3.31).

The Udaipur district is educationally the backward district of the state of Rajasthan, only 27.97 per cent of the population (age 7 years and above) have been found literate in the census 1991. However, some progress may have been made over the years, as the per cent literate in 1961 was only 13.96 per cent. There also seems to be a wide gender gap in literacy, with only 15.43% of females as against 40.07% per cent of males being literate.

Table 3.31. Per cent Distribution of Literates in Udaipur District

Census year	Male	Female	Total
1961	22.04%	5.35%	13.96%
1971	26.57%	7.82%	17.42%
1981	40.60%	15.45%	28.17%
1991	40.07%	15.43%	27.97%

Source: Prepared from table 3.25 and 3.32.

Table 3.32 *(See page 135)* reveals the literacy scenario of Udaipur district from 1961 to 1991.

In 1961, out of 0.37 lacs literate females 0.14 lacs literate females lived in rural areas while 0.23 lacs literate females lived in urban areas. In 1991, 2.19 lacs females including 0.99 rural females and 1.20 urban females were literate in Udaipur district.

It is an amazing fact that percentage of female literacy of Udaipur district has shown an increasing trend since 1961 to 1991 and vice versa in male literacy.

During 1961-1991, (Table 3.33, *See page 136*) percentage of female literate out of total literate in Udaipur district increased

Table 3.32. Gender-wise and Area-wise Literacy in Udaipur District

(Figures in lacs)

Census year	Rural			Urban			Total		
	Males	Females	Total	Males	Females	Total	Males	Females	Population
1961	1.10 (88.71%)	0.14 (11.29%)	1.24 (100%)	0.52 (69.33%)	0.23 (30.67%)	0.75 (100%)	1.62 (81.41%)	0.37 (18.59%)	1.99 (100%)
1971	1.70 (85.0%)	0.30 (15.0%)	2.00 (100%)	0.75 (65.79%)	0.39 (34.21%)	1.14 (100%)	2.45 (78.03%)	0.69 (21.97%)	3.14 (100%)
1981	2.64 (83.54%)	0.52 (16.46%)	3.16 (100%)	2.20 (63.22%)	1.28 (36.78%)	3.48 (100%)	4.84 (72.89%)	1.80 (27.11%)	6.64 (100%)
1991	4.01 (80.2%)	0.99 (19.8%)	5.00 (100%)	1.88 (61.04%)	1.20 (38.96%)	3.08 (100%)	5.89 (72.90%)	2.19 (27.10%)	8.08 (100%)

Source:

1. Census of India 1961, Volume XIV Rajasthan Part-IIA, General Population Tables, p. 207.
2. Census of India 1971, Series-18, Rajasthan Part-IIA, General Population Tables, p. 111, and Basic Statistics 1981, p. 223.
3. Census of India 1981, Series-1 India. Part-II B(i) p. 403.
4. Census of India 1991, Series-21, Rajasthan Part-XII A & B, district Udaipur p. 575.

Table 3.33. Female Population and Literacy in Udaipur District

(Figures in lacs)

Census year	Rural			Urban			Total		
	Total female	Literate Females	% of literate female to total rural female population	Total female	Literate females	% of literate female to total urban female population	Total female	Literate females	% of literate female to total female population
1961	6.35	0.14	2.20%	0.74	0.23	31.08%	6.91	0.37	5.35%
1971	7.79	0.30	3.85%	1.03	0.39	37.86%	8.82	0.69	7.82%
1981	9.98	0.52	5.21%	1.67	1.28	76.65%	11.65	1.80	15.45%
1991	11.86	0.99	8.35%	2.33	1.20	51.50%	14.19	2.19	15.43%

Source: Prepared from table 3.25 and 3.32.

Table 3.33 shows that in 1961 only 5.35% of females were literate to total female population, however in 1991 literacy increased up to 15.43%.

In rural area during 1961 to 1991, percentage of literate female to total female population increased from 2.20% to 8.35% while in urban area in the same period percentage of literate female to total female increased from 31.08% to 51.50%.

from 18.59% to 27.10%. Percentage of female literate in rural area increased from 11.29% to 19.80% while in urban area it increased from 30.67% to 38.96%.

Table 3.34 *(See page 138)* reveals that in the year of 1992-93, there were only 2,308 educational institutions in Udaipur district.

The overall analysis of table reflects that female lags behind male in educational line. There were only 1.10 lacs girls literate against 2.23 lacs boys. And when 0.07 lacs male teachers were providing their services to educational institutions at that time only 0.03 lacs female teachers were providing their service.

In the year of 1992-93 out of the 1.10 lacs girl students, S.T. and S.C. girl students were 0.24 lacs (21.81%) and 0.11 lacs (10%) respectively.

GENDER-WISE AND OCCUPATION-WISE DISTRIBUTION OF POPULATION IN UDAIPUR DISTRICT

According to 1991 census (Table 3.35 *See pages 139 to 142*) the total working population in the district was 12.51 lacs (43.30%) of the total population, out of which 9.54 lacs (33.02%) were main workers and 2.97 lacs (10.28%) were marginal workers. The occupation classification of the working population reflects greater predominance of agricultural sector (cultivations, Agricultural labourers, Ag. Allied activities) which accounts for 6.74 lacs (53.88%) of the total working force. It clearly indicates that district economy relies more on agriculture while the secondary and tertiary sector requires further development. In modern times, it is an accepted fact that highly developed economy always depends less on agriculture and more on secondary and tertiary sectors.

In 1961, there were 3.11 lacs female main workers against of 4.62 male main workers while in 1991 scene was different there were 1.87 lacs female main workers against of 7.67 lacs male main workers.

Table 3.34. Educational Institutions, No. of Students, and Teachers in Udaipur District (1992-93)

(Figures in lacs)

Classification of educational institution	Number of institutions			No. of total students			No. of S.C. Students			No. of ST students			No. of Teachers		
	Boys	Girls	Total	Boys	Girls	Total	Boys	Girls	Total	Boys	Girls	Total	Male	Female	Total
Primary	–	–	1603	1.04	0.52	1.56	0.08	0.05	0.13	0.48	0.17	0.65	0.03	0.01	0.04
Upper Primary	–	–	434	0.54	0.35	0.89	0.06	0.03	0.09	0.18	0.05	0.23	0.02	0.01	0.03
Secondary & Sr. Hr. Secondary	–	–	215	0.52	0.19	0.71	0.05	0.02	0.07	0.097	0.02	0.12	0.02	0.01	0.03
College for general education	–	–	8	0.04	0.02	0.06	0.001	0.0002	0.001	0.002	0.00007	0.002	–	–	–
College for professional education	–	–	13	0.03	0.008	0.04	0.004	0.0001	0.004	0.002	0.0001	0.002	–	–	–
University	–	–	1	0.03	0.004	0.03	0.001	–	0.001	0.001	–	0.001	–	–	–
School for vocational & professional education	–	–	16	0.02	0.008	0.03	0.005	0.002	0.007	0.004	0.001	0.005	–	–	–
Others	–	–	18	0.01	0.004	0.01	0.003	0.0005	0.004	0.005	0.001	0.006	–	–	–
Total	–	–	**2308**	**2.23**	**1.104**	**3.33**	**0.21**	**0.11**	–	**0.78**	**0.24**	**1.02**	**0.07**	**0.03**	**0.10**

Source: Gila Sankhyakhi Ruprekha, 1994, Gila Udaipur pp. 208, 214, 217, 220, 223 and 224.

Table 3.35. Occupation-wise and Gender-wise Population in Udaipur District

(*Figures in Lacs*)

Classification	Census year							
	1961				1971			
	Rural		Urban		Rural		Urban	
	Males	Females	Males	Females	Males	Females	Males	Females
1	2	3	4	5	6	7	8	9
1. Main workers	4.20	3.02	0.42	0.09	4.54	0.62	0.55	0.05
1.1 Cultivators	3.48	2.63	0.03	0.02	3.58	0.40	0.03	0.004
1.2 Agricultural labours	0.06	0.06	0.003	0.003	0.22	0.14	0.01	0.003
1.3 Livestock, forestry, fishing, hunting and plantations orchards and allied services	0.09*	0.07*	0.007*	0.002*	0.08	0.03	0.002	0.0004
1.4 Mining and quarrying					0.03	0.002	0.004	0.00007
1.5a Manufacturing, processing service and repairs in household industries	0.20	0.17	0.02	0.02	0.12	0.01	0.03	0.004
1.5b. Manufacturing, processing servicing and repairs in other than household industries	0.04	0.01	0.05	0.003	0.06	0.004	0.08	0.003

(*Contd...*)

(Table 3.35. Contd...)

1		2	3	4	5	6	7	8	9
1.6	Constructions	0.03	0.008	0.04	0.008	0.05	0.006	0.02	0.003
1.7	Trade and Commerce	0.11	0.008	0.08	0.01	0.14	0.003	0.12	0.004
1.8	Transport storage and communication	0.01	0.0002	0.04	0.0003	0.03	0.002	0.05	0.0006
1.9	Other services	0.18	0.05	0.15	0.03	0.23	0.002	0.20	0.03
1.10	Other worker (Total of 1.3 + 1.4 + 1.5(b) + 1.6 + 1.7 + 1.8 + 1.9)	–	–	–	–	–	–	–	–
2.0	Marginal workers	–	–	–	–	–	–	–	–
3.0	Non-workers	2.49	3.33	0.43	0.65	3.49	7.16	0.64	0.98

(Contd...)

(Table 3.35. Contd...)

(Figures in Lacs)

Classification	Census year										
	1981				1991						
	Rural		Urban		Rural		Urban		Total		
	Males	Females	Males	Females	Males	Females	Males	Females	Males	Females	Total population
1	2	3	4	5	6	7	8	9	10	11	12
1. Main workers	5.29	0.83	1.48	0.15	6.40 (52.94%)	1.69 (14.25%)	1.27	0.18 (7.72%)	7.67 (80.4%)	1.87 (19.6%)	9.54 (100%)
1.1 Cultivators	4.00	0.54	0.08	0.01	4.45	1.12	0.07	0.03	4.52 (79.7%)	1.15 (20.3%)	5.67 (100%)
1.2 Agricultural labours	0.22	0.16	0.01	0.007	0.52	0.42	0.02	0.01	0.54 (55.7%)	0.43 (44.3%)	0.97 (100%)
1.3 Livestock, forestry, fishing, hunting and plantations orchards and allied services	–				0.06	0.02	0.02	0.001	0.08 (80%)	0.02 (20%)	0.10 (100%)
1.4 Mining & quarrying	–				0.14	0.02	0.05	0.001	0.19	0.02	0.21
1.5a Manufacturing, processing service and repairs in household industries	0.13	0.02	0.04	0.009	0.10	0.02	0.02	0.009	0.12	0.03	0.15
1.5b Manufacturing, processing servicing & repairs in other than household industries	–				0.27	0.0098	0.24	0.01	0.51	0.02	0.53

(Contd...)

(Table 3.35. Contd...)

	1	2	3	4	5	6	7	8	9	10	11	12
1.6	Constructions	–				0.13	0.01	0.06	0.006	0.19	0.02	0.21
1.7	Trade & Commerce	–				0.28	0.008	0.32	0.01	0.6	0.02	0.62
1.8	Transport storage & communication	–				0.10	0.001	0.12	0.002	0.22	0.003	0.22
1.9	Other services	–				0.35	0.05	0.33	0.09	0.68	0.14	0.82
1.10	Other worker (Total of 1.3 + 1.4 + 1.5(b) + 1.6 + 1.7 + 1.8 + 1.9)	0.93	0.11	1.34	1.12	–	–	–	–	–	–	–
2.0	Marginal workers	0.13	2.07	0.003	0.04	0.13 (1.08%)	2.77 (23.36%)	0.009	0.06 (2.58%)	0.14 (4.7%)	2.83 (95.3%)	2.97 (100%)
3.0	Non-workers	4.62	7.29	1.64	2.55	5.56 (45.98%)	7.40 (62.39%)	1.33	2.09 (89.70%)	6.89 (42.0%)	9.49 (57.9%)	16.38 (100%)

Source:

1. Census of India 1961, Volume XIV Rajasthan Part II-A, General Population Tables, pp. 207 to 209.
2. Census of India 1971, Series-18, Rajasthan Part II-A, General Population Tables, pp. 112 to 115.
3. Census of India, 1981, Series-1, India. Part II B (i) pp. 404 to 407.
4. Statistical Abstract Rajasthan, 1997 pp. 25 and 26.
5. Census of India 1991. Series-21, Rajasthan, Part-XII A & B, District Udaipur, pp. 276 to 279.

Note:* It is the total of 1.3 and 1.4.

According to 1991 census, that total main workers in the district was 9.54 lacs out of which 1.87 lacs (19.6%) were female main workers on the other hand, out of 2.97 lacs marginal workers, 2.83 lacs (95.3%) were female marginal workers.

According to 1991 census, the total rural female population of the district was 11.86 lacs out of which 4.39 lacs (37.61%) females were working while in urban area out of 2.33 females only 0.24 lacs (10.3%) females were working.

It clearly indicates that work participation of women has been very high in rural area in comparison to urban area.

DEMOGRAPHIC PROFILE OF WOMEN IN DUNGARPUR DISTRICT

Dungarpur district is located on the Southern border of Rajasthan state between the parallels of 23°20′ and 24°.21′ north latitudes and 73°.21′ and 74°.23′ east longitudes. It is bounded on the east by Banswara district, on the north of Udaipur district and on the south and west by Sabarkanta and Panchmahal districts of Gujarat state. The district forms part of a tribal belt spreaded over Dungarpur, Banswara, and parts of Chittorgarh, and Udaipur district of Rajasthan and Jhabua district of Madhya Pradesh. The total area of the district is 3770 sq. km. The district consist of five blocks namely Aspur, Bichhiwara, Dungarpur, Sagwara, and Simalwara.

Dungarpur has a typical topography with mainly hilly terrain. As a result the area left for cultivation is quite meagre and cultivation is carried out only on land patches located in various valley. The average rainfall of the district is 76.17 cm. Administrative-wise, the district is divided into two sub-divisions and 4 tehsils and 5 blocks. The list of such divisions and blocks are as under:

Sub Divisions

1. Dungarpur
2. Sagwara

Blocks

1. Dungarpur
2. Simalwara
3. Sagwara
4. Aspur
5. Bichhiwara

GENDER-WISE AND AREA-WISE DISTRIBUTION OF POPULATION IN DUNGARPUR DISTRICT

The table 3.36 *(See page 145)* depicts female population of Dungarpur district was 0.50 lacs in 1901, and in 1991 reached upto 4.36 lacs.

From 1961 to 1991 female population in the district increased from 2.02 lacs to 4.36 lacs (115.84%). While rural female population increased from 1.92 lacs to 4.06 lacs (111.46%) population increased from 0.10 lacs to 0.30 lacs (200%).

According to 1991, census 95.05% female in Dungarpur district lives in rural area and the rest 4.95% in urban area. The urban female population increased from 1961 to 1991 (4.95% to 6.88%), resulting in consequent decrease of rural female population which was 95.05% in 1961 and came down to 93.12 in 1991.

DECADAL VARIATION OF FEMALES IN DUNGARPUR DISTRICT

The table 3.37 *(See page 146)* shows decadal variation of females in Dungarpur district. The very high decadal variation of 60% of female has been observed during 1901-1911 and the lowest decade variation observed in between 1941-1951 i.e. 14.1%. While in the decade of 1981-1991 variation of females has been 24.9%.

Table 3.36. Gender-wise and Area-wise Distribution of Population in Dungarpur District

(Figure in lacs)

Census year	Rural			Urban			Total		
	Males	Females	Total	Males	Females	Total	Males	Females	Population
1901			0.94			0.06	0.50 (50%)	0.50 (50%)	1.00 (100%)
1911			1.44			0.14	0.79 (49.7%)	0.80 (50.3%)	1.59 (100%)
1921			1.72			0.17	0.95 (50.3%)	0.94 (49.7%)	1.89 (100%)
1931			2.09			0.18	1.14 (50.2%)	1.13 (49.8%)	2.27 (100%)
1941			2.55			0.19	1.39 (50.7%)	1.35 (49.3%)	2.74 (100%)
1951			2.86			0.22	1.54 (50%)	1.54 (50%)	3.08 (100%)
1961	1.93 (50.1%)	1.92 (49.9%)	3.85 (100%)	0.11 (52.4%)	0.10 (47.6%)	0.21 (100%)	2.04 (50.2%)	2.02 (49.8%)	4.06 (100%)
1971	2.47 (49.5%)	2.52 (50.5%)	4.99 (100%)	0.16 (51.6%)	0.15 (48.4%)	0.31 (100%)	2.63 (49.6%)	2.67 (50.4%)	5.30 (100%)
1981	3.11 (48.7%)	3.28 (51.3%)	6.39 (100%)	0.23 (52.3%)	0.21 (47.7%)	0.44 (100%)	3.34 (48.8%)	3.49 (51.2%)	6.82 (100%)
1991	4.05 (49.9%)	4.06 (50.1%)	8.11 (100%)	0.34 (53.1%)	0.30 (46.9%)	0.64 (100%)	4.39 (50.2%)	4.36 (49.8%)	8.75 (100%)

Percentage has been given in bracket.

Source:

1. Census of India 1961, Volume XIV Rajasthan Part II-A, General Population Tables, p. 214.
2. Census of India 1971, Series-18, Rajasthan Part II-A, General Population Tables, p. 128.
3. Census of India 1981, Series-1 India, Part II B (i) pp. 408 and 409.
4. Census of India 1981, Series-18, Rajasthan Part II-A "General Population Tables pp. 85, 90, 117 and 169.
5. Census of India (PCA) NIC Udaipur.
6. Basic Statistics, Rajasthan, 1998, pp. 40 and 43.
7. Basic Statistics, Rajasthan, 1981 p. 38.

Table 3.37. Decadal Variation of Female in Dungarpur District

(Figures in lacs)

Census year	Total females	Decade variation
1901	0.50	—
1911	0.80	6.0%
1921	0.94	17.5%
1931	1.13	20.2%
1941	1.35	19.5%
1951	1.54	14.1%
1961	2.02	31.2%
1971	2.67	32.2%
1981	3.49	3.07%
1991	4.36	24.9%

Source:

1. Census of India 1981, Series-18 Rajasthan, Part II A, "General Population Tables, p. 169.
2. Basic Statistics, 1998 p. 40.

SEX COMPOSITION OF POPULATION IN DUNGARPUR DISTRICT

Sex ratio in Dungarpur district shows a lot of variation during 1901-1991 (Table 3.38). In 1901, sex-ratio in the district was perfectly balanced when 1000 females for 1000 males. In the year of 1911, 1951, 1971 and 1981 females were more than males and in the rest of the year females recorded less than males. In 1991, the highest sex-ratio have been recorded by Dungarpur district (996) among the state and districts, 897 females in urban areas and 1003 females in rural areas recorded for 1000 males.

Table 3.38. Sex Composition of Population in Dungarpur District

(Female per thousand male)

Census year	Rural	Urban	Sex ratio
1901	993	1123	1000
1911	1007	1070	1012
1921	990	961	987
1931	985	1023	988
1941	970	968	970
1951	1003	1001	1003
1961	995	930	991
1971	1021	931	1015
1981	1056	900	1045
1991*	1003	897	996

Source:

1. Census of India, 1981, Series 18, Rajasthan, Part II-A, "General Population Tables p. 164.

2*. Basic Statistics 1998, Rajasthan p. 40. and Rajasthan (Ecology culture and Society) 1999, Bhasin M.K. and Bhasin Veena, p. 25.

CASTE-WISE DISTRIBUTION OF POPULATION IN DUNGARPUR DISTRICT

According to 1991 census, out of the 4.35 lacs females 4.17 lacs (95.81%), 0.12 (2.76%) and 0.06 lacs (1.38%) women belongs to Hindu, Muslims, and Jain religion respectively (Table 3.39, *See page 148*). In Dungarpur district, 1991 census shows that Sikhs, Jain and Christians are from those community where men and women are equal in ratio, while Hindu, Muslim and Buddhist women are slightly neglected.

Table 3.39. Gender-wise and Caste-wise Distribution of Population in Dungarpur District

Religion	1971	1981	1991		
			Males	Females	Total
Hindus	5.06	6.52	4.18	4.17 (95.81%)	8.35 (95.70%)
Muslims	0.14	0.18	0.13	0.12 (2.76%)	0.25 (2.86%)
Sikhs	0.0001	0.0008	0.0004	0.00037	0.0008
Jain	0.097	0.12	0.06	0.06 (1.38%)	0.12 (1.38%)
Christians	0.003	0.006	0.002	0.002	0.004
Buddhist	–	0.00004	0.00014	0.00012	0.0002
Other not stated	0.0002	0.00005	0.00001	–	0.00001
Religion not stated	–	–	0.00009	0.00002	0.0001
Total	–	–	4.37	4.35	8.72

Source:

1. "Gila Sankhayakhi Ruprekha, 1994, District Dungarpur p. 30.
2. Basic Statistics, Rajasthan, 1988 pp. 41 and 42.
3. Census of India, 1991, series 21 Rajasthan, Part IV-B (ii), Religion Table C-9 pp. 68 and 69.

Gender wise and caste-wise population of S/C and S/T is shown in the table 3.40 *(See page 149)*. The district forms part of a tribal belt. In the state highest concentration of the scheduled tribes has been noticed in the district of Banswara and Dungarpur (73.5% and 65.8%) of the total population respectively. On the other hand, the lowest percentage of S/C has been recorded by Dungarpur district 4.6%.

According to 1991 census total female population was 4.36 lacs out of them 0.20 lacs (4.6%) belong to S.C. and 2.87 lacs (65.8%) females belong to S.T. Class. It may be mentioned that female population of S.C. and S.T. increased from 0.09 lacs and 1.21 lacs in 1961 to 0.20 and 2.87 lacs in 1991 in Dungarpur district.

Table 3.40. Gender-wise and Area-wise Population of Scheduled Castes and Scheduled Tribes in Dungarpur District

(Figures in lacs)

Census Year	S/C Population									S/T Population								
	Rural			Urban			Total			Rural			Urban			Total		
	Males	Females	Total	Males	Females	Total	Males	Females	Population	Males	Females	Total	Males	Females	Total	Males	Females	Population
1961	0.09 (52.9%)	0.08 (47.1%)	0.17 (100%)	0.007 (50%)	0.007 (50%)	0.014 (100%)	0.09 (50%)	0.09 (50%)	0.18 (100%)	1.22 (50.4%)	1.20 (49.6%)	2.42 (100%)	0.01 (52.6%)	0.009 (47.4%)	0.019 (100%)	1.24 (50.6%)	1.21 (49.4%)	2.45 (100%)
1971	0.09 (47.4%)	0.10 (52.6%)	0.19 (100%)	0.011 (55%)	0.009 (45%)	0.02 (100%)	0.10 (50%)	0.10 (50%)	0.20 (100%)	1.66 (49.8%)	1.67 (50.2%)	3.33 (100%)	0.02 (50%)	0.02 (50%)	0.04 (100%)	1.69 (50%)	1.69 (50%)	3.38 (100%)
1981	0.13 (48.1%)	0.14 (51.9%)	0.27 (100%)	0.02 (50%)	0.02 (50%)	0.04 (100%)	0.15 (48.4%)	0.16 (51.6%)	0.31 (100%)	2.11 (48.8%)	2.21 (51.2%)	4.32 (100%)	0.04 (57.1%)	0.03 (42.9%)	0.07 (100%)	2.16 (49.1%)	2.24 (50.9%)	4.4 (100%)
1991	0.18 (51.4%)	0.17 (48.6%)	0.35 (100%)	0.03 (50%)	0.03 (50%)	0.06 (100%)	0.20 (50%)	0.20 (50%)	0.40 (100%)	2.83 (50%)	2.83 (50%)	5.66 (100%)	0.06 (60%)	0.04 (40%)	0.10 (100%)	2.88 (50.1%)	2.87 (49.9%)	5.75 (100%)

Source:

1. Census of India 1961, Volume XIV Rajasthan Part II-A, General Population Tables, pp. 214 to 215.
2. Census of India 1971, Series-18, Rajasthan Part-IIA, General Population Tables, p. 129.
3. Census of India 1981, Series-18, Rajasthan. Part-IIB, p. 35.
4. Census of India 1991, (PCA) NIC Udaipur.

Table 3.41. Female Population of Scheduled Castes and Scheduled Tribes in Dungarpur District

(Figures in lacs)

Census year	Rural					Urban					Total				
	Total female population	S.C. female population	% of S.C. female population to total population	S.T. female population	% of S.T. female population to total population	Total female population	S.C female population	% of S.C. female population to total population	S.T. female population	% of S.T. female population to total population	Total female population	S.C. female population	% of S.C female population to total population	S.T. female population	% of S.T. female population to total population
1961	1.92	0.08	4.17%	1.20	62.5%	0.10	0.007	7%	0.009	9%	2.02	0.09	4.46%	1.21	59.90%
1971	2.52	0.10	3.97%	1.67	66.27%	0.15	0.009	6%	0.02	13.33%	2.67	0.10	3.75%	1.69	63.30%
1981	3.28	0.14	4.27%	2.21	67.38%	0.21	0.02	9.52%	0.03	14.29%	3.49	0.16	4.58%	2.16	61.89%
1991	4.06	0.17	4.19%	2.83	69.70%	0.30	0.03	10%	0.04	13.33%	4.36	0.20	4.59%	2.88	66.06%

Source: Prepared from Table 3.36 and 3.40.

Table 3.41 analysis female population of S.C. and S.T. in the district of Dungarpur. In 1961, S.C. female population was 0.09 lacs (4.46%) of the total female population which increased in 1991 to 0.20 lacs (4.59%). And S.T. female population increased from 1.21 lacs (59.90%) in 1961 to 2.88 lacs (66.06%) in 1991.

LITERACY AMONG FEMALES IN DUNGARPUR DISTRICT

Table 3.42 depicts per cent distribution of literates in Dungarpur district. First of all total percentage of literacy is very low in the districts. In 1991, only 24.45% per cent people are literate in Dungarpur district, when we focus our attention towards female literacy, the grip of women in this field is very untidy. In 1961, only 3.47% female were literate against of 17.16% males. In 1991, there were 12.39% females against of 36.45% males.

Table 3.42. **Per cent Distribution of Literates in Dungarpur District**

Census year	Male	Female	Total
1961	17.16%	3.47%	10.34%
1971	22.81%	5.99%	14.34%
1981	29.64%	8.02%	18.62%
1991	36.45%	12.39%	24.45%

Source: Prepared from table no. 3.36 and 3.43.

Table 3.43 *(See page 152)* castes a glance into sex-wise and area-wise literacy scene in Dungarpur district from 1981 to 1991.

In 1961, out of 2.02 lacs females only 0.07 lacs female (3.46%) were literate, from whom 0.04 lacs and 0.03 lacs belong to rural and urban areas respectively. In 1991, total female population was 4.36 lacs and total literate female population was only 0.54 lacs (12.39%) (0.39 of rural and 0.15 of urban areas).

Table 3.43 shows that in 1961 there were 16.7% females literate out of total literate, however, in 1991 percentage increase upto 25.2%. It envisage that norm of female education accepted

Table 3.43. Gender-wise and Area-wise Literacy in Dungarpur District

(Figures in lacs)

Census year	Rural			Urban			Total		
	Males	Females	Total	Males	Females	Total	Males	Females	Population
1961	0.29 (87.9%)	0.04 (12.1%)	0.33 (100%)	0.06 (66.7%)	0.03 (33.3%)	0.09 (100%)	0.35 (83.3%)	0.07 (16.7%)	0.42 (100%)
1971	0.50 (83.3%)	0.10 (16.7%)	0.60 (100%)	0.10 (62.5%)	0.06 (37.5%)	0.16 (100%)	0.60 (78.9%)	0.16 (21.1%)	0.76 (100%)
1981	0.83 (81.4%)	0.19 (18.6%)	1.02 (100%)	0.16 (64%)	0.09 (36%)	0.25 (100%)	0.99 (78%)	0.28 (22.0%)	1.27 (2.14%)
1991	1.36 (77.7%)	0.39 (22.3%)	1.75 (100%)	0.24 (61.5%)	0.15 (38.5%)	0.39 (100%)	1.6 (74.8%)	0.54 (25.2%)	2.14 (100%)

Source:

1. Census of India 1961, Volume XIV Rajasthan Part-IIA, General Population Tables, p. 215.
2. Census of India 1971, Series-18, Rajasthan Part-IIA, General Population Tables, p. 129.
3. Census of India 1981, Series-1, India, Part-II B(i) p. 409.
4. Census of India 1991, (PCA) NIC Udaipur.

by the society. During 1961 to 1991 in rural area, out of total literate percentage of female literate increased from 12.1% to 22.3%. While in urban area percentage of literate women increased from 33.3% to 38.5%.

Table 3.44 *(See page 154)* shows that in 1961, only 3.47% of females were literate to total female population however, in 1991 literacy increased upto 12.39%.

In rural area during 1961 to 1991, percentage of literate female to total female population increased from 2.08% to 9.61% while in urban area in same time period percentage of literate female to total female increased from 30% to 50%.

Table 3.45 *(See page 155)* displays that in 1992-93, 1096 total educational institutions were nourishing Dungarpur district.

In the year 1992-93, 0.94 lacs boys and 0.41 lacs girls were enrolled in educational institutions in Dungarpur district. Out of them 0.05 lacs boys and 0.02 lacs girls belonged to schedule caste group and 0.58 lacs boys and 0.24 lacs girls belonged to schedule tribe group.

In the year 1992-93, 0.04 lacs male and 0.01 female teachers providing their services for educational institutions.

GENDER-WISE AND OCCUPATION-WISE DISTRIBUTION OF POPULATION IN DUNGARPUR DISTRICT

The 1991 census (Table 3.46, *See page 156 to 159)* shows that total working population in the district was 3.9 lacs. Out of the main workers 0.20 lacs and 0.19 lacs females engaged as cultivators and agricultural labour respectively.

During 1961 to 1991, number of female main workers decrease from 0.95 lacs to 0.45 lacs while number of male main workers in increased from 1.14 lacs to 2.19 lacs and main workers was 2.64 lacs out of which 0.45 lacs (17%) were female main workers and out of 1.26 lacs marginal workers, 1.21 lacs (96%) were female marginal workers.

Table 3.44. Female Population and Literacy in Dungarpur District

(Figures in lacs)

Census year	Rural			Urban			Total		
	Total female	Literate Females	% of literate female to total rural female population	Total female	Literate females	% of literate female to total urban female population	Total female	Literate females	% of literate female to total female population
1961	1.92	0.04	2.08%	0.10	0.03	30%	2.02	0.07	3.47%
1971	2.52	0.10	3.97%	0.15	0.06	40%	2.67	0.16	5.99%
1981	3.28	0.19	5.79%	0.21	0.09	42.86%	3.49	0.28	8.02%
1991	4.06	0.39	9.61%	0.30	0.15	50%	4.36	0.54	12.39%

Source: Prepared from Table 3.43.

Table 3.45. Educational Institutions, No. of Students, and Teachers and Dungarpur District (1992)

(Figures in lacs)

Classification of educational institution	Number of institutions (Figures in Nos.)			No. of total students			No. of S.C. Students			No. of ST students			No. of Teachers		
	Boys	Girls	Total	Boys	Girls	Total	Boys	Girls	Total	Boys	Girls	Total	Male	Female	Total
Primary	-	-	804	0.48	0.25	0.73	0.022	0.011	0.033	0.35	0.17	0.52	0.01	0.005	0.02
Upper Primary	-	-	208	0.298	0.12	0.418	0.016	0.0099	0.026	0.14	0.05	0.19	0.01	0.003	0.02
Secondary and Sr. Hr. Secondary	-	-	80	0.15	0.04	0.19	0.01	0.0027	0.013	0.08	0.016	0.096	0.014	0.0016	0.005
College for general educational	-	-	1	0.01	0.001	0.011	0.0007	0.00003	0.0007	0.004	0.00008	0.00408	0.0004	0.0002	0.0006
College for professional education	-	-	1	0.0009	0.0004	0.0013	0.0002	0.00001	0.0002	0.0001	0.00003	0.00013	0.00003	0.00005	0.00008
University	-	-	-	-	-	-	-	-	-	-	-	-	-	-	-
School for vocational & professional education	-	-	1	0.002	0.00004	0.002	0.0002	0.00001	0.0002	0.001	0.00002	0.00102	0.00015	-	0.00015
Others	-	-	1	0.001	0.0006	0.002	-	-	-	-	-	-	-	-	-
Total	-	-	1096	0.94	0.41	1.35	0.05	0.02	0.07	0.58	0.24	0.82	0.035	0.0099	0.04

Source: (1) Gila Sankhayaki Ruprekha. 1994, Gila-Dungarpur pp. 164, 166, 168, 169, 171.

Table 3.46. Occupation-wise and Gender-wise Population in Dungarpur District

(Figures in Lacs)

Classification	Census year							
	1961				1971			
	Rural		Urban		Rural		Urban	
	Males	Females	Males	Females	Males	Females	Males	Females
1	2	3	4	5	6	7	8	9
1. Main workers	1.14	0.95	0.05	0.01	1.26	0.14	0.07	0.005
1.1 Cultivators	1.03	0.88	0.003	0.002	1.06	0.05	0.007	0.0002
1.2 Agricultural labours	0.02	0.02	0.0001	0.001	0.09	0.07	0.001	0.0003
1.3 Livestock, forestry, fishing, hunting and plantations orchards and allied services	0.02*	0.02*	0.0006*	0.0004*	0.005	0.004	0.0003	0.00005
1.4 Mining and quarrying					0.001	0.0002	0.001	–
1.5a Manufacturing, processing servicing and repairs in household industries	0.01	0.01	0.003	0.001	0.02	0.003	0.004	0.0007
1.5b Manufacturing, processing servicing and repairs in other than household industries	0.006	0.002	0.005	0.001	0.009	0.001	0.007	0.0003

(Contd...)

	1	2	3	4	5	6	7	8	9
1.6	Constructions	0.001	0.0001	0.005	0.0004	0.003	0.0001	0.002	0.0002
1.7	Trade and Commerce	0.02	0.001	0.01	0.002	0.02	0.0006	0.01	0.0003
1.8	Transport storage and communication	0.001	–	0.002	–	0.003	0.00006	0.005	0.00004
1.9	Other services	0.03	0.009	0.02	0.003	0.04	0.005	0.02	0.003
1.10	Other worker (Total of 1.3 + 1.4 + 1.5(b) + 1.6 + 1.7 + 1.8 + 1.9)	–	–	–	–	–	–	–	–
2.0	Marginal workers	–	–	–	–	–	–	–	–
3.0	Non-workers	0.79	0.98	0.06	0.09	1.20	2.38	0.09	0.14

(Contd…)

(Table 3.46. Contd...)

(Figures in Lacs)

Classification	Census year										
	1981				1991				Total		
	Rural		Urban		Rural		Urban				
	Males	Females	Males	Females	Males	Females	Males	Females	Males	Females	Total population
1	2	3	4	5	6	7	8	9	10	11	12
1. Main workers	1.52	0.24	0.09	0.009	2.04 (50.5%)	0.43 (10.6%)	0.15 (45.2%)	0.02 (6.5%)	2.19 (83%)	0.45 (17%)	2.64 (100%)
1.1 Cultivators	1.22	0.11	0.009	0.0006	1.55	0.20	0.01	0.001	1.56 (88.66%)	0.20 (11.4%)	1.76 (100%)
1.2 Agricultural labours	0.06	0.08	0.0007	0.0003	0.16	0.19	0.003	0.002	0.16 (45.7%)	0.19 (54.3%)	0.35 (100%)
1.3 Livestock, forestry, fishing, hunting and plantations orchards and allied services					0.01	0.002	0.003	0.0002	0.01 (83.3%)	0.002 (16.7%)	0.012 (100%)
1.4 Mining & quarrying					0.02	0.004	0.001	-	0.02 (83.3%)	0.004 (16.7%)	0.024 (100%)
1.5a Manufacturing, processing servicing and repairs in household industries	0.03	0.005	0.005	0.001	0.03	0.006	0.005	0.001	0.04 (85.1%)	0.007 (14.9%)	0.047 (100%)
1.5b Manufacturing, processing servicing & repairs in other than household industries					0.04	0.001	0.02	0.0006	0.06 (96.8%)	0.002 (3.2%)	0.062 (100%)

(Contd...)

	1	2	3	4	5	6	7	8	9	10	11	12
1.6	Constructions					0.02	0.002	0.01	0.0008	0.03 (90.9%)	0.003 (9.1%)	0.033 (100%)
1.7	Trade & Commerce					0.08	0.002	0.05	0.0001	0.13 (98.5%)	0.002 (1.5%)	0.132 (100%)
1.8	Transport storage & communication					0.02	0.00004	0.01	0.00007	0.03 (99.7%)	0.0001 (0.33%)	0.0301 (100%)
1.9	Other services					0.11	0.02	0.04	0.01	0.15 (83.3%)	0.03 (16.7%)	0.18 (100%)
1.10	Other worker (Total of 1.3 + 1.4 + 1.5(b) + 1.6 + 1.7 + 1.8 + 1.9)	0.20	0.04	0.08	0.007	–	–	–	–	–	–	–
2.0	Marginal workers	0.09	1.08	0.001	0.005	0.05 (1.2%)	1.198 (29.5%)	0.002 (0.6%)	0.008 (2.6%)	0.05 (4%)	1.22 (96.%)	1.26 (100%)
3.0	Non-workers	1.50	1.96	0.13	0.19	1.95 (48.3%)	2.43 (59.9%)	0.18 (54.2%)	0.28 (90.9%)	2.13 (44%)	2.71 (56%)	4.84 (100%)

Source:

1. Census of India 1961, Volume XIV Rajasthan Part II-A, General Population Tables, pp. 215 to 217.
2. Census of India 1971, Series-18, Rajasthan Part II-A, General Population Tables pp. 130 to 133.
3. Census of India 1981, Series-1 India. Part II B (i) pp. 410 to 413.
4. Statistical Abstract, Rajasthan, 1997. pp. 25 and 26.
5. Census of India 1991, (PCA) Rajasthan District, NIC, Udaipur

Note: *It is the total of 1.3 and 1.4

The 1991 census shows that the total rural female population of the district was 4.06 out of which, 1.63 lac (40.15%) females were working. While in urban area, out of 0.308% lacs females only 0.028 lacs (9.1%) females were engaged in work. Women participation in occupation is remarkably high in rural area in comparison to urban area.

COMPARATIVE STUDY OF DEMOGRAPHIC PROFILE OF WOMEN IN THE COUNTRY, STATE OF RAJASTHAN, UDAIPUR AND DUNGARPUR DISTRICT

Area-wise Distribution of Population

It has been tried to perform a comparative evaluation of female population of urban and rural areas in the country, State of Rajasthan as well as Udaipur and Dungarpur districts in table 3.47.

Proportion of rural females was remarkably high in Udaipur and Dungarpur district in comparison to the country and the state or Rajasthan.

In 1961 census year ratio of rural female was 83.02%, 83.96%. 89.56%, 95.05% of the country, State of Rajasthan, Udaipur and Dungarpur district respectively, and in 1991 the ratio of rural female decreased upto 74.77%, 77.53%, 83.58% and 93.12%. This trend of decreasing percentage shows rural female migrating to urban areas.

During last forty years (1961–91) growth of female population was high in Udaipur (100.14%) and Dungarpur district (115.84%) compared to the country (91.16%) while lower compared to the State of Rajasthan (118.56%).

Growth of rural female was higher in Dungarpur district (111.46%), Udaipur district (86.77%) and in the state of Rajasthan (101.81%) compared to the country (72.16%). Growth of urban female was also higher in Udaipur district (214.86%), Dungarpur district (200%) and State of Rajasthan (206.24%) compared to the country (184.12%).

Table 3.47. Female Population in the Country, State of Rajasthan, Udaipur and Dungarpur District

(Figures in lacs)

Census year	India			Rajasthan			Udaipur			Dungarpur		
	Number of rural women	No. of urban women	Total women	No. of rural women	No. of urban women	Total women	Number of rural	No. of urban women	Total women	Number of rural	No. of urban women	Total women
1961	1767.94 (83.02%)	361.47 (16.98%)	2129.42 (100%)	80.53 (83.96%)	15.38 (16.04%)	95.91 (100%)	6.35 (89.56%)	0.74 (10.44%)	7.09 (100%)	1.92 (95.05%)	0.10 (4.95%)	2.02 (100%)
1971	2138.51 (80.97%)	502.64 (19.03%)	2641.15 (100%)	101.61 (82.74%)	21.20 (17.26%)	122.81 (100%)	7.79 (88.32%)	1.03 (11.68%)	8.82 (100%)	2.52 (94.38%)	0.15 (5.62%)	2.67 (100%)
1981	2560.93 (77.42%)	746.93 (22.58%)	3307.86 (100%)	130.38 (79.46%)	33.7 (20.5%)	164.08 (100%)	9.98 (85.67%)	1.67 (14.33%)	11.65 (100%)	3.28 (93.98%)	0.21 (6.02%)	3.49 (100%)
1991	3043.70 (74.77%)	1027.02 (25.23%)	4070.72 (100%)	162.52 (77.53%)	47.10 (22.47%)	209.62 (100%)	11.86 (83.58%)	2.33 (16.42%)	14.19 (100%)	4.06 (93.12%)	0.30 (6.88%)	4.36 (100%)

Source: Prepared from table 3.2, 3.14, 3.25, 3.36.

DECADAL VARIATION OF FEMALES

During 1961-91, the decadal female variation rate in Dungarpur district was remarkably high in comparison to the Country, State of Rajasthan and Udaipur district in (Table 3.48 *See page 163*).

During 1971-81, decadal variation of females were remarkably high in the country (25.2%), state of Rajasthan (33.33%), Udaipur (32.09%) and Dungarpur district (30.07%) in comparison to the other decades while during 1981-91, decadal variation of females were low in Udaipur (21.80%) and Dungarpur districts (24.9%) compare to the state of Rajasthan (28.05%).

The decadal female variation was raising from the decade of 1951-61 to 1971 to 1981 in the country, State of Rajasthan and Udaipur district. In 1981-91, immensely fall in female growth rate is the effect of government's untiring effort to make people aware about the benefits of small family.

In Dungarpur district, female growth rate start falling from the decade of 1971-81 to 1981-91.

SEX COMPOSITION OF POPULATION

During 1961 to 1991, sex-ratio in Dungarpur and Udaipur district was very high in comparison to the country and the State of Rajasthan (Table 3.49 *See page 164)*

The sex-ratio of Dungarpur district was worthly of notice. In the year of 1971 and 1981, sex-ratio was 1015 and 1045 respectively. Sex-ratio of rural areas and urban areas outwardly high in Dungarpur district in comparison to the country, State of Rajasthan, and Udaipur district.

The lower sex-ratio in urban areas in comparison to rural areas is largely attributed to the migration of males to urban centres for educational and employment purposes.

Sex-ratio of rural female was remarkably low in the state in compare to the rural female of the Country, Udaipur and Dungarpur district.

Table 3.48. Decadal Variation of Females in the Country, State of Rajasthan, Udaipur and Dungarpur Districts

(Figures in lacs)

Census year	India		Rajasthan		Udaipur		Dungarpur	
	Total female	Decade variation	Total female	Decade variation	Total females	Decade variation	Total female	Decade variation
1961	2129.42	21.29%	96	24.68%	6.91	21.44%	2.02	31.2%
1971	2641.15	24.03%	123	28.13%	8.82	27.64%	2.67	32.2%
1981	3307.86	25.2%	164	33.33%	11.65	32.09%	3.49	30.7%
1991	4070.72	23.1%	210	28.05%	14.19	21.80%	4.36	24.9%

Source: Prepared from Table 3.3, 3.15, 3.26, 3.37.

Table 3.49. Composition of Population in the Country, State of Rajasthan, Udaipur and Dungarpur District

(Figures in lacs)

Census year	India			Rajasthan			Udaipur			Dungarpur		
	Rural	Urban	Total	Rural	Urban	Total	Rural	Urban	Total	Rural	Urban	Total
1961	963	845	941	913	882	908	949	865	940	995	930	991
1971	949	858	930	919	875	911	970	871	957	1021	931	1015
1981	951	878	934	930	877	919	995	886	977	1056	900	1045
1991	939	894	929	919	879	910	982	891	965	1003	897	996

Source: Prepared from table 3.4, 3.16, 3.27, 3.38.

CASTE-WISE DISTRIBUTION OF FEMALES

Table 3.50 reveals that Hindus accounted for the largest community (S.T and S.T. is the part of Hindu community).

Table 3.50. Caste-wise Females in the Country, State of Rajasthan, Udaipur and Dungarpur District (1991)

(Figures in lacs)

Religion	India	Rajasthan	Udaipur	Dungarpur
Hindus	3303.93 (81.9%)	186.58 (89.0%)	13.26 (90.20%)	4.17 (95.81%)
Muslims	489.64 (12.1%)	16.9 (8.0%)	0.45 (3.17%)	0.12 (2.76%)
Sikhs	76.49 (1.9%)	3.05 (1.45%)	0.01 (0.07%)	0.00037 (0.009%)
Jain	16.3 (0.40%)	2.79 (1.33%)	0.44 (3.10%)	0.06 (1.38%)
Christians	97.91% (2.4%)	0.24 (0.1%)	0.02 (0.14%)	0.002 (0.05%)
Buddhist	31.15 (0.8%)	0.016 (0.01%)	0.0004 (0.003%)	0.00012 (0.003%)
Others not stated	16.2 (0.4%)	0.005 (0.002%)	0.0002 (0.001%)	-
Religion not stated	1.95 (0.05%)	0.05 (0.02%)	0.002 (0.01%)	0.00002 (0.0005%)
	4033.68 (100%)	209.63 (100%)	14.183 (100%)	4.35251 (100%)

Source: Prepared from table 3.5, 3.17, 3.28 and 3.39.

Percentage of female population indicates that Hindu females were more in Dungarpur district (95.81%) and Udaipur districts (90.20%) compared to the state of Rajasthan (89.0%) and the country (81.9%).

Percentage of female population shows that Muslims, Sikhs, Christians and Buddhist were lower in both the districts compared to the country and the State of Rajasthan while percentage-wise females of Jain community was higher in both districts.

SC/ST FEMALE POPULATION

According to 1991 census, Udaipur and Dungarpur districts constitute 36.86% and 66.06% of S.T. female population, to the total female population, which is remarkably high in comparison to the country (8.20%) and the State of Rajasthan (12.58%). While regarding S.C. female population in Udaipur (8.25%) and Dungarpur districts (4.59%) situations is quite different because in the country percentage of S.C. female was (16.29%) and in the state of Rajasthan (17.17%) (Table 3.51).

Table 3.51. Scheduled Caste and Scheduled Tribe Females in the Country, State of Rajasthan, Udaipur and Dungarpur Districts

Census Year	India		Rajasthan		Udaipur		Dungarpur	
	S.C	S.T.	S.C.	S.T.	S.C.	S.T.	S.C.	S.T.
1961	314.99	148.41	16.12 (16.81%)	11.10 (11.57%)	0.62 (8.97%)	2.16 (31.26%)	0.09 (4.46%)	1.21 (59.90%)
1971	386.62 (14.64%)	188.34 (7.13%)	19.46 (15.85%)	15.07 (12.27%)	0.68 (7.71%)	2.98 (33.79%)	0.10 (3.75%)	1.69 63.30%
1981	505.44 (15.28%)	255.90 (7.74%)	27.86 (16.90%)	20.32 (12.38%)	0.95 (8.15%)	4.02 (34.51%)	0.16 (4.58%)	2.16 (61.89%)
1991	662.94 16.29%	333.95 (8.20%)	36.00 (17.17%)	26.38 (12.58%)	1.17 (8.25%)	5.23 (36.86%)	0.20 (4.59%)	2.88 (66.06%)

Source: Prepared from Table 3.7, 3.19, 3.30 and 3.41.

During last forty years (1961-1991) growth of S.C. female population was very low in Udaipur district (88.71%) as compare to Rajasthan State (122.33%), Dungarpur district (122.22%) and the country (110.46%). While growth of S.T. female population was quite high in Udaipur (142.13%), Dungarpur districts (138.01%) and State of Rajasthan (137.66%), compare to the country (125.02%).

LITERACY AMONG FEMALES

Table 3.52 analyses area-wise literacy among females in the country, State of Rajasthan, Udaipur and Dungarpur district.

The State of Rajasthan is educationally one of the most backward state of the country and state occupied the last

Table 3.52. Area-wise Females Literacy in the Country, State of Rajasthan, Udaipur and Dungarpur District

(Figures in lacs)

Census year	India			Rajasthan			Udaipur			Dungarpur		
	Rural	Urban	Total	Rural	Urban	Total	Rural	Urban	Total	Rural	Urban	Total
1961	151.04 + (8.54%)	124.75 - (34.51%)	275.79 * (12.95%)	2.14 + (2.7%)	3.47 - (22.6%)	5.61 * (5.85%)	0.14 + (2.20%)	0.23 - (31.08%)	0.37 * (5.35%)	0.04 + (2.08%)	0.30 - (30%)	0.07 * (3.47%)
1971	281.40 + (13.15%)	212.32 - (42.24%)	493.71 * (18.69%)	4.09 + (4.0%)	6.29 - (29.7%)	10.38 * (8.45%)	0.30 + (3.85%)	0.39 - (37.86%)	0.69 * (7.82%)	0.10 + (3.97%)	0.06 - (40%)	0.16 * (5.99%)
1981	444.51 + (17.4%)	352.96 - (47.3%)	797.47 * (24.11%)	7.12 + (5.5%)	11.61 - (34.5%)	18.73 * (11.42%)	0.52 + (5.21%)	1.28 - (76.65%)	1.80 * (15.45%)	0.19 + (5.79%)	0.09 - (42.86%)	0.28 * (8.02%)
1991	749.22 (24.62%)	548.25 - (53.4%)	1297.47 * (31.97%)	14.94 + (9.2%)	19.25 - (40.9%)	34.19 * (16.31%)	0.99 + (8.35%)	1.20 - (51.50%)	2.19 * (15.4%)	0.39 + (9.61%)	0.15 - (50%)	0.54 * (12.39%)

(+) Percentage of literate rural females source—prepared from table no. 3.19, 3.22, 3.33, 3.44.
(–) Percentage of literate urban females to total urban females
(*) Percentage of literate females to total female population.

position as per the ranking of major states of India with respect to 1991 female literacy.

In 1961, the percentage of literate female were 12.95%, 5.85%, 5.35% and 3.47 in the country, State of Rajasthan, Udaipur and Dungarpur district respectively, and in 1991 increased upto 31.97%, 16.31%, 15.43% and 12.39% respectively.

The female literacy is low in Udaipur and Dungarpur district in compare to the country and State of Rajasthan.

Female literacy is very low in rural areas compare to urban areas. Rural female of Udaipur and Dungarpur districts are more illiterate compare to the country and State of Rajasthan. Percentage of literacy is more in urban areas of Udaipur and Dungarpur districts compare to the state but low compared to the country.

GENDER-WISE DISTRIBUTION OF LITERATES

Table 3.53 *(See page 169)* shows gender-wise distribution of percentage of literates in the Country, State of Rajasthan, Udaipur and Dungarpur districts.

The Udaipur and Dungarpur districts are educationally backward districts of the State of Rajasthan, only 24.45% and 27.97% of the population have been found literate as compare to the Country (42.45%) and the state of Rajasthan (38.55%) in the census of 1991. There also seems to be a wide gender gap in literacy, Table clearly indicate that females of Udaipur and Dungarpur districts are more illiterate compare to females of the Country and the State of Rajasthan. According to 1991 census, 12.39%, 15.43%, 20.44% and 31.9% female are literate to the total female population respectively in Dungarpur, Udaipur State of Rajasthan and the Country.

OCCUPATIONAL DISTRIBUTION OF FEMALES

Table 3.54 *(See page 170 to 173)* shows that in 1961, the percentage of total female main workers (42.96%), (35.89%), (43.86%), and (47.28%) in the Country, State of Rajasthan, Udaipur and Dungarpur districts respectively, in the census year of 1991 female main workers in were decreased upto 15.93%, 13.3%, 13.18% and 10.31% respectively. In main workers most

Table 3.53. Gender-wise, Distribution of Literates (in percentage) in the Country, State of Rajasthan Udaipur and Dungarpur District

(Figures in lacs)

Census year	India			Rajasthan			Udaipur			Dungarpur		
	Male	Female	Total	Male	Female	Total	Male	Female	Total	Male	Female	Total
1961	34.44%	12.95%	24.02%	23.71%	5.84%	15.21%	22.04%	5.35%	13.96%	17.16%	3.47%	10.34%
1971	39.51%	18.4%	29.34%	28.74%	8.40%	19.07%	26.57%	7.82%	17.42%	22.81%	5.99%	14.34%
1981	45.51%	24.1%	35.18%	36.30%	11.42%	24.38%	40.60%	15.45%	28.17%	29.64%	8.02%	18.62%
1991	52.26%	31.9%	42.45%	54.99%	20.44%	38.55%	40.07%	15.43%	27.97%	36.45%	12.39%	24.45%

Source: Prepared from table no. 3.8, 3.20, 3.31, 3.42.

Table 3.54. **Occupational Distribution of Females in the Country, State of Rajasthan Udaipur and Dungarpur District**

S. No.	Classification	India											
		1961			1971			1981			1991		
		Rural	Urban	Total	Rural	Urban	Total	Rural	Urban	Total	Rural	Urban	Total
1.	Main workers	1668.93	172.03	1840.96 (42.96%)	311.12 (14.55%)	37.03 (7.37%)	348.15 (13.18%)	393.03 (16.0%)	53.70 (7.28%)	449.70 (13.99%)	(559.96 (18.57%)	82.78 (8.13%)	642.74 (15.93%)
2.	Marginal workers	–	–	–	–	–	–	177.85 (7.18%)	7.67 (1.04%)	185.52 (5.77%)	244.34 (8.10%)	10.59 (1.04%)	254.93 (6.32%)
3.	Non-workers	2024.51	420.03	2444.54 (57.04%)	1827.39 (85.45%)	465.61 (92.63%)	2293.0 (86.82%)	1901.66 (76.82%)	676.67 (91.68%)	2578.33 (80.23%)	2210.95 (73.33%)	924.97 (90.83%)	3135.92 (77.75%)
	Total	**3693.44**	**592.06**	**4285.5**	**2138.51 (100%)**	**502.64 (100%)**	**2641.15 (100%)**	**2475.54 (100%)**	**738.04 (100%)**	**3213.58 (100%)**	**3015.25 (100%)**	**1018.34 (100%)**	**4033.59 (100%)**

(Contd...)

S. No.	Classification	Rajasthan											
		1961			1971			1981			1991		
		Rural	Urban	Total	Rural	Urban	Total	Rural	Urban	Total	Rural	Urban	Total
1.	Main workers	32.88 (40.83%)	1.54 (10.01%)	34.42 (35.89%)	9.43 (9.28%)	0.82 (3.87%)	10.25 (8.35%)	13.8 (10.58%)	1.5 (4.45%)	15.3 (9.33%)	24.8 (15.26%)	2.53 (5.36%)	27.33 (13.03%)
2.	Marginal workers	–	–	–	–	–	–	18.78 (14.40%)	0.48 (1.43%)	19.26 (11.74%)	29.24 (17.99%)	0.87 (1.85%)	30.11 (14.36%)
3.	Non-workers	47.65 (59.17%)	13.84 (89.99%)	61.49 (64.11%)	92.18 (90.72%)	20.39 (96.13%)	112.57 (91.65%)	97.80 (75.01%)	31.71 (94.12%)	129.51 (78.93%)	108.49 (66.75%)	43.78 (92.79%)	152.27 (72.61)
	Total	**80.53 (100%)**	**15.38 (100%)**	**95.91 (100%)**	**101.61 (100%)**	**21.21 (100%)**	**122.82 (100%)**	**130.38 (100%)**	**33.69 (100%)**	**164.07 (100%)**	**162.53 (100%)**	**47.18 (100%)**	**209.71 (100%)**

(Contd...)

(Table 3.54. Contd...)

S. No.	Classification	Udaipur District											
		1961			1971			1981			1991		
		Rural	Urban	Total	Rural	Urban	Total	Rural	Urban	Total	Rural	Urban	Total
1.	Main workers	3.02 (47.56%)	0.09 (12.16%)	3.11 (43.86%)	0.62 (7.97%)	0.05 (4.85%)	0.67 (7.60%)	0.83 (8.31%)	0.15 (5.47%)	0.98 (7.70%)	1.69 (14.25%)	0.18 (7.72%)	1.87 (13.18%)
2.	Marginal workers	-	-	-	-	-	-	2.07 (20.72%)	0.04 (1.46%)	2.11 (16.57%)	2.77 (23.36%)	0.06 (2.58%)	2.83 (19.94%)
3.	Non-workers	3.33 (52.44%)	0.65 (87.84%)	3.98 (56.14%)	7.16% (92.03%)	0.98 (95.15%)	8.14 (92.40%)	7.09 (70.97%)	2.55 (93.07%)	9.64 (75.73%)	7.40 (62.36%)	2.09 (89.70%)	9.49 (66.88%)
	Total	6.35 (100%)	0.74 (100%)	7.09 (100%)	7.78 (100%)	1.03 (100%)	8.81 (100%)	9.99 (100%)	2.74 (100%)	12.73 (100%)	11.86 (100%)	2.33 (100%)	14.19 (100%)

(Contd...)

S. No.	Classification	Dungarpur District											
		1961			1971			1981			1991		
		Rural	Urban	Total	Rural	Urban	Total	Rural	Urban	Total	Rural	Urban	Total
1.	Main workers	0.95 (49.22%)	0.01 (10%)	0.96 (47.29%)	0.14 (5.56%)	0.005 (3.45%)	0.145 (5.44%)	0.24 (7.32%)	0.009 (4.41%)	0.249 (7.15%)	0.43 (10.60%)	0.02 (6.49%)	0.45 (10.31%)
2.	Marginal workers	–	–	–	–	–	–	1.08 (32.92%)	0.005 (2.45%)	1.085 (31.14%)	1.198 (29.52%)	0.008 (2.60%)	1.206 (27.62%)
3.	Non-workers	0.98 (50.78%)	0.09 (90%)	1.07 (52.71%)	2.38 (94.44%)	0.14 (96.55%)	2.52 (94.56%)	1.96 (59.76%)	0.19 (93.14%)	2.15 (61.71%)	2.43 (59.88%)	0.28 (90.91%)	2.71 (62.07%)
	Total	**1.93 (100%)**	**0.1 (100%)**	**2.03 (100%)**	**2.52 (100%)**	**0.145 (100%)**	**2.665 (100%)**	**3.28 (100%)**	**0.204 (100%)**	**3.484 (100%)**	**4.058 (100%)**	**0.308 (100%)**	**4.366 (100%)**

of the females are engaged as Agricultural labourers, cultivators and in manufacturing, processing servicing and repair in household industries. Indian economy is still an Agricultural based economy that's why, the ratio of rural female working population is high against of urban working population.

Female marginal workers are quite high in Dungarpur district in comparison to the Country, State of Rajasthan and Udaipur district. Female marginal worker shows the trend of increasing in ratio every census year except in the case of rural female of Dungarpur district.

Female non-workers are reducing in every census year. There is a wide gender gap in the work force participation too, as the percentage of female main workers was only 15.3%, 13.03%, 13.18% and 10.30% in the Country, State of Rajasthan, Udaipur and Dungarpur districts respectively as against 50.93%, 48.5%, 52.18% and 50.11% of male main workers in the Country, State of Rajasthan, Udaipur and Dungarpur districts respectively.

4 Banking Development in Udaipur and Dungarpur District

BANKING DEVELOPMENT IN UDAIPUR DISTRICT

I. Commercial Bank

Branch Expansion

Udaipur is an economically backward district of Rajasthan. Lack of adequate financial facilities was one of the important factor for its backwardness. Prior to 1969, banking development was very slow and unsatisfactory. The commercial banks had a strong rural bias and were almost the exclusive preserve of the urban elite. The bank had very few offices and operation in the rural areas and most of their activities were confined to the urban areas only.

After the nationalisation of 14 big commercial banks in 1969, the commercial banks launched a massive branch expansion programme in the district particularly in the rural and semi-urban areas. The expansion of branches in the rural and semi-urban areas not only enabled them in mobilising a larger amount of deposit, but also gave them the opportunity to credit in new fields and areas, thereby helping in the achievement of the goals and objectives of the nationalisation. Branch Expansion of Udaipur district after 1969 is shown in table 4.1. In 2000, Udaipur district

Table 4.1. **Branch Expansion by Commercial Banks in Udaipur District**

Year	1969	1970	1971	1972	1973	1974	1975	1976	1977	1978	1979	1980	1981	1982	1983	1984
1. Total no. of branches	25	33	41	46	48	49	52	61	72	80	84	98	115	118	123	124
2. Increase over the processing year	–	8	8	5	2	1	3	9	11	8	4	14	17	3	5	1

Year	1985	1986	1987	1988	1989	1990	1991	1992	1993	1994	1995	1996	1997	1998	1999	2000
1. Total no. of branches	124	129	125	NA	130	137	105	107	110	111	111	114	114	114	118	119
2. Increase over the processing year	–	5	-4	NA	5	7	-32	2	3	1	–	3	–	–	4	1

Source:

1. Banking statistics, R.B.I.
2. District Credit Plan of Udaipur from 1982 to 2000.
3. Annual Action Plan of Udaipur district from 1982 to 2000.

had 183 branches of banking and financial institution. Out of 183 branches commercial bank had 119 bank branches.

In the period between 1969 to 1990 bank branches of commercial bank increased from 25 to 137 and in 1991 branches declined to 105, this is due to formation of Rajasthan district from Udaipur district. Maximum branches opened in 1977, 1980 and 1981 i.e., 11, 14, 17 respectively. After 1990, very slow bank branch expansion occured in the district. After separation of Rajsamand district from Udaipur district, only 14 branches opened in the district.

Bank Group-wise Distribution of Branches

Bank group-wise distribution of branches of the commercial banks in Udaipur district is given in Table 4.2, *(See pages 178 & 179)* shows, in Dec. 1979, there were 63 branches of public sector banks and 21 branches of private sector banks functioning in the district and SBI group had maximum branches.

In the year of 1990-91, there were 100 branches of public sector banks and 37 branches of private sector banks functioning in the district. In 1991-92, due to the formation of Rajsamand district from Udaipur district, Public sector branches declined to 79 and Private sector branches were declined to 26.

The growth was steadily increasing till the end of 1990. But the formation of Rajsamand district was the only cause of decline in number of bank branches in the district. However, the trend of increasing the branches again started in 1993 but it was a slow increase. At the end of March 2000 there were 92 branches of public sector banks and 27 branches of private sector banks. Out of 27 branches, 1 branch of ICICI bank and 26 branches belongs to "The Bank of Rajasthan Ltd."

Center-wise Distribution of the Branches

Centre/Area-wise distribution of branches of commercial bank is given in Table 4.3. *(See page 180)* In 1969, 32% branches of commercial banks were functioning in urban areas of Udaipur district while at the end of March 2000, 44.54% branches were functioning in urban are. On the other hand in 1969, 68% branches of commercial banks were working in rural and semi-

Table 4.2. Bank Group-wise Distribution of Branches of Commercial Banks in Udaipur District

Sl. No.	Bank group and name of the bank	Dec. 79	Dec. 82	Dec. 84	June 87	1989-90	1990-91	1991-92	1992-93	1993-94	1995-96	31st March 1996-97	March 97	March 99	2000
(1)	**Public Bank**														
(A)	**SBI Group**	38	50	55	56	56	59	40	40	42	42	43	43	44	45
1.	SBBJ	35	47	51	52	52	55	36	36	38	38	39	39	40	40
2.	State Bank of India	3	3	4	4	4	4	4	4	4	4	4	4	4	5
(B)	**Nationalised Banks**	25	33	34	35	37	41	39	42	43	44	44	44	47	47
1.	Allahabad Bank	5	6	6	6	6	7	7	8	8	8	8	8	9	9
2.	Bank of Baroda	2	4	4	4	4	4	2	3	3	3	3	3	3	3
3.	Bank of India	1	1	1	2	2	2	2	2	2	3	3	3	3	3
4.	Canara Bank	1	1	1	1	1	1	1	1	1	1	1	1	1	1
5.	Indian Bank	1	1	1	1	1	1	1	1	1	1	1	1	1	1
6.	Central Bank of India	2	2	2	2	2	3	3	3	4	4	4	4	4	4
7.	Indian Overseas Bank	1	1	1	1	1	1	1	1	1	1	1	1	1	1
8.	Dena Bank	2	2	2	2	2	2	2	2	2	2	2	2	2	2
9.	Punjab National Bank	4	4	4	4	1	1	6	7	7	8	8	8	8	8
10.	Bank of Maharashtra	-	1	1	1	1	1	1	1	1	1	1	1	1	1

(Contd...)

Sl. No.	Bank group and name of the bank	Dec. 79	Dec. 82	Dec. 84	June 87	1989-90	1990-91	1991-92	1992-93	1993-94	1995-96	31st March 1996-97	March 97	March 99	2000
11.	Union Bank of India	4	4	4	4	4	4	4	4	4	4	4	4	4	4
12.	United Commercial Bank	1	1	2	2	2	2	2	2	2	2	2	2	2	2
13.	Syndicate Bank (Nationalised in 1980)	1	1	1	1	1	1	1	1	1	1	1	1	1	1
14.	Oriental Bank of Commerce	1	1	1	1	1	1	1	1	1	1	1	1	2	2
15.	Vijaya Bank of India	1	1	1	1	1	1	1	1	1	1	1	1	1	1
16.	New Bank of India	1	1	1	1	1	2	1	1	1	-	-	-	-	-
17.	Punjab Sindh Bank	1	1	1	1	5	5	1	1	1	1	1	1	1	1
18.	Andhra Bank	-	-	-	-	1	1	1	1	1	1	1	1	1	1
19.	United Bank of India	-	-	-	-	-	1	1	1	1	1	1	1	1	1
20.	Corporation Bank	-	-	-	-	-	-	-	-	-	-	-	-	1	1
(2)	Private Bank	21	32	34	35	37	37	26	25	25	25	27	27	27	27
1.	The Bank of Rajasthan Ltd.	17	32	34	35	37	37	26	25	25	25	27	27	26	26
2.	ICICI	-	-	-	-	-	-	-	-	-	-	-	-	1	1
	Total	-	-	-	-	**130**	**137**	**105**	**107**	**110**	**111**	**114**	**114**	**118**	**119**

Source: DCP and AAP of Udaipur district from 1982 to 2000.

Table 4.3. Centre-wise Distribution of Branches of the Commercial Banks in Udaipur District

(Percentage in Brackets)

Population group	Year										
	Dec. 1969	Dec. 1971	Dec. 1973	Dec. 1976	June 1978	Dec. 1980	Dec. 1982	Sept. 1987	March 1989	March 1999	March 2000
Rural	17 (68%)	28 (68.3%)	27 (60.87%)	29 (47.54%)	38 (51.35%)	64 (65.31%)	76 (66.08%)	88* (70.4%)	92* (70.8%)	57 (48.30%)	58 (48.74%)
Semi urban	-	-	5 (10.87%)	8 (13.11%)	9 (12.16%)	7 (7.14%)	8 (6.96%)			8 (6.78%)	8 (6.72%)
Urban	8 (32%)	13 (31.7%)	16 (28.25%)	24 (39.35%)	27 (36.49%)	27 (27.55%)	31 (26.96%)	37 (29.6%)	38 (29.2%)	53 (44.92%)	53 (44.54%)
Total	25 (100%)	41 100%)	48 (100%)	61 (100%)	74 (100%)	98 (100%)	115 (100%)	125 (100%)	130 (100%)	118 (100%)	119 (100%)

Source:

1. Annual reports of trends and progress of banking in India.
2. AAP of Udaipur district 1982-2000.
3. DCP of Udaipur district 1982-2000.

* It is the combined bank branches of rural and semi-urban areas.

urban areas which decreased to 55.46% at the end of March 2000.

Sector-wise Distribution of Branches

Sector-wise distribution of branches in Udaipur district is given in Table 4.4.

From Table 4.4, it is evident that the public sector banks accounted for most of the bank branches. In 2000, the public sector bank accounted for 77.31% of the total branches in the district.

Table 4.4. Sector-wise Distribution of Branches of Commercial Banks in Udaipur District

Year	No. of Public Sector Banks		No. of Private Sector Banks		Total	
1977	52	(72.22%)	20	(27.78%)	72	(100%)
1978	60	(75%)	20	(25%)	80	(100%)
1979	63	(75%)	21	(25%)	84	(100%)
1980	71	(71.43%)	27	(28.57%)	98	(100%)
1982	83	(72.26%)	32	(27.74%)	115	(100%)
1987	94	(72.87%)	35	(27.13%)	129	(100%)
1989	93	(71.54%)	37	(28.46%)	130	(100%)
1990	100	(72.99%)	37	(27.01%)	137	(100%)
1991	79	(75.24%)	26	(24.76%)	105	(100%)
1992	82	(76.64%)	25	(23.36%)	107	(100%)
1993	85	(77.27%)	25	(22.73%)	110	(100%)
1995	86	(77.48%)	25	(22.52%)	111	(100%)
March 96	87	(76.32%)	27	(23.68%)	114	(100%)
March 97	87	(76.32%)	27	(23.68%)	114	(100%)
March 98	88	(77.19%)	26	(22.81%)	114	(100%)
March 99	91	(77.12%)	27	(22.88%)	118	(100%)
March 2000	92	(77.31%)	27	(22.69%)	119	(100%)

Source: Prepared from Annual Reports of trends and progress of banking in India, R.B.I.

Block-wise Distribution of Branches

The Udaipur district is divided into three homogenous regions viz; the central eastern region, north-western region and the southern region. The district is divided into 18 blocks till the year of 1990. Rajsamand district has been separated in 1991 from Udaipur district, Now Udaipur district is divided into 11 blocks.

The central-eastern is the most developed region of the district. At the end of 1979 and 1993 there were 60 and 76 bank offices in this region, respectively. Table 4.5 *(See page 183)* shows region-wise distribution of branches in Udaipur district. The distribution of branches is quite uneven in the district. There are blocks like Mavli, Bhinder, Girwa and Sarada where the number of branches is in plenty. While in the blocks of Kotra, Jhadol, Gogunda and Dharyawad the number of offices is far below the required strength. This has created a disparity in the economic development of the district. The economic programme fail to succeed for want of branch net work.

Upto the end of 1979 and 1993, there were 84 and 110 offices in the district, out of them 60 and 76 were established in the central eastern region. The north western and southern regions had 6 and 28 branches respectively upto 1993.

The central-eastern (71.4 per cent) and 69.09 per cent), the north eastern (13.1 per cent and 5.45 per cent) and the southern region (15.5 per cent and 25.45 per cent) of the total branches in the district had at the end of 1979 and 1993 respectively.

At the end of March 2000, Northern western region had 11 offices and central eastern region had 133 offices and southern region had 49 offices of commercial bank, cooperative bank and RRB's.

Deposit Mobilisation and Credit Deployment

Another indicator of success of banking is the progress made in respect of deposit mobilisation and credit deployment. Rapid branch expansion has given sufficient impetus to banks in undertaking deposit mobilisation and credit deployment programmes.

The Commercial Bank mobilises rural deposits through attractive and effective schemes. It also tries to raise the rate of

Table 4.5. Block-wise and Region-wise Distribution of Branches of Commercial Banks in Udaipur District

Region and block		Number of bank offices						
		31.12.1979	30.9.1982	Dec. 1987	1990	1991	1993-94	1999-2000
Northern-western Region								
Block:	Amet	2	2	2	2	*	*	*
	Bhim	1	4	4	4	*	*	*
	Deogarh	1	2	2	2	*	*	*
	Gogunda	2	2	2	2	2	3	7
	Kotra	1	1	1	2	2	3	4
	Kumbhalgarh	4	4	5	5	*	*	*
Central-eastern Region								
Block	Badgaon	4	6	5	5	5	6	8
	Bhinder	4	6	81	8	8	9	14
	Girwa	32	37	46	46	46	51	86
	Khamnor	4	5	5	6	*	*	*
	Mavli	7	10	10	10	10	10	15
	Railmagra	4	4	4	4	*	*	*
	Rajsamand	5	8	8	8	*	*	*
Southern-Region								
Block:	Dhariwad	2	4	4	5	5	5	8
	Kherwara	2	5	5	5	5	7	13
	Jhadol	2	2	2	3	3	3	7
	Salumber	3	5	5	5	5	5	11
	Sarada	4	8	8	8	8	8	10
	Total	84	115	126	130	99	110	183

Source: Prepared from district credit plan, Udaipur district.
Note:
1. Upto Dec. 82, Agricultural bank/Gram Vikas Kendra included but from 1990 it is not included.
2. In 1999, April to March 2000 include all commercial co-operative and R.R.B.
3. From 1991, these (*) blocks are not included in Udaipur district.

savings of the district, because personal savings play a very vital role in the economic development of a country. In a country like India, where in addition to the need for mobilising personal savings for the purpose of putting them to productive purposes, there is all the more need at the present movement to funnel back into the economic main stream the large amounts placed in the hands of the people as a result of the rapid deficit financing that has been undertaken by the government for the past many years.

It is therefore right to assess the success of the commercial banking system by studying their credit deployment after the nationalisation.

After the nationalisation of the commercial banks deposit and advances of all scheduled commercial banks have shown a progressive trend as evident from Table 4.6 *(See page 185)*.

The amount of bank deposit was Rs. 532.00 lacs in Dec. 1969 which increased to Rs. 41,319 lacs at the end of March 1991. Then deposits slightly decrease at the end of March 92 i.e. Rs. 37,317 lacs because Rajasamand district formed from Udaipur district. From 1993, deposits again start increasing and at the end of March 2000 the amount of bank deposits was Rs. 1,56,520 lacs. The amount of bank credit was Rs. 186 lacs in 1969 which increased to Rs. 66,410 lacs in March 2000.

In 1969, the credit deposit ratio was only 33.9% which was the minimum and 63.5 (maximum) in Dec. 1982. It was only 42% in March 2000.

II. Co-operative Bank

1. THE UDAIPUR CENTRAL CO-OPERATIVE BANK

Branch Expansion

The branch expansion of the Udaipur Central Co-operative Bank in Udaipur district is given in the Table 4.7, *(See page 186)*.

The UCCB is the sole central financing agency in the district. It was functioning through 9 branches in the district at the end of March 2000. At the end of 1990, when Rajsamand district was the part of Udaipur district maximum branches has been recorded seventeen. Existing branches are quite insufficient to

Table 4.6. Growth of Deposits, Advances and Credit Deposit Ratio in Udaipur District

(Rs. in lacs)

Year	Deposit	Advances	Credit Deposit Ratio in %
1969	532	186	33.9%
1970	670	340	50.7%
1971	818	450	55.0%
1972	1034	599	57.9%
1973	192	532	44.6%
1974	1618	709	43.8%
1975	1766	960	54.3%
1976	2436	1173	48.1%
1977	3011	1614	53.6%
1978	3992	1847	46.2%
1979	4781	2502	62.9%
1980	5735	3313	57.7%
1981	6252	3617	57.8%
1982	7343	4667	63.5%
1983	10849	6317	58.2%
1984	13022	7863	60.4%
1985	15401	9417	61.1%
1986	18491	10662	57.6%
June 87	19873	10519	52.9%
Dec. 88	28843	12831	44.5%
Dec. 89	32389	14043	43.4%
Mar. 1991	41319	18278	44.2%
Mar. 1992	37317	19805	53.07
Mar. 95	69127	28238	41%
Mar. 96	74813	37983	51%
Mar. 97	88236	45870	52%
Mar. 98	105669	46894	44%
Mar. 99	127503	52367	41%
Mar. 2000	156520	66410	42%

Table 4.7. Branch Expansion by Udaipur Central Co-operative Bank in Udaipur District

Year	Branch Expansion																				
	June 71	June 72	June 73	June 74	Dec. 79	Dec. 82	Dec. 84	Dec. 85	Dec. 86	June 87	1989	1990	1991	1992-93	1993-94	1995-96	1996-97	March 97	March 98	March 99	Mar. 2000
Number of branches	5	5	6	7	14	16	16	16	17	17	17	17	10	8	8	8	8	9	9	9	9

Source: 1. Report of the study team on Agricultural Credit Institutions in Rajasthan RBI (2) DCP of Udaipur district.

effectly credit mobilisation in the district. It is therefore, urgently felt that the bank should open at least two branches in each block of the district so as to cover the areas which are not being served by commercial banks.

Block-wise Distribution of Branches

Block-wise offices of the UCCB are shown in Table 4.8 *(See page 188)*. In March 93, there were no branches of UCCB in the Badgaon, Kotra, Sarada, Dhariawad, Jhadol blocks while in Girwa block 3 branches of UCCB were functioning.

Deposits Mobilisation and Credit Development

The Deposit and Advances of the UCCB are given in Table 4.9, *(See page 189)*. The deposit and advances of the bank as on June 71 stood at Rs. 32. 57 lacs and Rs. 74.33 lacs respectively. The deposit and advances of the bank increased to Rs. 5681.45 lacs and Rs. 3154.17 lacs, respectively, at the end of March 2000. The advances of the bank decreased to Rs. 254.50 lacs at the end of June 87, due to drought in the district and at the end of March 92 again advances decreased to Rs. 650.95 lacs due to formation of Rajsamand district from Udaipur district.

2. PRIMARY LAND DEVELOPMENT BANK

There is only one Primary Land Development Bank functioning in the district. In 1990, there was 5 branches of PLDB functioning at Girwa, Rajsamand, Amet, Kotra and Salumbar but in 1991, branches of PLDB reduced to 3, due to the separation of Rajsamand district from Udaipur district. At the end of March 2000, there were still 3 branches functioning in the district. The number of PLDB is very small looking to the requirement of the district. Udaipur is consisting of 11 blocks at present in the district. It is suggested that the bank should have at least one branch in each block of the district, so that borrowers from remote rural areas may not have to come to the head office to apply for loans.

Advances and Deposit

The advances of the PLDB in Udaipur district are shown in Table 4.10, *(See page 190)*. The advances of the bank as on June 74 stood at Rs. 39.52 lacs which increased to Rs. 2846.68 lacs at the end of March 2000.

Table 4.8. Block-wise Branches of the Central Co-operative Bank in the Udaipur District

Name of the Block / Number of Branches	Amet	Bhim	Badgaon	Bhinder	Deogarh	Dhriawad	Girwa	Gogunda	Jhadol	Khamnor	Kher-wara	Kotra	Kumbhal-garh	Mavli	Railmagra	Rajsa-mand	Salumber	Sarada	Total
in Dec. 79	1	1	-	1	1	-	2	-	1	1	1	-	-	1	1	1	1	1	14
in Dec. 82	1	1	-	1	1	1	2	1	1	1	1	-	1	1	1	1	1	-	16
in Dec. 87	1	1	-	1	1	1	3	1	1	1	1	-	1	1	1	1	1	-	17
in 1990-91	1	1	-	1	1	1	3	1	1	1	1	-	1	1	1	1	1	-	17
in 1991-92	*	*	-	1	*	-	3	1	1	*	1	-	*	1	*	*	1	-	10
in 1993-94	*	*	-	1	*	-	3	1	-	*	1	-	*	1	*	*	1	-	8

Note: From 1991, these (*) blocks are not included in Udaipur district.

Table 4.9. Deposit and Advances of the UCCB in Udaipur District

(Amt. in Lacs of Rupees)

Year	Deposit	Advances
June 71	32.57	74.33
June 72	52.19	96.13
June 73	75.10	153.47
June 74	80.33	185.08
June 77	283.17	388.58
June 78	231.87	337.74
June 79	273.47	415.57
June 80	308.21	468.28
June 81	344.13	568.75
June 82	411.47	715.21
Dec. 83	N.A.	365.15
Dec. 84	533.98	371.98
Dec. 85	N.A.	377.94
Dec. 86	N.A.	279.19
June 87	N.A.	254.50
Dec. 88	1074.40	1492.18
Dec. 89	1242.43	1535.40
Mar. 91	1557.33	1009.48
Mar. 92	1205.34	650.95
Mar. 95	1943.37	1426.04
Mar. 96	2161.91	1834.76
Mar. 97	2974.77	2112.94
Mar. 98	3699.43	2624.77
Mar. 99	4371.77	2951.10
Mar. 2000	5681.45	3154.17

Source:

1. DCP of Udaipur district
2. Report of the study Team on Agricultural Credit Institution in Rajasthan.

Table 4.10. **Advances by the PLDB in Udaipur District**

(Amount in Lacs of Rupees)

Year	Advances
June 74	39.52
June 77	69.55
June 78	56.35
June 79	34.65
June 80	50.08
June 81	67.16
June 82	48.63
Dec. 83	68.14
Dec. 84	34.31
Dec. 85	84.13
Dec. 86	39.49
June 87	31.19
Dec. 88	—
Dec. 89	—
Mar. 91	—
Mar. 92	—
Mar. 95	1068.35
Mar. 96	1286.34
Dec. 96	1465.65
Mar. 98	1756.78
Mar. 99	2270.50
Mar. 2000	2846.68

Source:

1. Report of the study team on Agricultural Credit Institutions in Rajasthan, RBI.
2. DCP of Udaipur district.

In the co-operative field the long term loans are provided by this bank. Besides for minor irrigation purposes it also provides credit for a variety of purposes like farm mechanisation land reclamation development of horticulture and such other agricultural activities.

3. UDAIPUR URBAN CO-OPERATIVE BANK

The bank has 7 branches at the end of March 2000, in the district. Out of 7 branches, 5 branches of UUCB were functioning in the urban area and rest of the two in semi-urban area of the district.

The deposit and advances of this bank are given in Table 4.11, *(See page 192)*. In June 1977, deposit and advances were Rs. 4.49 lacs and Rs. 4.82 lacs in the district, which increased upto Rs. 7063.22 lacs and Rs. 4150.48 lacs, respectively in March, 2000.

The bank had been hitherto catering the needs of retail traders, artisans and the SSI in the city of Udaipur.

4. THE UDAIPUR MAHILA URBAN CO-OPERATIVE BANK

The Udaipur Mahila Co-operative bank came into existence on 28th September 1994. The management of this bank is vested in the hands of women and share holders of this bank are also women. The Udaipur Mahila Urban Co-operative Bank has only one branch and it is in the Udaipur city.

Main functions of the UMUCB are as follows:

1. For industrial development bank provide loan to small and cottage industries.
2. Bank provide loan and cash credit facilities to small and big business on securities of machine and material; and
3. Bank follow's the directive principal of R.B.I. and provide loan and advances to:
   - *(a)* Driver and road transporter for purchasing a vehicle;
   - *(b)* Retail businessmen who run a business of life utility commodities e.g. shop of fixed price;
   - *(c)* Professionals and self employed;
   - *(d)* For education;
   - *(e)* Residential loan;
   - *(f)* Consumer durable loan and
   - *(g)* Provide consumer loan to bank members.

Table 4.11. Deposit and Advances of Udaipur Urban Co-operative Bank

(Figures in Lacs of Rupees)

Year	Deposits	Advances
June 77	4.49	4.82
June 78	12.28	7.00
June 79	30.00	11.60
June 80	45.00	17.51
June 81	55.84	25.42
June 82	84.75	47.74
Dec. 87	—	44.86
Dec. 88	655.40	291.33
Dec. 89	792.54	394.99
Mar 91	1033.66	598.25
Mar. 92	1259.72	770.21
Mar. 95	2254.26	1462.73
Mar. 96	2872.20	2033.45
Mar. 97	4070.06	2788.67
Mar. 98	5111.19	3413.32
Mar. 99	6264.44	3807.53
Mar. 2000	7063.22	4150.48

Capital

The authorised capital of the bank is Rs. 50 lacs. In has been divided into 2 lacs shares of Rs. 25 each. The subscribed capital in 1999 was Rs. 44.9965 lacs (179986 share of Rs. 25 each).

Management

The management of the UMUCB is vested in the hands of Board of Directors. There are nine directors in the board of management. The board comprises on chairman, one vice chair person and seven managing directors.

Deposit and Advances

Table 4.12 and 4.13 are showing deposit and advances of UMUCB.

Table 4.12. Deposits of Udaipur Mahila Urban Co-operative Bank

(Amount in Lacs of Rupees)

S.No.	Type of Deposit	94-95	95-96	96-97	97-98	98-99
1.	Fixed Deposit	—	37.42	126.23	254.63	365.78
2.	Saving Bank	—	17.60	31.24	49.43	72.67
3.	Current Deposit	—	14.40	19.09	16.62	20.90
4.	Recurring Deposit	—	2.67	6.24	7.32	9.49
5.	Others	—	1.91	7.70	3.17	3.69
	Total		**74.00**	**190.50**	**331.17**	**472.53**

Source: Varshik Lekha-Jokha, The Udaipur Mahila Urban Co-operative Bank Ltd. (96-99).

Table 4.13. Loan and Advances by Udaipur Mahila Urban Co-operative Bank

(Amount of Lacs. of Rupees)

S.No.	Type of advance	94-95	95-96	96-97	97-98	98-99
1.	Medium term loan (secured)	—	13.43	48.83	160.57	222.65
2.	Medium term loan (unsecured)	—	5.93	1.05	1.71	0.39
3.	Cash credit	—	5.40	21.60	39.65	58.15
4.	Overdraft	—	1.94	4.19	1.93	8.09
5.	Loan against deposit	—	2.45	4.95	5.33	7.24
	Total	**24.00**	**29.15**	**80.62**	**209.19**	**296.52**

Source: Varshik Lekha-Jokha, The Udaipur Mahila Urban Co-operative Bank Ltd. (96-99).

The total deposit in 95-96 was Rs. 74.00 lacs, however in the year of Dec. 2000 deposits increased upto Rs. 669.10 lacs. The maximum deposit were of fixed deposit in UMUCB. In 1995-96, total loan and advances provided by bank was of Rs. 24 lacs increased in Dec. 2000 upto Rs. 375.50 lacs.

5. THE UDAIPUR MAHILA SAMRADHI URBAN CO-OPERATIVE BANK LTD

The Udaipur Mahila Samradhi Urban Co-operative Bank came into existence on 1st November 1994. The management of this bank is vested in the hands of women, share holders of this bank are also women and this bank provide loans only to women.

Bank provides loan only to women for following purposes:

1. Consumer loan for domestic goods, for 3 to 5 year period;
2. Loan to retail and small business for 3 to 5 years duration;
3. Loan for self employment and to establish service unit;
4. Loan for purchase and construction of house;
5. Loan to small Handicraft and cottage industry for 5 years;
6. 3 to 5 years loan for transportation; If jeep, car, truck, tampoo, auto riksha, loading tampoo etc. are buy for business purposes;
7. 75% loan against on National Saving Certificate and "Kisan Vikas Patra"; and
8. 85% loan against fixed deposit.

Capital

The authorised capital of the bank is Rs. 50 lacs. It has been divided into 5 lacs shares of Rs. 10 each.

Management

The management of the UMSUCB is vested in the Board of Directors. There are 10 Women directors in the board of management. The board comprises one chairman, one vice chairman and rest are managing directors.

Deposit and Advances

Table 4.14 and 4.15 depicts deposit and advances of UMSUCB.

Table 4.14. Deposits of Udaipur Mahila Samradhi Urban Co-operative Bank

(Amount in Lac of Rupees)

S.No.	Type of Deposit	96	March 97	March 98	March 99
1.	Fixed deposit		126.60	187.05	250.28
2.	Saving A/C		25.65	46.22	69.72
3.	Current A/C		15.58	18.12	31.67
4.	Recurring A/C		2.94	5.38	7.98
5.	Daily deposit		19.76	44.24	69.52
	Total	**109.35**	**190.53**	**301.01**	**429.25**

Source: "Varshik Lekha Avam Prativethan" (1995-1999)

Table 4.15. Loan and Advances by Udaipur Mahila Samrathi Urban Co-operative Bank

(Amount in Lacs of Rupees)

S.No.	Type of Loan	Year 96	96-97	97-98	98.99
1.	Medium term loan		52.85	104.75	134.87
2.	Medium term (unsecured)		—	0.04	—
3.	Cash credit		15.50	34.43	62.03
4.	Over draft		2.08	6.20	6.14
5.	Loan against deposit		2.86	1.17	2.87
	Total	**58.83**	**73.29**	**146.59**	**205.91**

Source: "Varshik Lekha Avam Prativedan" (1995-1999).

The deposits of UMSUCB was Rs. 109.35 lac in 96 increased upto Rs. 586.11 lacs in Dec. 2000.

The loan and advances provided of Rs. 58.83 Lac in March 96 increased in Dec. 2000 upto Rs. 349.23 lacs. In Co-operative sector, one branch of Madhav urban cooperative bank recently established in Udaipur city.

III. The Regional Rural Bank (R.R.B.)

Branch Expansion

The Mewar Aanchyalik Gramin Bank is the RRB operating in the district. It was sponsored by the Bank of Rajasthan Ltd. It started its operation in 1983 and since then there has been a rapid expansion in its number of branches. Upto the year of 1990, at that time 61 branches of RRB were functioning in the district. In 1991, separation of Rajsamand district from Udaipur district so branches of RRB decreased from 61 to 41. On March 2000, there were 41 branches of RRB functioning in the Udaipur district (Table 4.16 and 4.17).

Table 4.16. Branches of RRB in Udaipur District

Year	Branches
Dec. 1983	10
Dec. 1984	52
Dec. 1985	58
Dec. 1986	58
Dec. 1987	60
Dec. 1988	61
Dec. 1989	61
Dec. 1990	61
March 1991	41
March 1992	39
March 1993	40
March 1995	40
March 1996	40
March 1997	41
March 1998	41
March 1999	41
2000	41

Source:

1. 5th Annual Report of MAGB p. 2.
2. DCP of Udaipur district.

Table 4.17. Block-wise Branches of MAGB in Udaipur District

Block	Branches			
	Dec. 87	Dec. 89	1991	1993-94
Amet	3	2	*	*
Badgaon	1	1	1	—
Bhim	2	2	*	*
Bhinder	3	3	3	3
Deogarh	3	2	*	*
Dhariwad	3	3	3	3
Girwa	8	8	8	8
Gogunda	3	3	3	4
Jhadol	4	4	4	4
Khamnor	3	3	*	*
Kherwara	3	3	3	3
Kotra	4	4	4	4
Kumbhalgarh	2	2	*	*
Mavli	3	3	3	3
Rajasamand	5	5	*	*
Railmagra	2	2	*	*
Salumbar	3	3	3	3
Sarada	5	5	5	5
Total	60	58	40	40

Note:* These blocky are not included from 1991, in Udaipur district Blockwise branches of MAGB is given in Table 4.17.

Growth of Deposits, Advances and Credit Deposit Ratio of RRB

Growth of deposits advances and credit deposit ratio of RRB in Udaipur is given in Table 4.18.

Bank achieve encouraging growth in deposit mobilisation which is evident from the fact that the total deposit rose to Rs. 8379.29 lacs from Rs. 35.09 lacs during Dec. 1983 to March 2000. During the same period advances increase from Rs. 11.43 lacs to Rs. 2270.73 lacs. Credit deposit ratio is very low in last five years.

Table 4.18. Growth of Deposits, Advances and Credit Deposit Ratio of RRB in Udaipur District

(Amount in Lacs of Rupees)

Year	Deposits	Advances	Credit Deposit Ratio
Dec. 83	35.09	11.43	33%
Dec. 84	164.94	101.85	62%
Dec. 85	249.41	179.71	72%
Dec. 86	341.97	240.70	71%
Dec. 87	515.94	307.84	60%
Dec. 88	646.74	381.56	59%
Dec. 89	844.07	449.78	53%
Mar. 91	1214.60	625.35	51%
June 92	820.54	434.42	52.94%
Mar. 95	2058.29	730.23	41%
Mar. 96	3036.82	960.63	32%
Mar. 97	4389.49	1227.70	28%
Mar. 98	5766.73	1445.49	25%
Mar. 99	6967.70	1734.27	25%
Mar. 2000	8379.29	2270.73	27%

Source:

1. Annual Reports of MAGB.
2. DCP of Udaipur district.

BANKING DEVELOPMENT IN DUNGARPUR DISTRICT

I. Commercial Bank

Branch Expansion

Dungarpur is one of the economically backward district of Rajasthan. Lack of adequate financial facilities is one of the important factor for its backwardness. Prior to 1969, banking development was very slow and unsatisfactory. After the nationalisation of 14 commercial banks and beginning of the Lead Bank Scheme in 1969, commercial bank launched a massive branch expansion programme in the district, particularly in the rural and semi-urban areas. Though during the period 1969 to

2000. 34 branches were opened as shown in table 4.19, *(See page 200)*. Bankers had to face a lot of problems in undertaking its branch expansion programme, specially in view of the absence of the minimum infrastructural facilities like transportation and communication systems. Due to this they could not open the desired number of branches. Similarly they could not adopt a larger number of villages for financing purposes.

Branch expansion in Dungarpur district is given in table 4.19. Table 4.19 shows that at the end of March 2000, there were 41 branches of commercial banks functioning in the district.

Bank Group-wise Distribution of Branches

Bank group-wise distribution of branches shown in table 4.20, *(See page 201)*. Table 4.20 reveals the fact that the public sector banks account for most of the branches. On March 2000, the SBI Group Banks, Nationalised Banks and Private Sector Banks had 19.51 per cent, 70.73 per cent and 9.76 per cent branches in the district respectively. During Dec. 79 to March 2000 branches of SBI Group, Nationalised Banks and Private Sector Banks increased by 5, 18 and 3 respectively.

From Table 4.20, it can be concluded that the lead bank, Bank of Baroda and SBBJ have the highest number of Branches 28 and 5 at the end of March 2000.

Centre-wise Distribution of the Branches

Centre-wise distribution of the branches of commercial banks in Dungarpur district is given in table 4.21, *(See page 202)*.

At the time of nationalisation there was 7 branches in the district which increased upto 41 at the end of March 2000. The share of the rural branches increased from 28.57 per cent to 75.61 per cent during December 1969 to March 2000.

Sector-wise Distribution of Branches

Table 4.22 *(See page 203)* is evident that public sector banks account for most of the bank branches.

In March 2000 the public sector bank accounted for 90.24 per cent of the total branches in the district.

Table 4.19. Branch Expansion by Commercial Bank in Dungarpur District

Year	June 69	Dec. 72	Dec. 73	Dec. 74	Dec. 75	Dec. 76	Dec. 77	Dec. 78	Dec. 79	Dec. 80	Dec. 81	Dec. 82	Dec. 83
No. of Branches	7	8	10	10	10	13	14	14	15	15	26	31	32
Increasing over the preceding year	—	1	2	—	—	3	1	—	1	—	11	5	1

Year	Dec. 84	Dec. 85	Dec. 86	Dec. 87	Dec. 88	89	90	91	92	93	Dec. 94	95	March 96	97	March 98	99	2000
No. of branches	40	42	42	40	40	40	40	40	40	40	40	41	41	41	41	41	41
Increasing over the preceding year	8	2	—	-2	—	—	—	—	—	—	—	1	—	—	—	—	—

Source:

1. Banking Statistics, RBI
2. DCP of Dungarpur district.

Table 4.20. Bank Group-wise Distribution of Branches of the Commercial Banks in Dungarpur District

S.No.	Bank group and Name of the Bank	Number of Branches as on							
		Dec. 79	Dec. 82	Dec. 84	Dec. 87	March 1990	Dec. 94	March 98	March 2000
1.	**Public Sector Bank**								
	(A) SBI Group	3	5	7	7	7	7	8	8
	1. State Bank of Bikaner and Jaipur	3	3	4	4	4	4	5	5
	2. State Bank of India	—	2	3	3	3	3	3	3
	(B) Nationalised Bank	11	24	30	29	29	29	29	29
	1. Bank of Baroda	10	23	27	28	28	28	28	28
	2. Punjab National Bank	1	1	1	1	1	1	1	1
	3. Agricultural Development Branch	–	–	2	–				
2.	**Private Sector Bank**	1	2	3	4	4	4	4	4
	1. The Bank of Rajasthan Ltd.	1	2	3	4	4	4	4	4
	Total	**15**	**31**	**40**	**40**	**40**	**40**	**41**	**41**

Source: DCP of Dungarpur District.

Table 4.21. Centre-wise Distribution of Branches of the Commercial Banks in Dungarpur District

(Percentage in Brackets)

Population Group/Year	June 69	June 72	Dec 75	Dec 76	Dec 78	Dec 82	Dec 87	March 2000
Rural	2 (28.57%)	3 (37.50%)	4 (40%)	7 (53.85%)	8 (57.14%)	23 (74.19%)	33 (78.73%)	31 (75.61%)
Semi-urban	5 (71.43%)	5 (62.50%)	6 (60%)	6 (46.15%)	6 (42.86%)	8 (5.81%)	9 (21.43%)	10 (24.39%)
Total	7 (100%)	8 (100%)	10 (100%)	13 (100%)	14 (100%)	31 (100%)	42 (100%)	41 (100%)

Source: Annual report of trends and progress of banking in India, RBI.

Table 4.22. Sector-wise Distribution of Branches of the Commercial Banks in Dungarpur District

Year	No. of Public Sector Banks	No. of Private sector Banks	Total
Dec. 1980	14 (93.33%)	1 (6.67%)	15 (100%)
Dec. 1982	29 (93.55%)	2 (6.45%)	31 (100%)
Dec. 1987	36 (90.41%)	4 (9.52%)	40 (100%)
Dec. 1988	36	4	40
Mar. 1990	36	4	40
Dec. 1994	36	4	40
Mar. 1998	37 (90.24%)	4 (9.76%)	41 (100%)
Mar. 2000	37 (90.24%)	4 (9.76%)	41 (100%)

Source: DCP of Dungarpur District.

Block-wise Distribution of Branches

The block-wise distribution of bank branches is quite uneven in the district as table 4.23 depicts.

There are blocks like Sagwara and Dungarpur, where the number of branches in plenty, while in the block of Bicchiwara, Aspur and Simalwara the number of branches is below the required strength.

Table 4.23. Block-wise Distribution of Branches of Commercial Banks in Dungarpur District

Name of Block	No. of Branches					
	Dec. 80	Dec. 82	Dec. 87	March 1990	March 98	March 2000
1. Aspur	3	7	7	7	7	7
2. Bichhiwara	1	2	6	6	6	6
3. Dungarpur	4	6	9	9	10	10
4. Sagwara	4	10	11	11	11	11
5. Simalwara	3	6	7	7	7	7
Total	**15**	**31**	**40**	**40**	**41**	**41**

* DCP, Dungarpur, District.

DEPOSIT MOBILISATION AND CREDIT DEPLOYMENT

The growth of deposits and advances in Dungarpur district has been shown in table 4.24.

Table 4.24. Growth of Deposits, Advances and Credit Deposit Ratio in Dungarpur District

(Amount in Lacs of Rupees)

Year	Deposits	Advances	C.D.R.
Dec. 72	71	9	12.67%
Dec. 73	94	25	26.59%
Dec. 74	111	19	26.12%
Dec. 75	158	39	24.68%
Dec. 76	223	66	29.59%
Dec. 77	379	90	23.74%
Dec. 78	548	125	22.81%
Dec. 79	607	171	28.17%
Dec. 80	825	197	23.88%
June 81	883	242	27.40%
June 82	1160	321	27.67%
Feb. 84	2594	1243	47.92%
Feb. 85	3241	1528	47.14%
Feb. 86	4154	1876	45.16%
June 87	4655	2035	43.71%
Dec. 88	5817	2362	40.60%
Dec. 89	6308	2435	41.77%
* March 93	11,572	2877	24.86%
* March 94	14,166	3019	21.31%
* March 95	16,749	3287	19.65%
* March 96	19690	3860	19%
* March 97	23480	4050	17%
* March 98	27490	4870	18%
* March 99	32545	6495	20%
* March 2000	35443	6371	17.97%

*1. Source Banking Statistics, RBI.

*2. DCP, Dungarpur District.

The aggregate deposit growth has been risen from Rs. 71 lacs to Rs. 35443 lacs, over the span period between the Dec. 72 to March 2000. During this period, advances rose to Rs. 6371 lacs from Rs. 9 lacs. In other words during the period the deposits went up by 500 times while the advances increased by 708 times.

The Credit Deposit Ratio of the commercial banks in the district should be at least 60 per cent in terms of RBI guidelines. But the CDR was very low in Dungarpur district upto June 82, it was lower than 30 per cent after 1983 it was above than 43 per cent. It recorded highest (47.92 per cent) in the year of 1984 and lowest (12.67 per cent) in the year of 1972. From March 93 decline in CDR started, at the end of March 2000 CDR was only 18%. CDR shows that there was an out-flow of funds from the district. It is not a good sign for the development of the district.

II. Co-operative Banks

1. The Dungarpur Kendria Sahkari Bank (DKSB)

It was functioning through 9 branches in the district at the end of March 2000.

Block-wise Branches

Block-wise branches of the DKSB are given in Table—4.25.

Table 4.25. Block-wise Branches of the Central Co-operative Bank in Dungarpur District

Name of Block	No. of Branches				
	Dec. 82	Dec. 87	Nov. 90	Mar. 98	March 2000
Aspur	1	1	1	1	1
Bichhiwara	1	1	1	1	1
Dungarpur	2	2	2	2	2
Sagwara	3	3	3	3	3
Simalwara	2	2	2	2	2
Total	**9**	**9**	**9**	**9**	**9**

Loan and Advances

Advances disbursed by DKSB in Dungarpur district to shown in table 4.26. In 1978-79 advances of DCCB was Rs. 111.89 lacs reduced to Rs. 39.65 lacs at the end of June 87, which was the minimum advances visible in the table. However, at the end of Dec. 1999, advances of co-operative bank increased to Rs. 1200.15 lacs.

Table 4.26. Advances by Central Co-operative Bank in Dungarpur District

(Amount in Lacs of Rupees)

Year	Advances
1978-79	111.89
1979-80	65.09
1980	114.35
1981	122.29
Upto June 1982	116.54
1985	72.85
1986	43.18
June 87	39.65
1992-93	95.75
1993-94	114.25
1994-95	57.40
1995-96	239-93
1996-97	314.24
1997-98	550.27
1998-99	1105.00
Dec. 1999	1200.15

Source:

1. DCP, Dungarpur district.
2. **Institutional finance in TSP area by Ramakant Sharma.**

2. PRIMARY LAND DEVELOPMENT BANK

Upto December 83, only one branch of PLDB was functioning in Dungarpur block. Second branch of PLDB opened in the year of 1984 in Simalwara block. And till the end of March

2000, only 2 branches of PLDB were functioning in the district. The number of PLDB in very poor looking to the requirement of the district. Therefore, it is suggested that bank should have at least one branch in each block of the district.

Term loan disbursed by PLDB is shown in Table—4.27.

Table 4.27. Term Loan by PLDB in Dungarpur District

(Amount in Lacs of Rupees)

Year	Amount Advances
1978-79	68.69
1979-80	52.57
1980	37.68
1981	24.44
June 82	24.70
1985	31.83
1986	18.39
June 87	12.02
1992-93	86.25
1993-94	113.26
1994-95	88.80
1995-96	270.30
1996-97	308.98
1997-98	316.38
1998-99	389.69
Dec. 1999-2000	381.65

In 1979, Rs. 68.69 lacs advances given by bank, however at the end of December of 1999 loan amount increased upto Rs. 381.65 lacs.

III. Regional Rural Bank

In the year 1984 the major changes in the banking scene of the district has been taken place when of Dungarpur Banswara Kshetriya Gramin Bank established, sponsored by the Lead Bank (Bank of Baroda). At the end of March 2000, 21 branches of

DBKGB was functioning in Dungarpur district. Block-wise branches of RRB's given in Table—4.28.

Table 4.28. Block-wise Branches of the DBKGB in Dungarpur District

Name of the block	Year				
	June 85	June 86	Dec. 87	March 90	March 2000
Aspur	—	4	4	5	5
Bichhiwara	2	2	3	4	4
Dungarpur	3	3	4	5	6
Sagwara	2	2	3	3	2
Simalwara	1	2	2	4	4
Total	12	13	16	21	21

Source: DCP of Dungarpur District.

Table 4.29. Advances by RRB in Dungarpur District

(Amount in Lacs of Rupees)

Year	Advances
1985	19.64
1986	44.95
1987	19.01
1993	89.25
1994	64.49
1995	41.29
1996	119.67
1997	166.46
1998	474.19
March 1999	543.78
March 2000	329.86

Source: DCP of Dungarpur district advances distributed by DBKGB was Rs. 19.64 in 1985 however increased to Rs. 329.86 lacs in 1999.

COMPARATIVE STUDY OF BANKING DEVELOPMENT IN THE UDAIPUR AND DUNGARPUR DISTRICTS

I. Commercial Banks

Network of Branches

After the nationalsation of 14 commercial banks and the beginning of the LBS in 1969, commercial banks launched a massive branch expansion programme. Table 4.30 depicts the comparative performance of the commercial bank in the field of branch expansion in Udaipur and Dungarpur districts of Rajasthan.

Table 4.30. Branch Expansion Programme in Udaipur and Dungarpur District (1969-2000)

Year	No. of Commercial Bank	
	Udaipur District	Dungarpur District
1969	25	7
1975	52	10
1980	98	15
1985	124	42
1990	137	40
1991	105	40
1995	111	40
2000	119	41
% increase in branches	376%	485.71

Source: Prepared from table 4.1 and 4.19.

In Udaipur and Dungarpur district total number of branches in 1969 were 25 and 7 which increased to 119 (376%) and 41 (485.71%) at the end of March 2000, respectively. In Udaipur district, bank branches had increasing trend except in the year of 1991. This was due to the separation of Rajsamand district from Udaipur district. In Dungarpur district, 485.71% increase in bank branches shows that, the Lead Bank of Dungarpur district i.e. Bank of Baroda showed better performance in establishing bank branches then the Lead Bank of the Udaipur district, however, the performance of Lead Bank of Udaipur district, also not bad enough. The percentage has been fallen due to the separation of Rajsamand district from Udaipur district.

Centre-wise Distribution of Branches

The commercial bank launched a massive branch expansion programme particularly in rural and semi-urban areas (Table 4.31 *See page 211*). The expansion of the branches in the rural and semi-urban areas not only enabled them in mobilising of a large amount of deposits, but they could also extend credit facilities to new fields and areas, thus helping in the achievement of the goals and objectives of nationalisation.

In Udaipur district, share of rural and semi-rural branches decreased from 68% to 55.46% in the period of Dec. 1969 to March 2000. While the number of rural and semi-urban branches increased from 17 to 66 during the same period. On the other hand urban branches increased from 8 (32%) to 53 (44.54%).

In Dungarpur district all branches working in rural and semi-urban areas.

Sector-wise Distribution of Branches

Table 4.32, *(See page 212)* is evident that public sector bank accounted for most of the bank branches in Udaipur and Dungarpur District.

In 2000, the public sector bank accounted for 77.31% and 90.24% in Udaipur and Dungarpur district, respectively.

Block-wise Distribution of Branches

The distribution of branches is quite uneven in Udaipur and Dungarpur district. There are blocks like Girwa, Malvi, Bhinder, Kherwara in Udaipur district, and Sagwara and Dungarpur in Dungarpur district where the number of branches are plenty, while in the blocks of Kotra, Gogunda, Dhariwad and Jhadol in Udaipur district and Aspur, Bicchiwara and Simalwara in Dungarpur district, the number of branches is much below the

Table 4.31. Centre-wise Distribution of Branches in Udaipur and Dungarpur District

Population group/year	Udaipur					Dungarpur				
	1969	1976	1982	1987	2000	1969	1976	1982	1987	2000
Rural	17 (68%)	29 (47.54%)	76 (66.08%)	88* (70.4%)	58 (48.74%)	2 (28.57%)	7 (53.85%)	23 (74.19%)	33 (78.73%)	31 (75.61%)
Semi-urban	–	8 (13.11%)	8 (6.96%)		8 (6.72%)	5 (71.43%)	6 (46.15%)	8 (5.81%)	9 (21.43%)	10 (24.39%)
Urban	8 (32%)	24 (39.35%)	31 (26.96%)	37 (29.6%)	53 (44.54%)	–	–	–	–	–
Total	**25 (100%)**	**61 (100%)**	**115 (100%)**	**125 (100%)**	**119 (100%)**	**7 (100%)**	**13 (100%)**	**31 (100%)**	**42 (100%)**	**41 (100%)**

Source: Prepared from table 4.3 and 4.21.

* It is the combined bank branches of rural and semi-urban areas.

required strength. This unequal distribution of bank branches in every block created disparity in the economic and human resource development of the districts.

Table 4.32. Sector Wise Distribution of Branches of the Commercial Bank in Udaipur and Dungarpur District

Year	Udaipur		Dungarpur	
	Public sector bank	Private sector bank	Public sector bank	Private sector bank
1980	71 (71.43%)	27 (28.57%)	14 (93.33%)	1 (6.67%)
1987	94 (72.87%)	35 (27.13%)	36 (90.41%)	4 (9.52%)
1990	100 (72.99%)	37 (27.01%)	36 (90.41%)	4 (9.52%)
1991	79 (75.24%)	26 (24.76%)	36 (90.41%)	4 (9.52%)
2000	92 (77.31%)	27 (22.69%)	37 (90.24%)	4 (9.76%)

Source: Prepared from Table No. 4.4 and 4.22.

Deposit Mobilisation and Credit Deployment

The aggregate deposit of Udaipur and Dungarpur district (Table 4.33) rose from Rs. 532 lacs to Rs. 1,27,503 lacs and Rs. 39 lacs to 32,545 lacs, over the span of period between the nationalisation of the banks in 1969 and March 1999. During this period advances increased to Rs. 52,367 lacs from Rs. 186 lacs in Udaipur district and in Dungarpur district Rs. 6495 lacs from Rs. 6 lacks. In the other word during the same period deposits rose by 239.67 and 1017 times while the advances increased by 281.54 and 1082.5 times in Udaipur and Dungarpur district respectively.

The volume of deposits reflects efforts and potentiality of savings of a nation and gives a fair idea of the economic growth. During 31 years i.e. from 1969 to 2000 deposits in Dungarpur and Udaipur district increased to 23866.73% and 83348. 77% respectively.

Credit deposit ratio is yet another indicator of the progress made by banking sector in serving the society. Since the nationalisation of commercial banks, C.D.R. in the districts have not undergone any change. In the year of 1969 CDR in Udaipur and Dungarpur district was 34.9% and 15.38% respectively while in 1999 CDR was 41% and 20% in Udaipur and Dungarpur districts. The Lead Bank of Udaipur and Dungarpur district must try to stop the out-flow of funds and pay more attention to the local uses of funds.

Table 4.33. Growth of Deposits and Advances of the Commercial Banks and Credit Deposit Ratio in Udaipur and Dungarpur District

(Amount in Lacs of Rupees)

Year	Udaipur			Dungarpur		
	Deposit	Advances	CDR	Deposit	Advances	CDR
1969	532	186	34.9%	39	6	15.38%
1975	1766	960	54.3%	158	39	24.68%
1980	5735	3313	57.7%	825	197	23.88%
1985	15401	9417	61.1%	3241	1528	47.92%
1995	69127	28238	41%	16749	3287	19.65%
1999	127503	52367	41%	32545	6495	20.00%

Source: Prepared from table 4.6 and 4.24.

CO-OPERATIVE BANKS

1. District Central Co-operative Bank

The Co-operative Banks were set up with the intention of taking care of the bulk of the short term rural credit needs for purpose like crop loans processing of agricultural procedure and marketing of crops and consumption loans. They also issued medium term loans for purchases of agricultural machinery, pump sets, milch cattle and land conversions.

In June 1971, there were five branches of UCCB serving in Udaipur district. The trend of increase in branches continued till the year of 1990, and 17 branches of UCCB were functioning in the district but because of the separation of Rajsamand district (now an independent district) from Udaipur district, immensely fall in bank branches and came down to 10 in 1991. On March 2000, nine branches of UCCB were working in the Udaipur district. In Dungarpur district, there were 9 branches of DCCB working in December 1982, however, at the end of March 2000 there was no increase in branches still 9 branches were serving.

It is therefore urgently felt that the bank should open atleast two branches in each block of the district.

Upto the end of March 94, there was no branch of the UCCB in Badgaon, Kotra and Sarada blocks. And in Dhariwad and Jhadol blocks existed branches of UCCB had been closed in 1993-94.

Advances of UCCB increased by Rs. 74.33 lacs in June 1971 to Rs. 3154.17 lacs in March 2000. And the volume of deposit increased from Rs. 32.57 lacs in June 1971 to Rs. 5681.45 lacs in March 2000. While the Advances of DCCB reduced from Rs. 111.89 lacs in 1978-79 to Rs. 57.40 in 1995.

2. Primary Land Development Bank

There are three and two branches of PLDB functioning in the Udaipur and Dungarpur districts respectively. The number of PLDB's very small looking to the requirement of the district.

During the period of June 1974 to March 2000 PLDB's advances increases from Rs. 39.52 lacs to Rs. 2846.68 lacs in Udaipur district. While in Dungarpur district it increased to Rs. 68.69 lacs to Rs. 88.80 lacs in the period of 1978 to 1995.

3. The Urban Co-operative Bank

The bank has 7 branches at the end of March 2000, in the district. Out of 7 branches, 5 branches of UUCB were functioning in the urban area and rest of the two in semi-urban area.

4. The Udaipur Mahila Urban Co-operative Bank

The Udaipur Mahila Urban Co-operative Bank came into existence in 1994. The management of this bank is vested in the hands of women and shareholders of this bank are also women. The UMUCB has only one branch and working in proper Udaipur city.

During the period of March 95 to December 2000, deposit increase from Rs. 74 lacs to Rs. 669.10 lacs and advances increase from Rs. 24 lacs to Rs. 375.50 lacs.

This bank provide loan for consumer goods, business, profession, Residential loan and educational loan. In Dungarpur district yet no MUCB has been established.

5. The Mahila Samridhi Urban Co-operative Bank Ltd.

The Udaipur Mahila Samridhi Urban Co-operative Bank came into existence in November 1994. The management of the bank vested in the hands of women and shareholders are also women and this bank provides loan only to women. The bank provides loan for consumer durable, business, self-employment, residential loan facility etc.

During March 96 to December 2000 to deposit and advances increased from Rs. 109.35 lacs to Rs. 586.11 and Rs. 58.83 lacs to 349.23 lacs, respectively. In Dungarpur district yet no branch of MSUCB has been established.

III. Regional Rural Banks

The Mewar Aanchalik Gramin Bank (MAGB) and Dungarpur Banswara Kshetriya Gramin Bank (DBKGB) are the RRB's and operating in Udaipur and Dungarpur district respectively.

The MAGB is sponsored by the Bank of Rajasthan Ltd. It start its operation in 1983 and since then there has been a rapid expansion in branches. It start work with 10 branches in 1983 and in 1990 it reached to 61 bank branches in the district. Due to separation of Rajsamand district number of branches fallen to 41, and at the end of March 2000 there were 41 branches of MAGB working in the district.

During the period of December 83 to March 2000, Deposit and advances increase from 35.09 lacs to 8379.29 lacs and 11.43 lacs to 2270.73 lacs in the district respectively.

The DBKGB is sponsored by the Bank of Baroda. It started its operation in 1984 and since then there has been a rapid expansion in its number of branches which stood at 21 at the end of March 2000.

Advances disbursed by DBKGB is Rs. 19.64 lacs, Rs. 41.29 lacs, in the year of 1985, 1995, respectively.

5 Role of Banking Institutions in Economic Development of Women Under Development Programmes

After independence and beginning of the planned era for the economic development of our country, the government started various development programmes to bring out social and economic changes in the country. Many schemes and plans have been launched and implemented during the last five decades. Despite efforts made over the last five decades, poverty in the country continues to be significant. In the percentage terms, poverty levels have reduced from 56.44% of India's population in 1973-74 to 37.27% in 1993-94. The effects of such a large percentage of poor on the country's development is not difficult to appreciate. It is in this context that the self-employment programmes assume significance for, they can provide income to the poor on a sustainable basis. The credit plans were prepared for the financial year (April-March).

The banks and other institutions viz. Commercial banks, Regional Rural Banks, Cooperative Banks and non-banking financial institutions like State Financial Corporation, Khadi and Village Industries Board etc. are closely associated and involved in preparing these project report so as to avoid delays in sanctioning of loan and to ensure adequacy of financing.

The details of some important development schemes and programmes, are given below:

1. Integrated Rural Development Programme (IRDP)
2. Training to Rural Youth for Self Employment (TRYSEM)
3. Swarnajayanti Gram Swarozgar Yojana (SGSY)
4. The Swarna Jayanti Shahari Rozgar Yojana (SJSRY), and
5. Prime Minister Rozgar Yojana (PMRY).

1. INTEGRATED RURAL DEVELOPMENT PROGRAMME (IRDP)

To begin with IRDP was the only self-employment programme. Before this, multiplicity of agencies has been carrying on the task for providing rural employment. They include Employment Guarantee schemes, Food for work programme, Small Farmers Development Agency (SFDA), Marginal Farmers and Agricultural Labourers (MFAL), Drought Prone Area Programme (DPAP) and desert Development Programme (DDP), Command Area Development Programme etc. In the 6th plan such multiplicity of programmes replaced by one single integrated programme throughout the country. This programme has been named as the Integrated Rural Development Program (IRDP). The IRDP was initiated on October 2, 1980 in all the 5011 blocks in the country. Under the programme, identified the poor families (living below the poverty line) would be covered in a phased manner at the rate of 600 families per block per year i.e. 30 lacs families annually for the entire country and would be provided gainful employment in the form of subsidiary occupation with the help of financial assistance from the government in the form of subsidy and from the banks in the form of loan. The DRDA is the implementing agency and provides subsidy to the extent of 25% of the investment to small farmers, 33% to the marginal farmers and 50% to the S.C./S.T.

Table 5.1 shows the progress of IRDP in Udaipur district.

During the period of 1992-93 to 98-99, total beneficiaries were 32293 and loan and subsidy disbursed to them were

Table 5.1. Gender-wise Progress of I.R.D.P in Udaipur District

(Amount of Lacs of Rupees)

Financial year	Male		Female		Total		% of female to total beneficiaries	% of loan & subsidy disbursed to women
	Beneficiaries	Loan & subsidy disbursed	Beneficiaries	Loan & subsidy disbursed	Beneficiaries	Loan & subsidy disbursed		
1992-93	3658	267.09	1495	49.98	5153	317.07	29.01%	15.76%
1993-94	4896	324.95	710	46.99	5605	371.94	12.67%	12.63%
1994-95	4767	454.51	788	67.60	5555	522.11	14.19%	12.95%
1995-96	3787	487.97	1428	198.08	5215	686.05	27.38%	28.87%
1996-97	3594	784.83	512	112.86	4106	897.69	12.47%	12.57%
1997-98	2948	722.40	581	149.98	3529	872.38	16.46%	17.19%
1998-99	2162	649.31	968	282.65	3130	931.96	30.93%	30.33%
Total	**25812**	**3691.06**	**6482**	**908.14**	**32293**	**4599.2**	**20.07%**	**19.75%**

Source: DRDA, Udaipur district.

Rs. 4599.2 lacs. Out of these women beneficiaries were only 6482 (20.07%) and loan and subsidy disbursement was Rs. 908.14 lacs (19.75%).

Percentage of female beneficiaries recorded lowest in the year of 96-97 i.e. 12.47% while highest in 98-99 i.e. 30.93%.

The overall performance of females under IRDP scheme in Dungarpur district (Table 5.2 *See page 221*) is not quite satisfactory. Between the period of 1992-93 to 98-99 total IRDP beneficiaries were 14375 and loan disbursed to them of Rs. 1569.44 lacs. Out of these only 3748 (26.07%) were females and they benefitted by Rs. 340.38 lacs (21.69%) loan amount.

Progress of scheme regarding females declined very severely in 98-99, only 267 (16.88%) females were benefited out of 1582 beneficiaries and benefited by Rs. 51.41 lacs (13.97%) only.

2. TRAINING TO RURAL YOUTH FOR SELF EMPLOYMENT (TRYSEM)

In India most of the efforts have remained confined to the development of people through training in organised sectors. On the other hand, no efforts have been made for the rural mass. Government of India had launched a scheme to provide technical skills to rural youth in the year 1979. This scheme is known as "Training of Rural Youth for Self Employment (TRYSEM)".

The scheme work as a part of Integrated Rural Development Programme and aims at imparting training to about 2 lacs rural youth every year in the 5011 development blocks of the country and try to lift them above the poverty line.

Under this scheme, those rural youth who are in the age group of 18 to 35 years with annual family income from all sources should not be exceeding Rs. 8500 are eligible for selection. There is no minimum educational qualification prescribed under the scheme. Preference is given to S.C/S.T (50%), women (40%), and physically handicapped (3%).

Table 5.2. Gender-wise Progress of I.R.D.P in Dungarpur District

(Amount in Lacs of Rupees)

Financial year	Male		Female		Total		% of female to total beneficiaries	% of loan distributed to female
	Beneficiaries	Loan Amount (not subsidy)	Beneficiaries	Loan Amount (not subsidy)	Beneficiaries	Loan Amount (not subsidy)		
1992-93	1571	58.12	641	22.45	2212	80.57	28.98%	27.86%
1993-94	1777	87.42	768	32.11	2545	119.53	30.18%	26.86%
1994-95	1745	106.47	705	46.65	2450	153.12	28.78%	30.47%
1995-96	1955	155.5	569	42.13	2524	197.63	22.54%	21.32%
1996-97	1185	240.62	521	97.60	1706	338.22	30.54%	28.86%
1997-98	1079	264.23	277	48.03	1356	312.26	20.43%	15.38%
1998-99	1315	316.70	267	51.41	1582	368.11	16.88%	13.97%
Total	**10627**	**1229.06**	**3748**	**340.38**	**14375**	**1569.44**	**26.07%**	**21.69%**

Source: DRDA, Dungarpur district.

The selected beneficiaries are trained in the field of agriculture and allied activities, industrial, services and business activities.

The strategy for training includes apart from institutional training, through local servicing and industrial units, master craftsmen, artisans and skilled labour. The duration of training is generally six months but it largely depends upon the nature of the trade in which training is imparted. The syllabus of training includes not only technical and entrepreneurial skill, but it includes managerial, marketing and accounting skills. Trainees are paid a monthly stipend or daily allowance during the training period. A tool kit worth of rupees 800 is provided free to trainees after completion of training. The training institution is provided honorarium along with Rs. 75 per trainee per month for purchase of raw material. After completion of training the students are assisted in getting finance from the banks. A maximum of Rs. 35,000 can be sanctioned to a trained youth under this scheme as a complete loan. Trained youth are eligible to get subsidy by the government at the rate of 1/3 to ½ of the cost of the subject to set-up self-employment venture subject to the maximum subsidy limit of Rs. 6000. The trained youth are also provided marketing support for their finished products. The amount spent on this scheme is contributed by Centre and State Government in the proportion 50:50.

Progress of TRYSEM scheme in Udaipur and Dungarpur district are given as under.

Table 5.3 visualise that during 1993-94 to 1998-99 total 1728 (61.78%) females were trained out of 2797 trained youths.

It is evident that coverage of females in TRYSEM is quite above the earmarked level of 40%.

In TRYSEM scheme, overall performance of Dungarpur district is quite satisfactory regarding women. During 93-94 to 98-99 (Table 5.4), 1479 (92.32%) women benefited out of 1602 total beneficiaries. In the year of 1997-98, 118 (100%) women beneficiaries were benefited under the scheme.

Table 5.3. Gender-wise progress of TRYSEM in Udaipur

Financial year	No. of youth trained			% of female to total youth
	Male	Female	Total	
1993-94	97	291	388	75.00%
1994-95	—	—	—	—
1995-96	75	270	345	78.26%
1996-97	80	219	299	73.24%
1997-98	398	305	703	43.39%
1998-99	210	319	529	60.30%
1999-2000	209	324	533	60.79%
Total	1069	1728	2797	61.78%

Source: DRDA, Udaipur.

Table 5.4. Gender-wise Progress of TRYSEM in Dungarpur District

Financial year	No. of youths trained			% of female to total youth
	Male	Female	Total	
1993-94	67	428	495	86.46%
1994-95	27	366	393	93.13%
1995-96	10	211	221	95.48%
1996-97	4	203	207	98.07%
1997-98	—	118	118	100.0%
1998-99	15	153	168	91.07%
Total	123	1479	1602	92.32%

Source: DRDA, Dungarpur.

3. SWARNAJAYANTI GRAM SWAROZGAR YOJNA (SGSY)

Initially I.R.D.P. was the only self employment programme for rural poor. Beginning with Training of Rural Youth for Self

Employment (TRYSEM), a number of allied programmes have been added over the years such as Development of Women and Children in Rural Areas (DWCRA), Supply of Improved tool-kits to Rural Artisans (S.I.T.R.A) and Ganga Kalyan Yojana (GKY). The multiplicity of programmes being viewed as separate programmes in themselves, resulted in lack of proper social intermediation, absence of desired linkages among these programmses. To rectify the situation, government have decided to restructure the self-employment programmes. A new programme known as "Swarnajayanti Gram Swarozgar Yojna (SGSY)" has been launched from April 1999. This is a holistic programme covering all aspects of self-employment such as organisation of the poor into self help groups, training, credit, technology, infrastructure and marketing. With coming into force of SGSY, the earlier programmes IRDP, TRYSEM, DWCRA, SITA, GKY and MWS are no longer in operation. The unspent balances from 1.4.99 will be pooled under the head SGSY. SGSY will be funded by Centre and the State in the ratio of 75:25.

SGSY aims at establishing a large number of micro enterprises in the rural areas, building upon the potential of the rural poor. The assisted families (henceforth known as Swarozgaris) may be individuals or groups (Self Help Groups). Emphasis will be on the group approach. The objective under SGSY is to bring every assisted family above the poverty line in three years. In establishing the micro enterprises, the emphasis under SGSY is on the cluster approach. For this, 4-5 key activities will be identified for each block based on the resources, occupational skills of the people and availability of markets. Selection of key activities will be with the approval of the Panchayat Samities at the block level and the DRDA/ZP at the district level. SGSY will adopt a project approach for each key activity. Project reports will be prepared in respect of identified key activities.

The effort under SGSY is to cover 30% of the poor in each block in next five years through an efficient programme. SGSY will also focus on Group approach. This would involve organisation of the poor into Self Help Groups (SHGs) and their capacity building. *"Efforts would be made to involve women members in each SHG. Besides, exclusive women groups will be continue to be formed. At the level of the block, at least half of the groups will be exclusively women groups". Group activity will be given performance and progressively"*, majority of the funding will be for Self Help groups. The Gram Sabha will authenticate the list of families below the poverty line identified in the BPL (Below Poverty Line) census. SGSY is a credit cum subsidy programme. However, credit will be the critical component in SGSY, subsidy being only a minor and enabling element. SGSY will seek to promote multiple credit rather than a one time credit 'injection'. SGSY will seek to lay emphasis on skill development through well designed training courses. SGSY will ensure upgradation of the technology in the identified activity clusters and SGSY will also provide for promotion of marketing of the goods produced by the SGSY swarozgaris.

Subsidy under SGSY will be uniform at 30% of the project cost, subject maximum of Rs. 7500. In respect of ST/SCs, however, these will be 50%, 10000 respectively. SGSY will particularly focus on the vulnerable groups among the rural. *Accordingly the SC/STs will account for at least 50% of the Swarozgaris, women 40% and the disabled for 3%.*

SGSY, has been launched from April 1999. Because of new programme number of total beneficiaries was only 2378. Women beneficiaries was only 11.52% against the target of 40% women beneficiaries (Table 5.5, *See page 226*).

In the year 1999-2000, 55 (14.40%) were female beneficiaries out of 382 SGSY beneficiaries. And loan disbursed to them was Rs. 16.64 lacs (Table 5.6, *See page 226*).

4. THE SWARNAJAYANTI SHAHARI ROZGAR YOJANA (SJSRY)

This employment generation scheme was started from the year 1997-98. The scheme were earlier known as Nehru Rozgar Yojana and before Nehru Rozgar Yojana it was known as SETUP and SEPUP.

Table 5.5. Gender-wise Progress of SGSY in Udaipur District

(Amount in Lacs of Rupees)

Financial year	Male		Female		Total		% of female beneficiaries to total beneficiaries	% of loan subsidy disbursed to women
	Beneficiaries	Loan subsidy amount	Beneficiaries	Loan subsidy amount	Beneficiaries	Loan subsidy amount		
1999-2000	2104	527.66	274	68.24	2378	595.90	11.52%	11.45%

Source: DRDA, Udaipur district.

Table 5.6. Gender-wise Progress of SGSY in Dungarpur District

(Amount in Lacs of Rupees)

Financial year	Male		Female		Total		% of female beneficiaries to total beneficiaries	% of loan & subsidy disbursed to women
	Beneficiaries	Loan subsidy amount	Beneficiaries	Loan subsidy amount	Beneficiaries	Loan subsidy amount		
1999-2000	327	128.06	55	16.84	382	144.9	14.40%	11.62%

Source: DRDA, Dungarpur district.

The Swarna Jayanti Shahari Rozgar Yojana (SJSRY) shall seek to provide gainful employment to the urban unemployed or under employed poor through encouraging the setting up of self employment ventures or provision of wage employment. This programme will rely on creation of suitable community structures on the UBSP pattern and delivery of inputs under this programme shall be through the medium of urban local bodies and such community structures.

The Swarna Jayanti Shahari Rozgar Yojana (SJSRY) shall be funded on a 75:25 basis between the Centre and the States.

The SJSRY shall consist of two special schemes, namely;

1. The Urban Self Employment Programme (USEP)
2. The Urban Wage Employment Programme (UWEP)

1. THE URBAN SELF EMPLOYMENT PROGRAMME (USEP)

This programme will have three distinct parts:

1. Assistance to individual urban poor beneficiaries for setting up gainful self employment ventures.
2. Assistance to group of urban poor women for setting up gainful self employment ventures. This sub scheme may be called "The scheme for Development of Women and Children in the Urban Areas (DWCUA)".
3. Training of beneficiaries, potential beneficiaries and other persons associated with the urban employment programme for upgradation and acquisition of vocational and entrepreneurial skills.

The USEP will be applicable to all urban towns in India and target those living below the urban poverty line, *Special attention will be given to women. The percentage of women beneficiaries under this programme shall not be less than 30%.* SC and ST must be benefited at least the extent of the proportion of their strength in the local population. A special provision of 3% shall be reserved for the disabled under this programme. There will be no minimum educational, qualification for beneficiaries under this programme. However, to avoid an overlap with PMRY scheme, for the self employment, component, this scheme shall not apply to beneficiaries educated beyond the IX standard. Community structure like CDs will be involved in this task under the guidance of the Town urban poverty eradication cell/ Urban local body.

All other conditions being equal, women beneficiaries belonging to women headed households shall be ranked higher in priority than other beneficiaries. For purposes of this section, women headed household shall mean households which are headed by widows, divorcees, single women or even households where women are the sole earners.

(i) **Self Employment through setting up micro enterprises and skill development:** This programme encourages under employed and unemployed urban youth to set-up small enterprises relating to servicing, petty business and manufacturing, for which there is a lot of potential in urban areas. The maximum unit cost will be Rs. 50,000 and the maximum allowable subsidy will be 15% of the project cost, subject to a limit of Rs. 7500. The beneficiary is required to contribute 5% of the project cost as margin money. Skill development through appropriate training is another element of this programme. This unit cost allowed for training will be Rs. 2000 per trainee, including material cost, trainers fees, other miscellaneous expenses to be incurred by the training institution and the monthly stipend, to be paid to the trainee. The total training period for skill upgradation may vary from two to six months, subject to a minimum of 300 hours. Infrastructural support may also be provided to beneficiaries setting up micro enterprises in relation to marketing of their products etc. Tool kits may also be provided to trainees who complete the training satisfactorily. The cost of tool kit should not exceed Rs. 600.

(ii) **Development of women and children in urban areas (DWCUA):** This scheme is distinguished by the special incentive extended to urban poor women who decide to set-up self employment ventures in a group as opposed to individual effort. Groups of urban poor women shall take up an economic activity suited to their skill, training, aptitude and local conditions. To be eligible for subsidy under this scheme, the DWCUA group should consist of at least 10 urban poor women. The DWCUA group society shall be entitled to a subsidy of Rs. 1, 25,000 or 50% of the cost of project whichever is less. Where the DWCUA group sets itself up as thrift and credit society, in addition to its other entrepreneurial activity, the group/thrift and credit society shall also be entitled to a lumpsum grant of Rs. 25,000 as revolving fund at the rate of Rs. 1000 maximum per member. Revolving fund is meant for the use of the groups/society for purposes like purchases of raw materials and marketing, infrastructure support for income generation and other group activities, one time expense on child care activity, etc. A DWCUA group/thrift and credit society shall be entitled for payment of revolving fund not earlier than one year after its formation.

The Urban Wage Employment Programme (UWEP)

This programme shall seek to provide wage employment to beneficiaries living below the poverty line within the jurisdiction of urban local bodies by utilising their labour for construction of socially and economically useful public assets. The material labour ratio for works under this programme shall be maintained at 60:40. Gender-wise progress of SJSRY (NRY) in Udaipur and Dungarpur district during 1992-93 to 1999-2000 given in table 5.7 and 5.8.

The progress achieved under SJSRY (NRY) during 1992-2000 is given in the table 5.7. In this period 540 (20.38%) female were benefitted against 2110 (79.62%) male beneficiaries. The percentage of females is very low.

Table 5.7. Gender-wise Progress of SJSRY (NRY) in Udaipur District

Financial year	No. of beneficiaries			% of female to total beneficiaries
	Male	Female	Total	
N.R.Y.				
1992-93	622	137	759	18.05%
1993-94	239	83	322	25.78%
1994-95	408	52	460	11.30%
1995-96	233	99	332	29.82%
1996-97	306	71	377	18.83%
SJSRY				
1997-98	177	71	248	28.63%
1998-99	*	*	*	*
1999-2000	125	27	152	17.76%
Total	**2110**	**540**	**2650**	**20.38%**

Source: DUDA, Udaipur.

* Community development society has not been constituted in 98-99. That's why no work has been done.

Table 5.8. Gender-wise Progress of SJSRY (NRY) in Dungarpur District

Financial year	No. of beneficiaries			% of female to total beneficiaries
	Male	Female	Total	
N.R.Y.				
1992-93	75	52	127	40.94%
1993-94	50	39	89	43.82%
1994-95	70	48	118	40.68%
1995-96	56	42	98	42.86%
1996-97	56	40	96	41.67%
SJSRY				
1997-98	28	14	42	33.33%
1998-99	51	19	70	27.14%
1999-2000	65	22	87	25.29%
Total	**451**	**276**	**727**	**37.96%**

Source: DUDA, Udaipur.

The progress achieved under NRY/SJSRY in Dungarpur district during 1992-2000 is given in the table 5.8.

During 1992-2000, out of 727 beneficiaries female were only 276 (37.96%). The percentage of female beneficiaries to total beneficiaries was better in N.R.Y. scheme comparatively to SJSRY.

Prime Minister Rozgar Yojana (PMRY)

PMRY was initiated in October, 1993 to tackle the burning problem of educated unemployment. From 1994-95, the existing SEEUY scheme was subsumed in the PMRY. PMRY relates to setting up to self-employment ventures through industry, service and business routes. Any unemployed youth who is matric failed/passed or above or ITI passed is eligible for the benefits of the scheme, if he is between the age group of 18-35 yrs and his family income does not exceeds Rs. 40,000 per annum. The youth should also be the permanent resident of the area for at least last three years and he should not be defaulter to any bank or financial institution. The scheme envisages 22.5% reservation for SC/ST and 27% for OBCs and priority to women. A maximum loan of Rs. 1 lac per candidate is provided under this scheme, at the interest rate of 12.5% to 15.5%. The entrepreneur has to contribute 5% of project cost as margin money. No collateral security guarantee is asked on such loans. Period of repayment starts after a moratorium of six to eighteen months and ranges over 3 to 7 years. The government provides subsidy to the extent of 15% of the total loan disbursed, with a ceiling of Rs. 7,500 per entrepreneur. In case of a joint venture each partner may be provided a loan of Rs. 1 lac subsidy in such cases in calculated for each partner separately at the rate of 15% of his share in the project cost limited to Rs. 7500 for each partner.

The provision of compulsory training into entrepreneurship development is a salient feature of the scheme. Duration of this training is one month. Trainees are provided a stipend of Rs. 500 during the training period.

DIC is the nodal agency at district level for implementation of this scheme. The task force selects the youths and sponsors their applications to various banks for finance. DIC works under the overall guidance of District PMRY committee. The scheme is monitored at state level by state PMRY committee and at central level by high powered committee. Reputed NGOs are also involved in the implementation of the scheme.

Table 5.9 shows that in the absence of any reservation for women, coverage of women candidates under PMRY has been very small. During the period of 1993-94 to 1999-2000, only 194 (5.44%) beneficiaries belong to female group. The percentage is very low.

During the year 1993-94, out of 60 beneficiaries 4 (6.67%) were female beneficiaries. In 1999-2000, out of 774 youths, merely 58 (7.49%) were female. The lowest female beneficiaries has been recorded in 1996-97, out of 494 beneficiaries there were only 16 (3.24%) belonged to female group.

This low coverage of female is perhaps the result of no reservation for women candidates under PMRY.

Table 5.10 depicts gender-wise progress of PMRY scheme in Dungarpur district. Table 5.10, *(See page 234)* shows that very few females has access in this scheme. During 1993-94 to 1999-2000, out of 1296 beneficiaries only 62 (4.78%) were females.

In 1993-94, 100 per cent beneficiaries were males. In 1999-2000, there were 17 (6.59%) female beneficiaries against of 241 (93.41%) male beneficiaries. Maximum female beneficiaries recorded in the year of 1998-99, there were 18 (7.38%) female beneficiaries.

COMPARATIVE STUDY OF GOVERNMENT SCHEMES, SPONSORED/FINANCED BY BANKS IN UDAIPUR AND DUNGARPUR DISTRICT

Comparative evaluation of I.R.D.P. in Udaipur and Dungarpur district during 1992-93 to 1998-99 is shown in table no 5.11, *(See page 235)*.

During the period of 1992-93 to 1998-99, 2771 (19.42%) females benefited out of 14,272 total beneficiaries in Udaipur district, while in Dungarpur district during the span of same period 3748 (26.07%) females benefited out of 14375 total beneficiaries.

Table 5.9. Gender-wise Progress of PMRY in Udaipur District

(Amount in lacs of Rupees)

Financial year	Male		Female		Total		% of female to total beneficiaries	% of loan amount disbursed to female
	Beneficiaries	Amount	Beneficiaries	Amount	Beneficiaries	Amount		
1993-94	56	46.89	4	2.25	60	49.14	6.67%	4.58%
1994-95	389	240.16	16	9.22	405	249.38	3.95%	3.70%
1995-96	468	273.65	20	11.87	488	285.52	4.10%	4.16%
1996-97	478	330.06	16	11.82	494	341.88	3.24%	3.46%
1997-98	597	391.19	28	16.19	625	407.38	4.48%	3.97%
1998-99	671	406.61	52	31.65	723	438.26	7.19%	7.22%
1999-2000	716	489.43	58	43.27	774	532.70	7.49%	8.12%
Total	**3375**	**2177.99**	**194**	**126.27**	**3569**	**2304.26**	**5.44%**	**5.48%**

Source: DIC, Udaipur district.

Table 5.10. Gender-wise Progress of PMRY in Dungarpur District

(Amount in Lacs of Rupees)

Financial year	Male		Female		Total		% of female to total beneficiaries	% of loan amount disbursed to female
	Beneficiaries	Amount	Beneficiaries	Amount	Beneficiaries	Amount		
1993-94	3	0.93	–	–	3	0.93	0%	0%
1994-95	127	39.01	2	0.45	129	39.46	1.55%	1.14%
1995-96	224	89.24	9	2.41	233	91.65	3.86%	2.63%
1996-97	173	70.25	10	4.01	183	74.26	5.46%	5.40%
1997-98	240	105.24	6	1.87	246	107.17	2.44%	1.74%
1998-99	226	94.55	18	7.39	244	101.94	7.38%	7.25%
1999-2000	241	109.99	17	4.64	258	114.63	6.59%	4.05%
Total	**1234**	**509.21**	**62**	**20.77**	**1296**	**529.98**	**4.78%**	**3.92%**

Source: DIC, Dungarpur district.

Table 5.11. Progress of I.R.D.P. in Udaipur and Dungarpur District

(Amount in Lacs of Rupees)

Financial year	Udaipur						Dungarpur					
	Total		Female		% of female to total beneficiaries	%of loan amount disbursed to female	total		Female		% of female to total beneficiaries	% of loan amount disbursed to female
	Beneficiaries	Amount	Beneficiaries	Amount			Beneficiaries	Amount	Beneficiaries	Amount		
1992-93	5153	317.07	1495	49.98	29.01%	15.76%	2212	80.57	641	22.45	28.98%	27.86%
1993-94	5605	371.94	710	46.99	12.67%	12.63%	2545	119.53	768	32.11	30.18%	26.86%
1994-95	5555	522.11	788	67.60	14.19%	12.95%	2450	153.12	705	46.65	28.78%	30.47%
1995-96	5215	686.05	1428	198.08	27.38%	28.87%	2524	197.63	569	42.13	22.54%	21.32%
1996-97	4106	897.69	512	112.86	12.47%	12.57%	1706	338.22	521	97.60	30.54%	28.86%
1997-98	3529	872.38	581	149.98	16.46%	17.19%	1356	312.26	277	48.03	20.43%	15.38%
1998-99	3130	931.96	968	282.65	30.93%	30.33%	1582	368.11	267	51.41	16.88%	13.97%
Total	**14272**	**3885.37**	**2771**	**796.41**	**19.42%**	**20.50%**	**14375**	**1569.44**	**3748**	**340.38**	**26.07%**	**21.69%**

Source: Prepared from table 5.1 and 5.2.

When we compare number of female beneficiaries, performance of Dungarpur district is better in comparison to Udaipur district but Dungarpur females benefited by less loan amount in comparison to Udaipur district females.

The overall analysis of Table 5.12 *(See page 237)* reveals that more representation to females has been given under TRYSEM schemes in Dungarpur district. However, both district cover the target of 40% women beneficiaries. During the period of 1993-94 to 1998-99 female beneficiaries in Dungarpur district were 1479 (92.32%); whereas in Udaipur district during the same time period 1404 (62.01%) females were benefited.

Table 5.13, *(See page 238)* shows coverage of females under SGSY scheme. Female representation is quite poor in both of the district, against the target to 40% female beneficiaries were 14.40% and 11.52% in Dungarpur and Udaipur district respectively. Performance of Dungarpur is better in comparison to Udaipur district.

Table 5.14, *(See page 239)* shows that Dungarpur district has showed very good performance regarding coverage of female under NRY/SJSRY scheme.

During the year 1992-93 to 1996-97 (NRY scheme period) total 442 (19.64%) females has been benefited out of 2250 total beneficiaries in Udaipur district. During the same period in Dungarpur district total 221 (41.86%) females benefited out of 528 total beneficiaries.

In SJSRY scheme coverage of females during the year 1997-98 to 1999-2000, was 27.64% and 24.50% in Udaipur and Dungarpur district, respectively.

It has been tried to perform a comparative evaluation of progress of PMRY scheme in the Udaipur and Dungarpur district in Table 5.15, *(See page 240, 241)*.

During the period of 1993-94 to 1999-2000, female beneficiaries in Udaipur district was 194 (5.45%) benefited by Rs. 126.27 lacs (5.48%) of loan amount, whereas in Dungarpur district during the same period 62 (4.78%) females benefited by Rs. 20.77 lacs (3.92%) of loan amount.

Table 5.12. Progress of TRYSEM in Udaipur and Dungarpur District

(Amount in Lacs of Rupees)

Financial year	Udaipur			Dungarpur		
	Total Beneficiaries	Female	% of female to total youth	Total beneficiaries	Female	% of female to total youth
1993-94	388	291	75.00%	495	428	86.46%
1994-95	–	–	–	393	366	93.13%
1995-96	345	270	78.26%	221	211	95.48%
1996-97	299	219	73.24%	207	203	98.07%
1997-98	703	305	43.39%	118	118	100.0%
1998-99	529	319	60.30%	168	153	91.07%
Total	**2264**	**1404**	**62.01%**	**1602**	**1479**	**92.32%**

Source: Prepared from Table No. 5.3 and 5.4.

Table 5.13. Progress of SGSY in Udaipur and Dungarpur District

(Amount in Lacs of Rupees)

Financial year	Udaipur						Dungarpur					
	Total		Female		% of female to total beneficiaries	% of loan disbursed to female	Total		Female		% of female to total beneficiries Beneficiaries	% of loan amount disbursed to female
	Beneficiaries	Amount	Beneficiaries	Amount			Beneficiaries	Amount	Beneficiaries	Amount		
1999-2000	2378	595.90	274	68.24	11.52%	11.62%	382	144.9	55	16.84	14.40%	11.62%

Source: Prepared from table no. 5.5 and 5.6.

Table 5.14. Progress of SJSRY/NRY in Udaipur and Dungarpur District

(Amount of Lacs of Rupees)

Financial year	Udaipur			Dungarpur		
	Total Beneficiaries	Female	% of female to total youth	Total beneficiaries	Female	% of female to total youth
NRY						
1992-93	759	137	18.05%	127	52	40.94%
1993-94	322	83	25.78%	89	39	43.82%
1994-95	460	52	11.30%	118	48	40.68%
1995-96	332	99	29.82%	98	42	42.86%
1996-97	377	71	18.83%	96	40	41.67%
SJSRY						
1997-98	248	71	28.63%	42	14	33.33%
1998-99	*	*	*	70	19	27.14%
1999-2000	152	27	17.76%	87	22	25.29%
Total	**2650**	**540**	**20.38%**	**727**	**276**	**37.96%**

Source: Prepared from Table 5.7 and 5.8.

* Community Dev. society has not been constituted in 1998-99. That's why no work has been done.

Table 5.15. Progress of PMRY in Udaipur District

(Amount in Lacs of Rupees)

Financial Year	Udaipur					
	Total		Female		% of female to total Beneficiaries	% of loan amount disbursed to female
	Beneficiaries	Amount	Beneficiaries	Amount		
1993-94	60	49.14	4	2.25	6.67%	4.58%
1994-95	405	249.38	16	9.22	3.95%	3.70%
1995-96	488	285.52	20	11.87	4.10%	4.16%
1996-97	494	341.88	16	11.82	3.24%	3.46%
1997-98	625	407.38	28	16.19	4.48%	3.97%
1998-99	723	438.26	52	31.65	7.19%	7.22%
1999-2000	774	532.70	58	43.27	7.49%	8.12%
Total	**3569**	**2304.26**	**194**	**126.27**	**5.44%**	**5.48%**

Source: Prepared from Table No. 5.9 and 5.10.

Table 5.15. Progress of PMRY in Dungarpur District

(Amount in Lacs of Rs.)

Financial Year	Dungarpur					
	Total		Female		% of female to total Beneficiaries	% of loan amount disbursed to female
	Beneficiaries	Amount	Beneficiaries	Amount		
1993-94	3	0.93	0	0	0%	0%
1994-95	129	39.46	2	0.45	1.55%	1.14%
1995-96	233	91.65	9	2.41	3.86%	2.63%
1996-97	183	74.26	10	4.01	5.46%	5.40%
1997-98	246	107.17	6	1.87	2.44%	1.74%
1998-99	244	101.94	18	7.39	7.38%	7.25%
1999-2000	258	114.63	17	4.64	6.59%	4.05%
Total	**1296**	**529.98**	**62**	**20.77**	**4.78%**	**3.92%**

Source: Prepared from Table No. 5.9 and 5.10.

6 A Case Study of Banking Habits Among the Women in Udaipur and Dungarpur Districts of Rajasthan

To examine banking habits among the women and impact of banks on women following schedule was prepared and used for collection of primary data.

THE SCHEDULE FOR WOMEN BANK ACCOUNT HOLDERS

In present era of time banking institutions play very vital role in Human Resource Development. With this point in consideration it was decided to meet and interview the women bank account holders of various bank branches were prepared. Then 100 beneficiaries were selected random from Udaipur and Dungarpur districts, so in all 200 women were selected for this study.

Awareness and opinion of the selected beneficiaries was shared on the bank deposit scheme, lending scheme, social schemes, services provided by bank, investment mode of respondent, reasons for visiting banks, frequency of visit regarding operation and nature of a/c, interest rate on a/c, time taken in various bank services, problems faced in banking operation and suggestion for improvement of bank services etc.

along with social, economical and educational status of respondents.

THE DETAILS OF SCHEDULE OF WOMEN BANK ACCOUNT HOLDERS

Table 6.1. Age-wise Distribution of Respondents

Districts		14 to 18	19 to 30	31 to 40	41 to 50	51 to 60	Above 60 years	Total
Udaipur	N	–	31	39	16	14	–	100
	%	–	31	39	16	14	–	100
Dungarpur	N	–	35	32	29	3	1	100
	%	–	35	32	29	3	1	100

In Udaipur district, maximum account holders (39%) were in between the age group of 31 and 40 years whereas in Dungarpur district, majority (35%) were belong to the age group of 19 and 30 years and 70% and 67% women account holders were in between the age group of 19 and 40 years in Udaipur and Dungarpur_districts, respectively. There were no account holders in the age group of 14 to 18 years in both of the districts. In the category of above 60 years of age only one respondent was in Dungarpur district. And in the age of 51 group to 60, there were 14 respondents in Udaipur district and only 3 in Dungarpur district.

Table 6.2. Caste-wise Distribution of Respondents

Districts		Hindu	Muslim	Jain	Christians	S.C. & S.T.	O.B.C.'s	Others	Total
Udaipur	N	54	6	28	3	7	2	–	100
	%	54	6	28	3	7	2	–	100
Dungarpur	N	40	–	12	–	44	4	–	100
	%	40	–	12	–	44	4	–	100

The data regarding religion of beneficiaries showed that Hindus (54%) were prominent in Udaipur district, whereas, S.C./S.T. (44%) were prominent in Dungarpur district. Second, leading religion in Udaipur district was of Jain (28%) while in Dungarpur it was Hindu (40%). There were no Christians and Muslim beneficiaries in Dungarpur district.

Table 6.3. Educational Status of Respondents

Districts		Illiterate	Upto Primary	Below Secondary	Senior Hr. Secondary	Graduate	Post Graduate	Technical	Total
Udaipur	N	-	4	7	6	30	30	23	100
	%	-	4	7	6	30	30	23	100
Dungarpur	N	7	22	8	20	22	21	-	100
	%	7	22	8	20	22	21	-	100

In Udaipur district 83% women were Graduate, Post-graduate and technical qualified, whereas, in Dungarpur district only 43% women were Graduate and Post-graduate. In Udaipur district, 17% women were educated upto senior Hr. Secondary, whereas, in Dungarpur district 50% women were studied upto senior Hr. Secondary. There were no illiterate a/c holders in Udaipur district while 7% women were in Dungarpur district.

The investigation showed in Table 6.4 about the residential status of respondents in Udaipur district respondents constitute most of the urban population (73%), on the contrary, Dungarpur district constitute most of the rural (49%) and semi-urban (40%) population.

Table 6.4. Area-wise Distribution of Respondents

Districts		Rural	Semi-rural	Urban	Total
Udaipur	N	10	17	73	100
	%	10	17	73	100
Dungarpur	N	49	40	11	100
	%	49	40	11	100

The occupation wise distribution (Table 6.5) showed that more than half respondents in both district were working which formed an over-whelming majority. It also indicated the increasing importance of being women employed in the Indian society. In Udaipur district, majority of working respondent engaged in teaching (35%) and service (11%) while in Dungarpur district majority of occupied respondent engaged in teaching (24%) and as agricultural labour (11%).

Table 6.5. Occupation-wise Distribution of Respondents

Districts		Non-working women or Housewives	Agricultural Labour	Educational Field	Professional	Own Business	Family Business	Service	Others	Total	Total
Udaipur	N	42	-	35	2	4	6	11	-	58	100
	%	42	-	35	2	4	6	11	-	58	100
Dungarpur	N	48	11	24	-	8	5	4	-	52	100
	%	48	11	24	-	8	5	4	-	52	100

An important aspect of family life involved the co-operation of the working respondent with other members of the family. Hence, it was considered important to look into this aspect of the respondents family life and data in this regard (Table 6.6, *See page 246*) revealed that in nuclear family majority of working respondent in both district (28 in Udaipur and 20 in Dungarpur district out of 32 and 24, respectively) were getting supportive co-operation from their husband while 4 respondent in both district were doing hard. In joint family, too, in general attitude of husband, in-law and parent were co-operative towards the respondent in both districts.

Table 6.7, *(See page 247)* revealed that in Udaipur district 27 respondents husband had low annual income (Rs. 10 thousand to Rs. 1 lac) and 57 respondents husband had high annual income in between Rs. 1 lac and more than Rs. 2 lacs, while, in Dungarpur district 47 respondents husband had low annual income (Rs. 10 thousand to Rs. 1 lac) and 37 respondents husband had high annual income in between Rs. 1 lac and more than Rs. 2 lacs.

Out of 58 working respondents of Udaipur district 40 had income in low group i.e. Rs. 10,000 to 1 lac. While in Dungarpur district out of 52 working respondents 44 had income in low group. 18 working respondents belong to high income group (Rs. 1 lac to more than 2 lacs) in Udaipur district and in Dungarpur district 8 working women belongs to high income group.

Table 6.6. Family Status and Extent of Co-operation Between Working Women and Family Members

Districts		(Co-operation from) Nuclear Family							(Co-operation from) Joint Family						
		Husband							Husband						
		Always	Frequ.	Normally	Rarely	Never	N.A.	Total	Always	Frequ.	Normally	Rarely	Never	N.A.	Total
Udaipur	N	21	1	6	1	3	68	100	7	5	3	1	–	84	100
Dungarpur	N	10	6	4	4	–	76	100	8	–	3	5	–	84	100
Udaipur	N	21	1	6		3	68	100	7	5	3	1	–	84	100
Dungarpur	N	100	6	4	4	–	76	100	8	–	3	5	–	84	100
		Joint Family							Joint Family						
Districts		Co-operation From In-Law							Co-operation from Parents						
		Always	Frequ.	Normally	Rarely	Never	N.A.	Total	Always	Frequ.	Normally	Rarely	Never	N.A.	Total
Udaipur	N	4	3	6	2	1	84	100	15	6	2	–	–	77	100
Dungarpur	N	–	–	16	–	–	84	100	–	–	8	3	–	89	100

Table 6.7. Income-wise Distribution of Respondent's and their Husband (Income in Rupees)

Respondent's Annual Income

District		Non-Working	Upto 10,000	10,001 to 25,000	25,001 to 50,000	50,000 to 1,00,000	1,00,000 to 1,50,000	1,50,000 to 2,00,000	Above 2,00,000	Total
Udaipur	N	42	–	5	10	25	9	6	3	100
Dungarpur	N	48	23	–	4	17	4	4	–	100

Respondent's Husband Annual Income

District		Upto 10,000	10,001 to 25,000	25,001 to 50,000	50,001 to 1,00,000	1,00,000 to 1,50,000	1,50,000 to 2,00,000	Above 200,001	Not Applicable	Total
Udaipur	N	–	–	4	23	27	21	9	16	100
Dungarpur	N	–	15	19	13	22	8	7	16	100

It was evident from the data that more than half respondents in Dungarpur district taken up employment to supplement family income because their husband had low income, however the respondents of Udaipur district taken up employment due to supplement family income and to maintain high standard in their life.

Table 6.8 shows the distribution of beneficiaries by the type of accounts with bank. The survey found that every women had S.B a/c with bank. The other popular a/c, in Udaipur District was F.D. a/c, S.D.L. a/c. and loan a/c. In Udaipur district out of 100 women a/c holders, 51 women had F.D. a/c, 46 women had S.D.L. a/c, and 34 women had loan a/c. While in Dungarpur district popular a/c was F.D. a/c, S.D.L. a/c and R.D. a/c. Out of 100 women a/c holders, 36 women had F.D. a/c, 39 had S.D.L. a/c and 13 women had R.D. a/c.

The table 6.8 also indicate that among women current a/c, NRI a/c were not popular.

Table 6.8. Bank Account-wise Distribution of Respondents

District		Out of 100 Respondents							
		S.B a/c	C. a/c	F.D. a/c	R.D. a/c	N.R.I.	Safe Deposit Locker a/c	Loan a/c	Others
Udaipur	N	100	5	51	3	2	46	34	–
Dungarpur	N	97	2	36	13	4	39	12	–

Table 6.9 clearly indicates that, 73% and 64% women of Udaipur district and 56% and 57% women of Dungarpur district visit bank for withdrawal and deposit of savings, respectively. Nearly, one-third women visited bank to operate safe lockers, issue of cheque book and completion of passbook in both the districts. Another reason to visit bank branch for loan by 22% respondents of Udaipur district and 7% of Dungarpur district. In Udaipur district, respondents also visit for issue draft (11%), to get technical advice (4%), to seek information on bank scheme (7%), and to repay loan (6%), while; in Dungarpur district, no respondent had bank visit for these purpose.

Table 6.9. Reason and Frequency of Bank Visit

District		Frequency of Bank visit									
		Twice a week	Once a week	Fortnightly	Once in a month	Once in a quarter	Once in 6 months	Yearly	More than one year	Only go to open a/c	Total
Udaipur	N	2	11	7	40	14	7	9	4	6	100
Dungarpur	N	–	3	9	36	15	9	16	12	–	100

Out of 100 women, 13% women in Udaipur district and 3% women in Dungarpur district at least visited bank, once in a week, while 47% women in Udaipur district and 45% women in Dungarpur at least visited bank once in a month. Nearly, 14% women in both the district visited their bank branch in a quarter. 19% women in Udaipur district and 28% women in Dungarpur district not visited their branch even in last one year.

The above analysis clearly showed that frequency of Udaipur district women was more in comparison to women of Dungarpur district. At least 60% women of Udaipur district and 48% women of Dungarpur district visited their bank once in a month.

Table 6.10 revealed that 43% women a/c holders of Udaipur district and only 24% of Dungarpur district yet visited at regional office of any bank. While 10% female a/c holder of Udaipur district and no account holder of Dungarpur district yet visited at head office of any bank.

Table 6.10 Did Respondent Visit Ever at Regional Office/ Head Office?

District		Regional Office			Head Office		
		Yes	No	Total	Yes	No	Total
Udaipur	N	43	57	100	10	90	100
Dungarpur	N	24	76	100	–	100	100

The beneficiaries were asked about the various bank deposit scheme. (Table 6.11) Maximum beneficiaries were well aware about Fixed deposit scheme (95% in Udaipur district and 72% in Dungarpur district) and Recurring deposit scheme (64% in Udaipur district and 53% in Dungarpur district). Monthly pension scheme, Cash Certificate Scheme and Insurance linked deposit scheme were known by 42%, 31% and 22% respondents of Udaipur district, respectively, while in Dungarpur district only 20%, 11% and 15% respondents, respectively knew about the scheme. Very few respondents know about the scheme of Annuity deposit, Deposit under permanent income plan, Reinvestment deposit, and scheme for N.R.I. in both the districts.

Table 6.11. Awareness of Respondents About Bank Deposit Schemes

District		Cash Certificate Scheme	Monthly Pension Scheme	R.D. Scheme	F.D. Scheme	Annuity Deposit	Deposit under permanent Income Plan	Rent investment Deposit	Insurance Linked Deposit Scheme	Scheme for N.R.I
Udaipur	N	31	42	64	95	11	12	12	22	14
Dungarpur	N	11	20	53	72	8	7	7	15	5

Table 6.12. Awareness of Respondents About Bank Lending Scheme

Districts		Finance to small scale units	Overdraft against approved securities	Export Finance	Scheme for Agriculture Activities	Loans for failed ag. Activities	Loans for Artisans	Loan For Marriage	Loan against Deposit
Udaipur	N	60	37	40	52	42	29	33	56
Dungarpur	N	36	15	20	57	47	20	12	44

Districts		Loan for Housing	Loan for Vechicle	Loan against Gold Ornaments	Loan for consumer Durables	Loan for Childrens Education
Udaipur	N	83	80	31	63	41
Dungarpur	N	70	73	20	55	31

The survey showed that, near about two-third women a/c holders were aware about bank lending scheme of Housing and Vehicle in both the districts. About half of the beneficiaries had awareness about bank lending scheme of consumer durables, SSI, loan against deposit and for agricultural activities, in both the districts. Many respondents also had knowledge about following bank lending scheme, Loan for allied activities, children education, Export finance, overdraft against approved securities, Marriage, on gold ornaments and for artisans, in both the districts.

Women of Udaipur district had more knowledge about following schemes, Loan for housing, Vehicle, consumer durables, Small scale industries, Loan against deposits, children education, Export, Overdraft against approved securities, Marriage, on gold ornaments, Land loan for artisans in comparison to Dungarpur district. While women a/c holders of Dungarpur district had more knowledge about bank lending scheme of finance to agricultural activities allied agricultural activities in comparison to Udaipur district.

In present era banks provide different types of facilities to their customer for eg. credit card, gift cheque, ATM facilities, Demate facilities, stock investment, Quantum deposit and safe deposit locker etc. (Table 6.13) When we inquire to our respondents regarding knowledge about these schemes study revealed that a large number of women had knowledge about safe deposit lockers, credit card, Travellers Cheque and Gift Cheque scheme in both the districts. Women a/c holders also had awareness about MT/TT/DD, ATM, standing instruction to bank and stock investment scheme in both the district. Women of Udaipur district had more knowledge in comparison to Dungarpur district women about different bank service/scheme. In Udaipur district few respondents also had knowledge of Technical cell, Quantum deposit and Demate facilities. In Udaipur district ICICI, IDBI, The Bank of Rajasthan Ltd. and PNB were providing such type of facilities, while in Dungarpur district, no bank was providing such type of facilities to public. Maximum number of women 46% in Udaipur district and 39% in Dungarpur district were availing the facilities of safe deposit locker provided by banks. Another facilities availing by the women a/c holders were Gift Cheque and MT/TT/DD, in both

Table 6.13. Awareness and Uses of Bank Services by Respondent

Districts		Credit card	Traveller's Cheque	Gift Cheque	Technical Cell	MT/TT DD	Safe Deposit Locker	Standing instructions to make Regular payment	ATM Facilities	Quantum Deposit	Demate Facilities	Stock Inv.
Udaipur	F	68	55	63	7	43	81	32	46	10	19	31
Dungarpur	F	45	36	44	–	31	40	16	11	–	–	7
Uses of Bank and Services by Respondent												
Udaipur	N	5	19	22	–	13	46	1	14	6	5	6
Dungarpur	N	3	3	12	–	15	39	4	–	–	–	–

the district. Very few beneficiaries enjoy the facilities of Travellers Cheque, credit card and standing instructions to bank for regular payment in both the districts. The respondents of Udaipur also enjoying the facilities of ATM, Demate, Quantum deposit and stock investment.

Table 6.14 revealed that nearly, two-third females were aware about PMRY scheme, in both districts. Nearly, one-third women a/c holders had knowledge about N.R.Y. SGSY, SJSRY and I.R.D.P. scheme, in both the districts. Very few beneficiaries were aware about TRYSEM, National rural employment programme, Credit to minority communities, Differential rate of interest rate scheme, Lead bank scheme, Priority sector lending scheme, and credit Authorisation scheme. There were 8 respondents of Udaipur district and 11 of Dungarpur district who did not aware about any single scheme. Udaipur district women a/c holders had more knowledge in comparison to Dungarpur district a/c holders in the following schemes, N.R.Y., TRYSEM, National rural employment programme, Credit to minority communities, Differential interest rate scheme, Priority sector lending, Credit authorisation scheme. On the contrary, Dungarpur district respondent had more knowledge about, Lead bank scheme and twenty point programme in compare to Udaipur district respondents.

Table 6.14. Social Scheme and Respondents

Districts		20 point Programme	Differential interest rate scheme	SGSY	SJSRY	PMRY	I.R.D.P.	TRYSEM
Udaipur	N	35	19	30	29	65	28	28
Dungarpur	N	48	7	32	28	64	29	12

Districts		N.R.Y.	Lead Bank Scheme	Credit Authorisation Scheme	National Rural Employment Programme	Priority Sector Lending	Credit to Minority Communities
Udaipur	N	43	17	13	25	16	22
Dungarpur	N	28	25	–	7	8	16

The investigation clearly showed (Table 6.15) that Cent per cent beneficiaries of both the districts had first choice to invest their saving in bank because of more liquidity and safety of money. Second choice, of investment of money respondents prefer Post Office (50% in Udaipur, 45% in Dungarpur District) L.I.C. is also one of the favourite mode of investment revealed by respondents (35% of Udaipur district beneficiaries and 24% Dungarpur district beneficiaries) because it provide the security of Life time insurance and after the death of L.I.C. holder, dependents will be provided aid by the insurance amount. 31% and 22% respondents of Udaipur and Dungarpur district, respectively keep some money in the form of cash for transaction and precautionary motive. Less than one-fourth of respondents invest money in gold/property, share and debentures while some keep it with friends and relatives, in both the district. In Udaipur district, respondent also like to invest their saving in UTI (18%) and co-operatives (11%). In both the district, no respondent like to invest money with chit funds because much better mode of invest money already available to them.

Table 6.15. Where Respondent Invest their Savings?

Districts		Post Office	NSCs	Shares Bonds, Debentures	Gold/ Property	Chit Funds	Bank
Udaipur	N	50	16	15	15	–	100
Dungarpur	N	45	25	7	17	–	100

Districts		Unit Trust of India	Co-operatives	L.I.C.	Friends, Relatives, Others	Keep in Cash
Udaipur	N	18	11	35	14	31
Dungarpur	N	–	–	24	3	22

In table 6.16 the survey revealed that about 57% beneficiaries in Udaipur district and 31% beneficiaries in Dungarpur district respectively, were approach for their loan requirement to banks and 18% and 24% beneficiaries were approach for their loan requirement to their friends/neighbour/relative, in Udaipur and Dungarpur district respectively, while very few respondents approach to money lenders for their Loan requirement in both the district.

Table 6.16. For Loan Requirement Respondent Approach to Whom

Districts		Friends/ Neighbours Relatives	Private Money Lenders	Bank	Do not Approach yet now	Total
Udaipur	N	18	3	57	22	100
	%	18	3	57	22	100
Dungarpur	N	24	4	31	41	100
	%	24	4	31	41	100

Table 6.17 revealed that 18 women of Udaipur district and 49 women of Dungarpur district did not like to invest their saving other than banks. The beneficiaries who prefer other institution than bank mainly because of simple procedure, more interest on saving, better security, less interest on loan and tax incentives by 22, 27, 30, 18 and 16 respondents of Udaipur district and 25, 20, 20, 11 and 16 by Dungarpur district respondents, respectively. 25 respondents of Udaipur district revealed that they get better service in private financial institution. Another reason of preference to other financial institution due to more liquidity, desired services, No knowledge about bank lending scheme and Faster loan by other institutions by 6, 4, 1 and 21 respondents of Udaipur and 11, 3, 12 and 5 by respondent of Dungarpur district respectively.

Table 6.17. Why Respondents Approach to Other Institution than Bank for Deposit of Money and Loan Requirement

District		Simple Procedure	No Knowledge About Bank Lending Schemes	Better Services	Desired Services	Faster Loan
Udaipur	N	22	1	25	4	21
Dungarpur	N	25	12	–	3	5

Districts		Less interest on Loan	More interest on savings	Tax-incentives	More Liquidity	Do not Prefer other institution
Udaipur	N	18	27	16	6	18
Dungarpur	N	11	20	16	11	49

Table 6.18 showed that, majority of women a/c holders (56%) in Udaipur district and more than one third in Dungarpur district were aware about the customer service centre scheme. On the Contrary, in Dungarpur district nearly two-third of women a/c holders (63%) and nearly 44% women a/c holders in Udaipur district were not know about this scheme.

Table 6.18. Whether Respondents Know About the Customer Service Centre Scheme?

District		Yes	No	Total
Udaipur	N	56	44	100
	%	56	44	100
Dungarpur	N	37	63	100
	%	37	63	100

Branch Manager, Zonal Manager, Regional Manager, Chairman and even Managing Director meet Customers on a specific day to solve their grievance but majority of women bank a/c holders did not know about this fact in both the district. (Table 6.19)

Table 6.19. Whether Respondent know that Higher Authority Meet them About their Grievances?

District		Yes	No	Total
Udaipur	N	40	60	100
	%	40	60	100
Dungarpur	N	28	72	100
	%	28	72	100

Table 6.20 clearly indicate that 72% and 60% women bank a/c holders in Udaipur and Dungarpur district, respectively, were not know that one day in a week is for non-business working for rural branches of banks and bank officials supposed to meet their customers on that day.

Table 6.20. Whether Respondents Know about Non-business Working Day for Rural Branches?

Districts		Yes	No	Total
Udaipur	N	28	72	100
	%	28	72	100
Dungarpur	N	40	60	100
	%	40	60	100

Table 6.21. Problems Faced by Respondents During Banking Operation

Districts		Non-Availability of the staff on their seats	Behaviour of staff is not upto the mark	Delay in service	More paper work
Udaipur	N	17	15	30	32
Dungarpur	N	8	11	16	45

We shared views and opinion of the selected women on above accounts with the help of schedule. The details of different accounts are given below.

(A) OPERATION OF SAVING ACCOUNT BY WOMEN

Table 6.22. Respondents Having Number of S.B a/c's with Banks

Districts		0	1	2	3	4	5	6	Total A/c Holder	Total No. of S.B A/c	Average S.B. A/c
Udaipur	N	–	65	20	13	–	–	2	100	156	1.56
	%	–	65	20	13	–	–	2	100		
Dungarpur	N	3	89	4	4	–	–	–	100	109	1.09
	%	3	89	4	4	–	–	–	100		

The study regarding respondent having number of S.B a/c revealed that in Udaipur district 65% women had only one S.B. a/c with bank, whereas, in Dungarpur district 89% women had only one S.B. a/c and 3% respondents had no S.B. a/c with bank. 35% women a/c holders of Udaipur district and 8% women of Dungarpur district had more than one S.B a/c. In Udaipur district, every woman had 1.56 S.B. a/c while in Dungarpur district every woman had only 1.09 S.B. a/c.

According to 32 and 45 respondents of Udaipur and Dungarpur district, respectively, revealed that more paper work in banking operation was the main problem.

30 women a/c holders of Udaipur district and 16 of Dungarpur district admitted that bank employees do work very slowly.

Non availability of the bank staff on their seats also one major problem of banking industry, 17 respondents of Udaipur district and 8 respondents of Dungarpur district agree with above statement while according to 15 women a/c holders of Udaipur district and 11 of Dungarpur district revealed that behaviour of bank staff was not polite. Above analysis shows that women a/c holders of Udaipur district were less satisfied with bank service compare to women a/c holders of Dungarpur district.

The composition of women bank accounts in both the districts are similar, generally women operated these accounts with the banks:

(*a*) Saving Account

(*b*) Current Account

(*c*) Recurring Deposit Account

(*d*) Fixed Deposit Account

(*e*) Non-Resident Account

(*f*) Safe Deposit Locker Account

(*g*) Loan and Advance Account

Bank-group wise classification of S.B a/c revealed (Table 6.23) that in Udaipur and Dungarpur district women had 74.36% and 55.05% S.B. a/c with the public sector banks, respectively. In private sector banks 16.03% and 18.35% S.B. a/c belong to women in Udaipur and Dungarpur district, respectively. In Udaipur district, women had 7.69% and 1.92% S.B. a/c with Co-operative Banks and Regional Rural Bank, respectively, while, in Dungarpur district women had 11.01% and 15.60% a/c with Co-operative and Regional Rural Bank, respectively. The above analysis clearly indicate that in Udaipur district Public Sector Bank were more popular in women while in Dungarpur district Private Sector Bank, Regional Rural Bank and Co-operative Banks were more popular.

Table 6.23 showed that in Udaipur and Dungarpur district women had 116 and 60 S.B. a/c with public sector banks. In both the districts most of the women had their S.B. a/c with S.B.B.J., BOB, P.N.B. and S.B.I. In Udaipur district, many women had 25

Table 6.23. Bank Group-wise and Bank-wise Distribution of S.B. A/c

District	Bank Group Wise	Public Sector Bank														
	Bank wise	SBBJ	BOB	CBI	PNB	SBI	OBC	Cenara Bank	Allahabad	PSB	UBI	Indian Bnak	BOI	UCO	Andhra Bank	Vijaya Bank
Udaipur	N	18	17	12	16	11	9	5	6	2	4	1	4	3	2	4
	%	11.54	10.90	7.69	10.26	7.05	5.77	3.21	3.85	1.28	2.56	0.64	2.56	1.92	1.28	2.56
Dungarpur	N	15	21	*	16	8	*	*	*	*	*	*	*	*	*	*
	%	13.76	19.27	*	14.68	7.34	*	*	*	*	*	*	*	*	*	*

District	Bank Group Wise	Private Sector Bank					Co-operative Bank			Regional Bank Rural		Total
	Bank wise	IOB	Total	The Bank of Rajasthan Ltd.	ICICI	Total	UCCB/ DCCB	MUCB	Total	MAGB/ DBKGB	Total	
Udaipur	N	2	116	7	18	25	8	4	12	3	3	156
	%	1.28	74.36	4.49	11.54	16.03	5.13	2.56	7.69	1.92	1.92	100
Dungarpur	N	*	60	20	*	20	12	*	12	17	17	109
	%	*	55.05	18.35	*	18.35	11.01	*	11.01	15.60	15.60	100

S.B a/c with Private Sector Bank i.e ICICI (18) and The Bank of Rajasthan Ltd. (7), while in Dungarpur district women had 20 S.B. a/c with Private Sector Bank i.e BOR.

In both the districts women had 12 S.B a/c in Co-operative Banks. In Udaipur district, women had only 3 a/c with R.R.B. in MAGB while in Dungarpur district women had 17 a/c with DBKGB.

Table 6.24. Why Respondents Prefer S.B. a/c with Bank

District		To Earn Interest	More Liquidity	Safety of Money	Others (Salary deposited ATM, Demate)
Udaipur	N	42	60	107	3
Dungarpur	N	41	48	53	–

Table 6.24 revealed that 107 respondents of Udaipur district and 53 of Dungarpur district had S.B. a/c with bank because bank provide more safety to their money. According to 60 respondents of Udaipur district and 48 respondents of Dungarpur district bank provide more liquidity to their funds so they had S.B a/c with banks. While, 42 and 41 respondents of Udaipur and Dungarpur district, respectively, revealed that they prefer S.B a/c with banks to earn interest. Only 3 respondents of Udaipur district had S.B. a/c with Bank because bank provide special facilities i.e. ATM, Demate etc.

Table 6.25. Reasons for Opening S.B. a/c with Particular Bank Branch

District		Near to Residence	Near to Working Place	Bank Employees Friend/ Relative	Salary Deposited	On request of Husband/ Father	Special Facilities (For payment of instalment of housing Loan ATM)	Others (Employed in same Bank,) 24 hour open for operation
Udaipur	N	45	10	28	23	36	12	5
Dungarpur	N	40	8	28	4	24	3	–

In Udaipur district 45 and in Dungarpur district 40 women account holders open their a/c because that particular bank branch was near to their residence. 36 and 24 women of Udaipur and Dungarpur district, respectively, open their a/c on the request of their husband. And 28 respondents of both the districts had open their a/c in particular bank branch because they had good relations with bankers. In Udaipur district, 23 respondents open their a/c because of salary deposited in that bank. While in Dungarpur district only 3 respondents opened their a/c in particular bank branch because bank was near to their working place special facilities like ATM, Demate provided by bank and because respondent had loan a/c so they also opened S.B. a/c in that bank, and because the respondent employed in the same bank branch etc.

Table 6.26. Whether Respondents have Individual or Joint S.B. a/c with Bank

District		Individual Joint A/c with						
		A/c	Husband	Father	Son/ Daughter	Brother/ Sister	Others	Total
Udaipur	N	73	75	2	3	3	–	156
Dungarpur	53	53	56	–	–	–	–	109

The study revealed that in both the district women had more than 50% S.B. a/c as Joint with their husband. While in Udaipur district females also had some joint a/c with their father, son, daughter, brother and sister.

Table 6.27 showed that in Udaipur district nearly half S.B a/c was operated by a/c holder themselves while rest half S.B. a/c was operated by respondent's husband and by their son/daughter while in Dungarpur district nearly two-third S.B. a/c were operated by respondents husband/father/son, daughter and brother, sister. Only one-third S.B. a/c was operated by women themselves.

Table 6.27. S.B. a/c is Operated by Whom

Districts		Respondent	Husband	Son/ Daughter	Father	Brother/ Sister
Udaipur	N	87	80	9		
Dungarpur	N	44	60	3	13	4

Table 6.28 shows that 79 (50.64%) S.B. a/c of Udaipur district and 44 (40.37%) S.B. a/c of Dungarpur district last time operated their a/c within a month. 34 (21.79%) and 37 (33.95%) S.B. a/c of Udaipur and Dungarpur district, respectively, operated by women during last one year. There were 22 (14.11%) S.B. a/c of Udaipur district and 28 (25.69%) S.B. a/c of Dungarpur district not operated by women within two years and amazingly, that 21 (13.46%) S.B. a/c of Udaipur district were never operated by women.

Table 6.28. Last Time when Respondent Operate their S.B. a/c

Districts		Within 15 Days	Before a month	Before a Quarter	Before 6 months	Before one year	Before two years	More than two years	Once in a life	Total
Udaipur	N	47	32	14	13	7	5	17	21	156
	%	30.13	20.51	8.97	8.33	4.49	3.21	10.90	13.46	100
Dungarpur	N	15	29	20	8	9	1	27	-	109
	%	13.76	26.61	18.35	7.34	8.26	0.92	24.77	-	100

The above analysis clearly indicate that women of Udaipur district operate their S.B. a/c frequently compare to the women of Dungarpur district but on the other hand number of non-operating S.B. a/c were more in Udaipur district compare to Dungarpur district.

Table 6.29, visualized that in Udaipur and Dungarpur district 97 (62.18%) and 77 (70.64%) women respectively were not going bank for deposit money and 97 (62.18%) and 64 (58.72%) women respectively were not going bank for withdraw of money from their S.B. a/c. In Udaipur district, 124 (79.49%) and 96 (61.54%) women were never gone bank for deposit of cheque for collection and for completion of passbook, respectively, while, in Dungarpur district 101 (92.67%) and 88 (80.74%) women were never going for same purpose respectively.

For issue of cheque book and issue of Draft 101 (64.75%) and 144 (91.67%) women a/c holder respectively, never approach bank in Udaipur district while in Dungarpur district 81 (74.31%) and 84 (75.07%) women were never approach bank for issue of cheque book and issue of draft, respectively.

Table 6.29. Operation of Account by Respondent

Districts		Deposit of Money						Withdrawn of Money						Cheque for		
		Always	Frequently	Normally	Rarely	Never	Total	Always	Frequently	Normally	Rarely	Never	Total	Always	Frequently	Normally
Udaipur	N	8	13	38	37	60	156	12	15	32	46	51	156	4	3	25
	%	5.13	8.33	24.36	23.72	38.46	100	7.69	9.62	20.51	29.49	32.69	100	2.56	1.92	16.03
Dungarpur	N	-	20	12	57	20	109	-	16	29	44	20	109	-	-	8
	%	-	18.35	11.01	52.29	18.35	100	-	14.68	26.61	40.37	18.35	100	-	-	7.34

Districts		Collection			Completion of Pass Book						
		Rarely	Never	Total	Always	Frequently	Normally	Rarely	Never	Monthly Report send by Bank	Total
Udaipur	N	44	80	156	19	5	30	20	76	6	156
	%	28.21	51.28	100	12.18	3.21	19.23	12.82	48.72	3.85	100
Dungarpur	N	33	68	109	8	–	13	36	52	–	109
	%	30.28	62.39	100	7.34	–	11.93	33.03	47.71	–	100

(Contd...)

(Table 6.29 Contd...)

Districts		Issue of Cheque Book							Issue of Draft					
		Always	Freq.	Normally	Rarely	Never	Not Adding	Total	Always	Frequently	Normally	Rarely	Never	Total
Udaipur	N	10	–	35	46	55	10	15	2	–	11	39	104	156
	%	6.41	–	22.44	29.49	35.26	6.41	100	1.28	–	7.05	25.00	66.67	100
Dungarpur	N	–	–	16	12	45	36	109	–	–	25	24	60	109
	%	–	–	14.68	11.01	41.28	33.03	100	–	–	22.94	22.02	55.05	100

Table 6.30 Time Taken in Depositing and Withdrawing of Money

Districts		Depositing of Money						Withdrawing of Money					
		Upto 5 Minutes	6 to 10 Minutes	11 to 15 Minutes	More than 15 Minutes	More than ½ hour	Total	Upto 5 Minutes	6 to 10 Minutes	11 to 15 Minutes	More than 15 Minutes	More than ½ hour	Total
Udaipur	N	20	52	46	31	7	156	23	30	49	38	16	156
	%	12.82	33.33	29.48	19.87	4.49	100	14.74	19.23	31.41	24.36	10.26	100
Dungarpur	N	32	24	18	19	16	109	17	24	34	9	25	109
	%	29.36	22.02	16.51	17.43	14.68	100	15.60	22.01	31.19	8.26	22.94	100

In the opinion of nearly two-third respondents of Udaipur and Dungarpur districts they deposit and withdraw money within fifteen minutes from bank.

The above analysis clearly indicate that in both district women were generally not visit their banks for deposit of money and cheque, withdraw of money from S.B. a/c for completion of cheque book, for issue cheque book and to issue of draft etc. although frequency of women of Udaipur district were quite good in comparison to women of Dungarpur district.

Table 6.31 Clearly indicate that in both district cent per cent women maintain minimum balance in the S.B. a/c.

Table 6.31. Whether Respondent Maintain Minimum Balance in their S.B. A/c

Districts		Yes	No	Total
Udaipur	N	156	–	156
	%	100	–	100
Dungarpur	N	109	–	109
	%	100	–	100

Table 6.32 : Whether Respondents know about Balance and Interest they are Getting on their S.B. A/c? And their Opinion about the Rate of Interest

District		Respondent Knowledge About Their Balance in S.B. A/c					Knowledge about the Rate of Interest they are getting		
		Always	Generally	Occasionally	Never	Total	Yes	No	Total
Udaipur	N	75	41	24	16	156	63	93	156
	%	48.08	26.29	15.38	10.26	100	40.38	59.62	100
Dungarpur	N	36	44	21	8	109	57	52	109
	%	33.03	40.37	19.27	7.34	100	52.29	47.71	100

Districts		Opinion About the Rate of Interest					
		Very Less	Less	Sufficient	More	Don't know or can't say	Total
Udaipur	N	59	44	27	–	26	156
	%	37.82	28.21	17.31	–	16.67	100
Dungarpur	N	24	52	16	–	17	109
	%	22.02	47.71	14.68	–	15.60	100

Table 6.32 revealed that in both the district, nearly three-fourth S.B. a/c holder's generally knew about the balance in their S.B. a.c. 40.38% women S.B. a/c holders of Udaipur district and 52.29% of Dungarpur district know about the rate of interest they were getting on their S.B. a/c. When respondents were asked about their opinion regarding the rate of interest they were getting on S.B. a/c, nearly two-third women a/c holders of both the district had opinion that bank were providing very less interest on S.B. a/c.

Table 6.33 clearly showed that women had availed cheque book facilities on their 93% and 66% S.B. a/c in Udaipur and Dungarpur district respectively.

Table 6.33. Whether Cheque Facility are Being Availed by Respondents?

Districts		Yes	No	Total
Udaipur	N	145	11	156
	%	92.95	7.05	100
Dungarpur	N	72	37	109
	%	66.06	33.94	100

Table 6.34. Whether Pass Book is Checked by Respondent after Completion

Districts		Always	Frequently	Normally	Rarely	Never	Total
Udaipur	N	55	14	35	24	28	156
	%	35.26	8.97	22.44	15.38	17.95	100
Dungarpur	N	28	12	25	12	32	109
	%	25.69	11.01	22.94	11.01	29.36	100

When respondents were asked about the availability of bank employees in the banks most of the women S.B a/c holders were satisfied with their availability in both the district. (Table 6.35)

In general behaviour of male and female employees were satisfactory in both the districts. But 7.69% women respondents in Udaipur and 7.34% women respondents in Dungarpur district were not satisfied by the behaviour of male bankers. About the behaviour of female banker 13.46% women S.B. a/c holders of Udaipur district were not satisfied.

In the opinion of women S.B. a/c holders, overall bankers were very helpful and Co-operative in both the district.

Table 6.35. Opinion of Respondents about Availability

Districts		Availability of Bank employees							Behaviour of male employees						
		Always	Freq.	Normally	Rarely	Never	Can't Say	Total	Very Satis-factory	Satis-factory	Normal	Un-satisfac-tory	Rude	Non Opening A/c	Total
Udaipur	N	47	16	71	4	2	16	156	26	61	49	4	8	8	156
	%	30.13	10.26	45.51	2.56	1.28	10.26	100	16.67	39.10	31.41	2.56	5.13	5.13	100
Dungarpur	N	32	13	64	–	–	–	109	32	45	24	5	3	–	109
	%	29.36	11.93	58.72	–	–	–	100	29.36	41.28	22.02	4.59	2.75	–	100

District		Behaviour of Female Employees								Overall Experience with Bank						
		Very Satis-factory	Sati-sfac-tory	Normal	Unsatis-factory	Rude	No females There	Non opening A/c	Total	Very Satis-factory	Satis-factory	Normal	Unsatis-factory	Rude	Non open-ing-A/c	Total
Udaipur	N	30	35	60	12	9	12	8	156	23	48	76	3	2	4	156
	%	19.23	22.4	38.46	7.69	5.77	7.69	5.13	100	14.74	30.77	48.72	1.92	1.28	2.56	100
Dungarpur	N	5	–	7	–	–	–	97	109	36	33	31	4	5	–	109
	%	4.59	–	6.42	–	–	–	88.99	100	33.03	30.28	28.44	3.67	4.59	–	100

(B) OPERATION OF CURRENT ACCOUNT BY WOMEN

Table 6.36. Respondents Having Number of Current A/c with Banks

Districts		0	1	2	3	Total Account Holder	Total Current Account	No. of Average Total a/c per women
Udaipur	N	–	5	–	–	5	5	0.05
Dungarpur	N	–	2	–	–	2	2	0.02

The study regarding respondent having number of current a/c revealed that out of 100 women in Udaipur district only 5 women and in Dungarpur district only 2 women had only one current a/c with bank. In Udaipur district, every women had 0.05 current a/c while in Dungarpur district every women had only 0.02 current a/c.

Table 6.37. Bank Group-wise and Bank-wise Distribution of Current A/c

District	Bank Group wise	Public Sector Bank					Private Sector Bank	Co-operative Bank	Regional Rural Bank	Total
	Bank Group wise	BOB	PSB	PNB	SBBJ	Total				
Udaipur	N	2	1	1	1	5	–	–	–	5
Dungarpur	N	1	*	–	1	2	–	–	–	2

Bank group-wise classification of current a/c revealed that in Udaipur and Dungarpur district women had cent per cent current a/c with the public sector bank.

The above analysis clearly indicate that in both the districts Public Sector Bank were popular in women.

Table 6.37 showed that in both the districts women had their current a/c with BOB, SBBJ. In Udaipur district women also had current a/c with PSB and PNB.

Table 6.38. Why Respondents Prefer Current A/c with Bank

District		Provide Cash Credit Facility	Provide Overdraft Facility	Provide facilities of collection of cheque	No Restriction on transaction	Others	Total
Udaipur	N	–	5	–	–	–	5
Dungarpur	N	–	2	–	–	–	2

Table 6.38 clearly indicate that in both the district, cent per cent women prefer current a/c with bank because bank provided overdraft facilities to current a/c holders.

Table 6.39. Reasons for Opening Current A/c with Particular Bank Branch

District		Near to Reside-nce	Near to Working Place	Bank Employee are Friend Relative	Suffici-cent overdraft facilities	On request of Husband/ Father	Limit Facility Provided By Bank	Being employed in the same Bank	To-tal
Udaipur	N	–	–	–	–	1	3		5
Dungarpur	N	–	–	–	–	2	–	–	2

In Udaipur district, one and in Dungarpur district two women current a/c holders open their a/c with particular bank on the request of husband. One respondent of Udaipur district opened her a/c because respondent was employed in the same bank. And 3 respondents of Udaipur district were opened their a/c due to limit facility provided by bank.

Table 6.40. Respondents have Individual or Joint Current A/c with Bank

District		Individual A/c	Joint A/c with				Total
			Husband	Father	Son/ Daughter	Brother/ Sister	
Udaipur	N	5	–	–	–	–	5
Dungarpur	N	1	1	–	–	–	2

The investigation revealed that in Udaipur district all women current a/c holders had individual current a/c, whereas, in Dungarpur district, one woman had individual current a/c and one woman had joint a/c with her husband.

Table 6.41. Current A/c is Operated by Whom?

District		By Respondent themselves	Husband	Father	Son/ Daughter	Brother/ Sister	Others	Total
Udaipur	N	2	1	–	2	–	–	5
Dungarpur	N	–	2	–	–	–	–	2

Table 6.41 showed that in Udaipur district one current a/c was operated by beneficiaries husband while in Dungarpur district, all current a/c were operated by respondent husband. Two current a/c in Udaipur district were operated by respondents themselves rest of the two were operated by respondents son.

The above analysis clearly indicate that in both the districts women had mostly individual current account but operated by their husband or son.

Table 6.42. Frequency of Operation of Current A/c

District		Always	Frequently	Normally	Rarely	Never	Total
Udaipur	N	1	1	1	–	2	5
Dungarpur	N	–	–	–	1	1	2

Table 6.42 shows that 3 women current a/c holders of Udaipur district were operating their a/c regularly. While, all respondents of Dungarpur district and 2 respondents of Udaipur district were not operating their current a/c.

In the opinion of 60% respondents of Udaipur district they deposit and withdraw money with in 5 minutes for their bank and for issuing of cheque generally time taken by bank was 16 to 30 minutes while the two respondents of Dungarpur and Udaipur district each admitted that their current a/c were operated by their husband so they were not knowing how much time has been taken in depositing, withdrawing of money and issue of cheque book from bank.

Table 6.43. Operation of Account by Respondents

Districts		Depositing of Money							Withdrawing of Money		
		Upto 5 Minute	6 to 10 Minutes	11 to 15 Minutes	More than 15 Minutes	More than ½ hour	Do not Know	Total	Upto 5 Minutes	6 to 10 Minutes	11 to 15 Minutes
Udaipur	N	–	3	–	–	–	2	5	–	1	2
Dungarpur	N	–	–	–	–	–	2	2	–	–	–

Districts		Money			Issuing of Cheque Book					
		More than 15 Minutes	Do not Know	Total	Within 15 Minutes	16 to 30 Minutes	31 to 60 Minutes	61 to 120 Minutes	Do Not Know	Total
Udaipur	N	–	2	5	–	3	–	–	2	5
Dungarpur	N	–	2	2	–	–	–	–	2	2

Table 6.44. Cash Credit Facilities Availing by Respondent and their Limit

Districts		Respondent Availing cash facility			Limit of cash credit			Total
		Yes	No	Total	Less than 1 lac	1 to 2 lacs	2 to 3 lacs	
Udaipur	N	5	–	5	1	2	2	5
Dungarpur	N	2	–	2	–	2	–	2

Table 6.44 clearly indicate that cent per cent women current a/c holder had cash credit facility, in both the districts. Mostly respondents of both the districts had cash credit limit between Rs. 1 lac and 3 lacs.

Table 6.45. Overdraft Facilities Availing by Respondents

Districts		Respondents Availing Overdraft Facility			Limit of Overdraft		
		Yes	No	Total	Upto 10,000	Do Not know	Total
Udaipur	N	5	–	5	1	4	5
Dungarpur	N	2	–	2	–	2	2

Table 6.45 revealed that cent per cent respondents of both the districts had overdraft facilities from bank but they were ignorant about the maximum limit of overdraft.

Table 6.46. Did Respondents Pay Charges for Facilities of Current A/c

Districts		Yes	No	Total
Udaipur	N	–	5	5
Dungarpur	N	–	2	2

Table 6.46 clearly indicates that in both the districts, no respondent were paying any incidental charges for the facility of current a/c.

Table 6.47. Whether Respondents Know about their Balance in Current A/c

Districts		Always	Generally	Occasionally	Never	Total
Udaipur	N	2	1	2	–	5
Dungarpur	N	–	–	–	2	2

Table 6.47 showed that in Udaipur district (60%) women current a/c holder were aware about their balance, whereas in Dungarpur district no women had knowledge regarding balance in their current a/c.

Table 6.48. Whether Respondents Maintain Minimum Balance in their Current A/c?

Districts		Yes	No	Total
Udaipur	N	5	–	5
Dungarpur	N	2	–	2

Table 6.48 showed that in both the district cent per cent women current a/c holders was maintaining minimum balance in their current a/c.

Table 6.49. Whether Statement/Passbook is Checked by Respondents after Completion

Districts		Always	Frequently	Normally	Rarely	Never	Total
Udaipur	N	2	1	–	–	2	5
Dungarpur	N	–	–	–	1	1	2

In Udaipur district 3 respondents always check their statement/passbook after its completion while 2 respondents of Udaipur and Dungarpur district each admitted that they did not check their statement/passbook after completion.

Impact of current a/c is visualize in Table 6.50. One–third beneficiaries of Udaipur district and half of Dungarpur district admitted that their income-level sufficiently increased while rest of the beneficiaries were not positively affected by the increase in income level. In the opinion of (40%) respondents of Udaipur district and cent per cent beneficiaries of Dungarpur district their property increase upto sufficient level. 60% women current a/c

Table 6.50. Impact of Current A/c

Districts		Income level Increased					Property owned increased				
		High Increase	Sufficient Increase	Low Increase	No effects	Total	High Increase	Suffici. Increase	Low Increase	No Effects	Total
Udaipur	N	–	2	1	2	5	–	2	–	3	5
Dungarpur	N	–	1	1	–	2	–	2	–	–	2

Districts		Living Standard improved				
		Highly Increase	Sufficiently Increase	Low Increase	No Effects	Total
Udaipur	N	–	3	–	2	5
Dungarpur	N	–	–	2	–	2

Table 6.51. Opinion of Respondent About Availability and Behaviour of Bank Employees and their Overall Experience with Bankers

District		Behaviour of Male employees						Behaviour of female employees			
		Very Satisfactory	Satisfactory	Normal	Unsatis-factory	Rude	Total	Very satisfactory	Satisfactory	Normal	Unsatis-factory
Udaipur	N	–	5	–	–	–	5	–	2	2	–
Dungarpur	N	2	–	–	–	–	2	–	–	–	–

Districts		Female	Total	Very Satisfactory	Satisfactory	Normal	Unsatisfactory	Rude	Total
Udaipur	N	1	5	3	2	–	–	–	5
Dungarpur	N	2	2	2	–	–	–	–	2

holders of Udaipur district admitted that living standard sufficiently improved by operation of current a/c. While in Dungarpur district and cent per cent women admitted that their living standard slightly improved by operation of current a/c.

In the opinion of women current a/c holders, male and female employees were very helpful for them and their overall experience with bank was very satisfactory.

(C) OPERATION OF RECURRING ACCOUNT BY WOMEN

As Table 6.52 showed that R.D. a/c was more popular among women in Dungarpur district, out of 100 women 13 women had R.D. a/c with bank, where as in Udaipur district only 3 women had R.D. A/c. In both the districts no women had more than one R.D. a/c. In Dungarpur district every woman had average 0.13 R.D. a/c. While in Udaipur district, every woman had average 0.03 R. A/c.

Table 6.52. Respondents Having Number of R.D. A/c with Banks

Districts		0	1	2	3	4	Total A/c Holder	Total no. of R.D a/c	Average R.D. A/c Per Woman
Udaipur	N	–	3	–	–	–	3	3	0.03
Dungarpur	N	–	13	–	–	–	13	13	0.13

Table 6.53 visualise us by Bank Group-wise and Bank wise distribution of R.D A/c. Bank Group-wise distribution showed that in Udaipur and Dungarpur district beneficiaries had 66.67% and 38.46% R.D. a/c with public sector banks, respectively. In private sector bank, 33.33% and 15.38%, respondents had R.D. a/c in Udaipur and Dungarpur district, respectively. In Co-operative bank, 46.15% respondents of Dungarpur district had R.D. a/c while no respondent of Udaipur district had R.D. a/c with Co-operative bank. In both the districts, no beneficiaries had R.D. a/c with Regional rural bank.

Bank-wise distribution of R.D. A/c clearly indicate that in Udaipur district 2 (66.67%) respondents had R.D. A/c with

Table 6.53. Bank Group-wise and Bank-wise Distribution of R.D A/c

District	Bank Group wise	Public Sector				Private Sector Bank		Co-operative Bank		RRB		Grand Total
	Bank wise	SBBJ	BOB	Syndicate Bank	Total	The Rajasthan Bank Ltd.	Total	UCCB/ DCCB	Total	MAGB/ DBKGB	Total	Grand Total
Udaipur	N	–	–	2	2	1	1	–	–	–	–	3
	%	–	–	66.67	66.67	33.33	33.33	–	–	–	–	100
Dungarpur	N	2	3	*	5	2	2	6	6	–	–	13
	%	15.38	23.08	*	38.46	15.38	15.38	46.15	46.15	–	–	100

Syndicate Bank and 1 (33.33%) respondents had R.D. a/c with the Bank of Rajasthan Ltd. In Dungarpur district 6 (46.15%) respondents had R.D. a/c with Dungarpur Central Co-operative Bank while 3 (23.08%), 2 (15.38%) and (15.38%) respondents had R.D. a/c with SBBJ, BOB and The Bank of Rajasthan Ltd., respectively.

Table 6.54 showed that Udaipur district respondents prefer R.D. a/c due to regular saving (2), to earn interest (2), to get lump sum amount after maturity (3), and because loan facility available on R.D. a/c (1) while in Dungarpur district all 13 respondents prefer R.D. a/c with bank because R.D. a/c was the best mode of regular savings.

Table 6.54. Why Respondents Prefer R.D. A/c with Bank?

Districts		Regular Saving	To Earn Interest	To get Lump Sum Amount After Maturity	Loan Facilities Available on R.D. a/c	Others
Udaipur	N	2	2	3	1	–
Dungarpur	N	13	–	–	–	–

Table 6.55 revealed that in Udaipur district 2 (66.67%) respondents open their a/c with particular bank because bank branch was near to their working place and 1 (33.33%) respondents revealed that bank (Syndicate) provide door to door service for collection of money.

Table 6.55. Reasons for Opening R.D. A/c with Particular Bank Branch

Districts		Near to Residence	Near to Working place	Bank Employees are Friend/ Relative	On request of Husband Father	Banker are coming door to door	Total
Udaipur	N	–	2	–	–	1	3
Dungarpur	N	9	–	–	4	–	13

In Dungarpur district, 9 (69.23%) beneficiaries open their R.D. a/c with particular bank branch because bank branch was near to their residence and 4 (30.77%) open R.D. a/c on the request of their husband.

More than two-third women R.D. a/c holders had joint a/c with their husband as shown in Table 6.56 in both the districts. Rest women had individual R.D. a/c.

Table 6.56. Whether Respondents have Individual or Joint R.D. A/c with Bank

District		Individual A/c	Joint A/c with						Total
			Husband	Father	Son/ Daughter	Brother/ Sister	Others	Total	
Udaipur	N	1	2	–	–	–	–	2	3
	%	33.33	66.67	–	–	–	–	66.67	100
Dungarpur	N	3	10	–	–	–	–	10	13
	%	23.08	76.92	–	–	–	–	76.92	100

Table 6.57 revealed that cent per cent R.D. a/c in Udaipur district had been operated by respondents themselves. While in Dungarpur district only 3 (23.08%) R.D. account were operated by respondents themselves.

Table 6.57. R.D. A/c is Operated by Whom?

Districts		By Respondent	Husband	Son/ Daughter	Father	Brother/ Sister	Others	Total
Udaipur	N	3	–	–	–	–	–	3
	%	100	–	–	–	–	–	100
Dungarpur	N	3	10	–	–	–	–	13
	%	23.08	76.92	–	–	–	–	100

Table 6.58 showed that duration of R.D. a/c of Udaipur district respondents had in between two and three years, while all respondents of Dungarpur district had R.D. of 5 years.

About 62% respondents depositing monthly instalment of more than Rs. 1000 in both the districts. Rest of the respondents were depositing monthly instalment in between Rs. 300 and Rs. 1000.

Table 6.58. Duration of R.D. A/c and Monthly Instalment

Districts		Duration of R.D. A/c							Monthly instalment deposited by respondent				
		One Year	Two Year	Three Year	Four Year	Five Year	More Than five Year	Total	Rs. 300	Rs. 301 to Rs. 500	Rs. 501 to Rs. 1000	More than Rs. 1000	Total
Udaipur	N	–	1	2	–	–	–	3	–	–	1	2	3
	%	–	33.33	66.67	–	–	–	100	–	–	33.33	66.67	100
Dungarpur	N	–	–	–	–	13	–	13	–	3	2	8	13
	%	–	–	–	–	100	–	100	–	23.08	15.38	61.54	100

Table 6.59 showed very amazing fact that cent per cent women were depositing monthly instalment very regularly in both the districts.

Table 6.59. Whether Respondents Depositing their Instalment Regularly?

Districts		Always	Frequently	Normally	Rarely	Never	Total
Udaipur	N	3	–	–	–	–	3
Dungarpur	N	13	–	–	–	–	13

Table 6.60 showed that cent percent women R.D. a/c holders of Udaipur district had awareness about the rate of interest what they were getting. On the contrary, in Dungarpur district cent per cent respondents were not aware about the concerning fact. In the opinion of 2 (66.67%) respondents of Udaipur district rate of interest provided by banks on R.D. a/c was less, whereas, in the opinion of three/fourth respondents of Dungarpur district it was sufficient.

Table 6.60. Whether Respondents Know that how Much Interest they are Getting on their R.D. A/c? And their Opinion about the Rate of Interest

District		Respondents Knowledge about the Rate of Interest			Opinion about the rate of interest				
		Yes	No	Total	Very less	Less	Sufficient	More	Total
Udaipur	N	3	–	3	1	1	1	–	3
	%	100	–	100	33.33	33.33	33.33	–	100
Dungarpur	N	–	13	13	–	3	10	–	13
	%	–	100	100	–	23.08	76.92	–	100

Table 6.61. Whether Respondents Avail Loan Facilities Against R.D. A/c?

Districts		Yes	No	Total
Udaipur	N	–	3	3
	%	–	100	100
Dungarpur	N	–	13	13
	%	–	100	100

As table 6.61 clearly indicates that in both the districts no women taken loan on their R.D. A/c.

Table 6.62. Experience of Respondents with Banks

Districts		Very Satisfactory	Satisfactory	Normal	Unsatisfactory	Rude	Total
Udaipur	N	–	1	2	–	–	3
	%	–	33.33	66.67	–	–	100
Dungarpur	N	5	8	–	–	–	13
	%	38.46	61.54	–	–	–	100

In general respondents of both the districts were satisfied with bankers. 5 (38.46%) respondents of Dungarpur district were highly impressed by the behaviour of bankers.

(D) OPERATION OF FIXED DEPOSIT ACCOUNT BY WOMEN

Table 6.63. Respondent Having Number of F.D. A/c's with Banks

Districts		0	1	2	3	4	Total Account Holder	Total no. of F.D. a/c	Average F.D a/c per woman
Udaipur	N	–	29	18	–	4	51	81	0.81
	%	–	56.86	35.29	–	7.85	100	–	–
Dungarpur	N	–	24	12	–	–	36	48	0.48
	%	–	66.67	33.33	–	–	100	–	–

The analysis regarding beneficiaries having number of F.D. a/c revealed that in Udaipur district 56.86% women had only one F.D. a/c with bank whereas in Dungarpur district 66.67% women had only one F.D. a/c. One-third F.D. a/c holders of Udaipur and Dungarpur district had two F.D. a/c with banks. There were 7.85% women in Udaipur district who had 4 F.D. a/c with banks. In Udaipur district, every woman had average 0.81 F.D. a/c whereas, in Dungarpur district every woman had only average 0.48 F.D. a/c.

Bank group wise analysis of F.D. a/c revealed that in Udaipur and Dungarpur district women had 70.37% and 50% F.D. a/c with Public Sector Bank. In Private Sector Bank 17.28%

and 25% F.D. a/c belong to women in Udaipur and Dungarpur district, respectively. In Udaipur district women had 9.88% and 2.47% F.D. a/c with Co-operative Banks and Regional Rural Bank, respectively. Where as, in Dungarpur district women had 22.92% and 2.08% F.D. a/c with Co-operative Bank and Regional Rural Bank, respectively.

Co-operative Banks, Regional Rural Bank and even Private Sector Bank give more interest on F.D a/c compare to Public Sector Banks, Even then women had less account in Dungarpur district and Udaipur district. In Udaipur district women had more F.D. a/c with Public Sector Banks while less a/c in private sector bank and co-operative banks.

Table 6.64, *(See page 286)* revealed that in Udaipur and Dungarpur district women had 57 and 24 F.D. a/c with public sector Banks, respectively. In both the district most of the women had their F.D. a/c with SBBJ, BOB, and SBI. In Udaipur district many women also had their F.D. a/c with CBI, Allahabad Bank, UBI and Indian Bank. In Udaipur district, women had 14 F.D. a/c with Private Sector Bank i.e. ICICI (11) and The Bank of Rajasthan Ltd. (3), while in Dungarpur district women had 12 F.D. a/c with Private Sector Banks i.e. The bank of Rajasthan Ltd. In Udaipur district total 8 women had F.D. a/c in Co-operative Banks i.e. in UUCB (5) and MUCB (3) while in Dungarpur district 11 women had F.D a/c in DCCB. In Udaipur district, women had only 2 a/c in RRB i.e. in MAGB while in Dungarpur district women had only one F.D. a/c in RRB (DBKGB).

Table 6.65, *(See page 287)* showed that 38 respondents of Udaipur and 31 respondents of Dungarpur district had F.D. a/c with bank because bank provide more interest on F.D. a/c. According to 41 respondents of Udaipur district and 10 of Dungarpur district, F.D. a/c was the best mode of safety of money. While 9 and 7 respondents of Udaipur and Dungarpur district, respectively, revealed that bank provide more liquidity to their funds. 7 respondents of Udaipur district and 3 of Dungarpur district had F.D. a/c with bank because at the time of need they easily get loan from bank. And only 2 and 5 respondents of Udaipur and Dungarpur district, respectively had F.D. a/c with bank because there S.B. a/c was also there.

Table 6.64. Bank Group-wise and Bank-wise Distribution of F.D.

District	Bank Group-Wise	Public Sector Bank								Private Sector Bank		
	Bank wise	SBBJ	SBI	CBI	BOB	Allahabad	UBI	Indian Bank	Total	The Bank of Rajasthan Ltd.	ICICI	Total
Udaipur	N	14	2	27	8	3	1	2	57	3	11	14
	%	17.28	2.47	33.33	9.88	3.70	1.23	2.47	70.37	3.70	13.58	17.28
Dungarpur	N	3	1	*	20	*	*	*	24	12	*	12
	%	6.25	2.08	*	41.67	*	*	*	50.00	25.00	*	25.00

Districts	Bank group-wise	Co-operative Bank			Regional Rural Bank		Grand Total
	Bank wise	UUCB/ DCCB	MUCB	Total	MAGB/ JBKGB	Total	
Udaipur	N	5	3	8	2	2	81
	%	6.17	3.70	9.88	2.47	2.47	100
Dungarpur	N	11	*	11	1	1	48
	%	22.92	*	22.92	2.08	2.08	100

Table 6.65. Why Respondents Prefer F.D. A/c with Bank

District		Interest Rate is High	To get Loan	More Liquidity	Safety of money	S.B. a/c is there
Udaipur	N	38	7	9	41	2
	%	31	3	7	10	5

In Udaipur district, 24 and in Dungarpur district 17 women F.D. a/c holders open their a/c because bank branch was near to their residence. 17 and 23 women of Udaipur and Dungarpur district, respectively, open their a/c on the request of their husband. 22 and 2 women of Udaipur and Dungarpur district, respectively, open their F.D. a/c in that particular bank branch because their salary deposited in that bank. Only 3 respondents of Udaipur district and 5 of Dungarpur district open their F.D. a/c in that particular bank because that bank branch was near to their working place. And 5 respondents of both the district had open their F.D. a/c in that particular branch because their S.B. a/c was already there. In Udaipur district 11 women open their a/c in particular bank branch because they had good relation with bankers. And 5 women revealed that the reason of opening F.D. a/c in that particular bank branch because high rate of interest paid by particular bank branch on F.D. in comparison to other banks.

Table 6.66. Reasons for Opening F.D. A/c with Particular Bank Branch

Districts		Near to Residence	Near to Working place	Bank Employees are Friend Relative	High Interest paid by Bank	On request of Husband/ Father	Salary Deposited	S.B. a/c is there
Udaipur	N	24	3	11	5	17	22	5
	%	17	5	–	–	23	2	5

Table 6.67, revealed that 64.2% and 83.33% women of Udaipur and Dungarpur district, respectively had joint a/c with their family members. Only 35.80% and 16.67% women of Udaipur and Dungarpur district respectively, had individual F.D. a/c.

Table 6.67. Whether Respondents have Individual or Joint F.D. A/c with Bank

District		Individual A/c	Joint A/c with Husband	Father	Son/ Daughter	Brother/ Sister	Mother	Total
Udaipur	N	29	34	–	5	3	10	81
	%	35.80	41.98	–	6.17	3.70	12.35	100
Dungarpur	N	8	31	9	–	–	–	48
	%	16.67	64.58	18.75	–	–	–	100

Table 6.68 indicate that in Udaipur district 55 beneficiaries were operating their F.D. a/c by themselves while in Dungarpur district only 12 F.D. a/c were operated by beneficiaries themselves. 26 and 36 F.D. a/c in Udaipur and Dungarpur district respectively, were operated by beneficiaries Husband/ Father/Son/Daughter.

Table 6.68. F.D. A/c is Operated by Whom?

District		By Respondent	Husband	Father	Son/ Daughter	Brother/ Sister	Others	Total
Udaipur	N	55	24	–	2	–	–	81
Dungarpur	N	12	27	9	–	–	–	48

In Table 6.69, the above analysis clearly indicate that in Udaipur district mostly F.D. a/c were operated by respondents themselves while in Dungarpur district mostly F.D. a/c were operated by beneficiaries Husband/Father.

Duration-wise classification of F.D. a/c indicate that, one-third respondents in both the districts had F.D. upto 6 months to 1 year maturity. In Udaipur district 41 (50.62%) respondents and 31 (64.58%) Dungarpur district respondents had F.D. upto 3 year maturity. While in Udaipur district 10 (12.35%) women had invested their money in bank F.D. for 5 year period.

Amount wise classification of F.D. a/c showed that, 36 (44.45%) respondents of Udaipur district and 36 (75%) respondents of Dungarpur district Phad F.D. upto Rs. 20 thousand while in Udaipur district 41 (50.62%) respondents and 12 (25%) respondents of Dungarpur district had F.D. of Rs. 0.5

to Rs. 1 lac amount. In Udaipur district 3 (3.7%) women had F.D. of Rs. more than 1 lac.

Table 6.69. Duration-wise and Amount-wise Distribution of F.D.

Districts		Duration of F.D.							
		Upto 45 days	46 days to 90 days	91 days to 179 days	180 days to 1 year	upto 2 years	upto 3 years	5 years	Total
Udaipur	N	–	2	–	25	3	41	10	81
	%	–	2.47	–	30.87	3.70	50.62	12.35	100
Dungarpur	N	–	–	–	17	–	31	–	48
	%	–	–	–	35.42	–	64.58	–	100

Districts		Amount of F.D.						
		Upto 5000	5001 to 10,000	10,001 to 20,000	20,001 to 50,000	50,001 to 1 lac	More than 1 lac	Total
Udaipur	N	5	10	21	30	11	3	81
	%	6.17	12.35	25.93	37.04	13.58	3.70	100
Dungarpur	N	9	3	24	12	–	–	48
	%	18.75	6.25	50.00	25	–	–	100

Table 6.70. Whether Respondents Know that How Much Interest They are Getting on their F.D A/c and their Opinion about the Rate of Interest

Districts		Respondents knowledge About the rate of interest			Opinion about the rate of interest					
		Yes	No	Total	Very Less	Less	Sufficient	More	Can't Say	Total
Udaipur	N	53	28	81	3	54	15	–	7	81
	%	65.43	34.57	100	3.70	66.67	18.52	–	8.64	100
Dungarpur	N	32	16	48	4	32	12	–	–	48
	%	66.67	33.33	100	8.33	66.67	25	–	–	100

Table 6.70 revealed that about 65% respondents in both the districts had knowledge about the rate of interest they were

getting on their F.D. a/c. When respondents were asked about their opinion regarding the rate of interest they were getting on their F.D. a/c, nearly, two-third women F.D. a/c holders of both the districts had opinion that bank were providing very less rate of interest.

Table 6.71. Whether Respondents Avail Loan Facilities Against F.D. A/c

Districts		Yes	No	Total
Udaipur	N	18	63	81
	%	22.22	77.78	100
Dungarpur	N	7	41	48
	%	14.58	85.42	100

Only 22.22% respondents in Udaipur district and 14.58% respondents in Dungarpur district had taken loan against F.D. a/c while the rest of the beneficiaries had not taken loan against F.D. a/c.

Table 6.72. Whether Respondents Renew their F.D. Just after Maturity?

Districts		Yes	No	Total
Udaipur	N	61	20	81
	%	75.31	24.69	100
Dungarpur	N	37	11	48
	%	77.08	22.92	100

As Table 6.72 reveals, in both the district generally three-fourth F.D. a/c holders renewed their F.D. just after maturity.

Table 6.73. Experience of Respondents with Bankers

Districts		Very Satisfactory	Satisfactory	Normal	Unsatisfactory	Rude	Do not know	Total
Udaipur	N	12	37	25	–	1	6	81
	%	14.81	45.68	30.86	–	1.23	7.41	100
Dungarpur	N	24	13	11	–	–	–	48
	%	50	27.08	22.92	–	–	–	100

In both the districts women were generally satisfied with the behaviour of Bankers. About 14.81% respondents of Udaipur district and 50% respondents of Dungarpur district were highly impressed by good behaviour of bankers.

(E) OPERATION OF NON-RESIDENT ACCOUNT BY WOMEN

Table 6.74. Respondents Having Number of N.R.I. A/c with Bank

Districts		0	1	2	3	4	Total No. of N.R.I. a/c	Average a/c per women
Udaipur	N	–	2	–	–	–	2	0.02
Dungarpur	N	–	4	–	–	–	4	0.04

As Table 6.74 clearly indicate that in both the districts very few women had N.R.I. a/c with banks. Out of 100 beneficiaries 2 women of Udaipur district and 4 of Dungarpur district had N.R.I. a/c with bank and no woman had more than one N.R.I. a/c. In Udaipur district every woman had average 0.02 N.R.I. a/c while in Dungarpur district every woman had average 0.04 N.R.I. a/c.

Table 6.75. Bank Group-wise and Bank-wise Distribution of N.R.I. A/c

Districts		Public Sector Bank				Private Sector Bank	Co-operative Bank	Regional Rural Bank	Total
		BOB	PNB	SBBJ	Total	–	–	–	
Udaipur	N	–	1	1	2	–	–	–	2
Dungarpur	N	2	1	1	4	–	–	–	4

Table 6.75 revealed that Bank Group-wise and Bank-wise distribution of N.R.I. a/c. in both the district cent per cent women had N.R.I. a/c with public sector bank.

In public sector bank, women had their a/c with PNB and SBBJ in both the district while in Dungarpur district women also had N.R.I. a/c in BOB.

Table 6.76. Reasons for Opening N.R.I. A/c with Particular Bank

Districts		Near to Residence	Near to working place	Bank Employees are Friend/ Relative	On request of Husband/ Father	Bank are paying more Interest	Total
Udaipur	N	1	–	1	–	–	2
Dungarpur	N	1	–	2	1	–	4

Table 6.76 analyse that one woman N.R.I. a/c holder of Udaipur district and two of Dungarpur district opened their N.R.I. a/c with particular bank branch because they had good relations with bankers. And 1 respondent of both district open their N.R.I. a/c in particular bank branch because bank was near to their residence. In Dungarpur district one respondent open her a/c on the request of husband.

Table 6.77. Whether Respondents have Individual or Joint N.R.I. A/c with Bank

District		Individual A/c	Joint A/c with						Total
			Husband	Father	Son/ Daughter	Brother/ Sister	Others	Total	
Udaipur	N	1	–	–	1	–	–	1	2
Dungarpur	N	–	2	–	2	–	–	4	4

As Table 6.77 showed that 50% N.R.I. a/c in Udaipur district and cent per cent N.R.I. a/c in Dungarpur district were joint with Son/Daughter/Husband.

Table 6.78. N.R.I A/c is Operated by Whom

Districts		By Respondent	Husband	Father	Son/ Daughter	Brother Sister	Others	Total
Udaipur	N	1	–	–	1	–	–	2
Dungarpur	N	–	2	–	2	–	–	4

In Udaipur district, one N.R.I. a/c was operated by respondent herself and one was operated by respondent's son.

While in Dungarpur district 2 (50%) a/c were operated by respondent's Son/Daughter and rest 2 (50%) were operated by respondent's Husband.

Table 6.79 showed that 50% respondents of both the districts lastly operated their N.R.I. a/c with in a month and rest 50% N.R.I. in both the districts operated by women during last six months.

Table 6.79. Last Time When Respondent Operate their NRI A/c

Districts		Within 15 Days	Before a Month	Before a Quarter	Before Six Month	Before One year	Before Two Years	More than two years	Total
Udaipur	N	–	1	1	–	–	–	–	1
Dungarpur	N	1	1	1	1	–	–	–	4

Table 6.80 revealed that 50% respondents of both the districts were getting foreign currency from their husband and rest 50% were getting from their son.

In Udaipur district, all respondents were getting currency from U.S.A. (dollars) while in Dungarpur district 2 respondents were getting currency from Saudi Arabia (Rial) and 1 was getting from Tanzania (Shillings).

Table 6.80. Respondents Getting Foreign Currency by Whom and from Which Country?

Districts		Source of Currency				
		Husband	Father	Son	Brother/Sister	Total
Udaipur	N	1	–	1	–	2
Dungarpur	N	2	–	2	–	4

According to table 6.81 50% NRI a/c holders of both the districts generally had knowledge of their balance while rest 50% N.R.I. a/c holders of both the districts occasionally had knowledge of their balance. All women N.R.I. a/c holders of Udaipur district and 2 (50%) of Dungarpur district had knowledge about the rate of interest they were getting on their

Table 6.81. Whether Respondent Know About Balance and Interest they are Getting on their N.R.I. A/c? And their Opinion About the Rate of Interest

District		Knowledge of respondent about their balance in N.R.I a/c					Knowledge about the rate of interest they are getting on N.R.I. a/c			Opinion about the rate of interest				
		Always	Generally	Occasionally	Never	Total	Yes	No	Total	Very less	Less	Sufficient	More	Total
Udaipur	N	–	1	1	–	2	2	–	2	1	1	–		2
Dungarpur	N	–	2	2	–	4	2	2	4	1	3	–		4

N.R.I. a/c. And cent per cent respondents of both the districts felt that bankers were providing less interest on N.R.I. A/c.

Table 6.82. Experience of Respondents with Bankers

Districts		Very Satisfactory	Satisfactory	Normal	Unsatisfactory	Rude	Total
Udaipur	N	1	1	–	–	–	2
Dungarpur	N	2	1	1	–	–	4

In the opinion of women N.R.I. a/c holders, male and female employees of banks were very helpful and their overall experience with bank was satisfactory.

(E) OPERATION OF SAFE DEPOSIT LOCKER ACCOUNT BY WOMEN

Table 6.83 visualising respondent having number of Safe Deposit Locker A/c with bank. In Udaipur district 100% women had only one S.D.L a/c with bank, whereas in Dungarpur district, 97.44% women had only on S.D.L. a/c. In Dungarpur district, 1 (2.56%) women had 3 S.D.L a/c. In Udaipur district, every woman had average 0.46 S.D.L. a/c while in Dungarpur district every woman had only 0.41 S.D.L. a/c.

Table 6.83. Respondents Having Number of Safe Locker A/c with Bank

District		0	1	2	3	Total A/c Holder	Total No. of S.D.L. A/c	Average S.D.L. a/c
Udaipur	N	–	46	–	–	46	46	0.46
	%	–	100	–	–	100		
Dungarpur	N	–	38	–	1	39	41	0.41
	%	–	97.44	–	2.56	100		

Bank group-wise classification of S.D.L. a/c (Table 6.84) showed that in Udaipur and Dungarpur district women had 84.78% and 51.22% S.D.L. a/c with Public Sector Bank, respectively. In Private Sector Bank, 8.70% and 21.95% S.D.L. a/c belong to women in Udaipur and Dungarpur district, respectively. Only 6.52% women had S.D.L. a/c with

Table 6.84. Bank Group-wise and Bank-wise Distribution of Safe Deposit Locker A/c

Districts	Bank-wise	Bank group-wise public sector Bank												
		BOB	SBBJ	SBI	CBI	PNB	Maharashtra Bank	BOI	UBI	IOB	PSB	OBC	A' Bad	Total
Udaipur	N	5	5	2	4	4	2	2	2	2	3	4	4	39
	%	10.87	10.87	4.35	8.70	8.70	4.35	4.35	4.35	4.35	6.52	8.70	8.70	84.78
Dungarpur	N	15	3	–	*	3	*	*	*	*	*	*	*	21
	%	36.59	7.32	–	*	7.32	*	*	*	*	*	*	*	51.22

Districts	Bank-wise	Private Sector Bank		Bank group-wise Co-operative Bank		Regional Rural Bank		Grand Total
		The Bank of Rajasthan Ltd.	Total	UUCB/ DCCB	Total	MAGB/ DBKGB	Total	
Udaipur	N	4	4	3	3	–	–	46
	%	8.70	8.70	6.52	6.52	–	–	100
Dungarpur	N	9	9	–	–	11	11	41
	%	21.95	21.95	–	–	26.83	26.83	100

Co-operative Bank (UCCB), in Udaipur district. While in Dungarpur district no woman had S.D.L. a/c with Co-operative Bank. In Dungarpur district, 26.83% woman had S.D.L. a/c with R.R.B. (DBKGB) whereas no woman had S.D.L. a/c with R.R.B. in Udaipur district.

The above analysis clearly indicate that in Udaipur district women had more S.D.L. A/c with Public Sector Bank and Co-operative Bank while in Dungarpur district women had more S.D.L. a/c with Private Sector Bank and Regional Rural Bank.

Table 6.84 revealed that in Udaipur and Dungarpur district women had 39 and 21 S.D.L. a/c with Public Sector Bank. In both the districts most of the women had their S.D.L. a/c with BOB, SBBJ, and PNB. In Udaipur district, many women also had S.D.L. a/c with CBI, SBI, Maharashtra Bank, BOI, UBI, IOB, PSB, OBC and A'Bad Bank in Private Sector Bank, 4 women of Udaipur district and 9 of Dungarpur district had S.D.L. a/c with The Bank of Rajasthan Ltd. In Udaipur district 3 women had S.D.L. a/c with Udaipur Central Co-operative Bank (Co-operative Banks). While in Dungarpur district 11 respondents had S.D.L. a/c with DBKBG (RRB).

Table 6.85. Reason's for Opening Safe Deposit Locker A/c with Particular Bank Branch

Districts		Near to Residence	Near to Working Place	Bank Employees Friend/ Relative	Low Locker Charges	On Request of Husband/ Father	Locker Were available only in that Bank	Service in same bank
Udaipur	N	18	–	14	1	14	2	3
Dungarpur	N	9	4	21	5	23	–	–

Table 6.85 investigate that 18 respondents of Udaipur district and 9 of Dungarpur district had S.D.L. a/c with particular bank branch because that branch was close to their residence. 14 and 23 women of Udaipur and Dungarpur district, respectively, open their a/c on the request of their husband. And 14 and 21 women had good relation with bankers that was sufficient reason for them to open their S.D.L a/c with particular bank branch. The other reasons for opening S.D.L a/c with particular bank branch were low locker charges, near to working place, service in the same branch and lockers were available only in that branch.

Table 6.86. Purpose for Uses Locker Facilities

District		To keep Jewelley	To keep Documents	To keep Cash	Others
Udaipur	N	45	10	2	–
Dungarpur	N	43	5	–	–

Table 6.86 clearly indicate that most of the women of both the districts used locker facility to keep their jewellery. While 10 women of Udaipur district and 5 of Dungarpur district also used locker facility to keep their important and confidential documents. In Udaipur district 2 respondents also used locker facility to keep their cash.

Table 6.87. Whether Respondents have Individual or Joint Safe Deposit Locker A/c with Banks?

Districts		Individual	Joint A/c with				Total
			Husband	Father	Son/ Daughter	Brother Sister	Mother/ Mother in-law	
Udaipur	N	–	36	–	2	1	7	46
Dungarpur	N	–	40		1	–	–	41

The study revealed that in both the district nearly cent per cent women had joint S.D.L a/c. Most of the women had joint S.D.L. a/c with their husband and upto some extent with their mother-in-law, Son, Daughter, Brother and Sister.

Table 6.88. Safe Deposit Locker A/c is Operated by whom?

Districts		Respondent	Husband	Mother	Son/ Daughter	Brother/ Sister	Daughter in-Law
Udaipur	N	32	26	–	3	1	1
Dungarpur	N	16	39	4	–	1	–

Table 6.88 envisage that in Udaipur district 32 S.D.L a/c and 16 S.D.L. a/c in Dungarpur district was operated by a/c holder themselves 31 and 44 a/c in Udaipur and Dungarpur district, respectively, were operated by respondents husband mother/son/daughter-in-law etc.

Table 6.89. Frequency of Operation of Safe Deposit Locker A/c

Districts		Once in a year	Twice in a year	Thrice in a year	Four Times	5 to 8 Times	9 to 12 Times	13 to 24 Times	Total
Udaipur	N	8	5	10	5	6	7	5	46
	%	17.39	10.87	21.74	10.87	13.04	15.22	10.87	100
Dungarpur	N	9	3	23	–	5	1	–	41
	%	21.95	7.32	56.10	–	12.20	2.44	–	100

Table 6.89 clearly indicate that women of Udaipur district operated more lockers compare to women of Dungarpur district.

In Udaipur district 5 (10.87%), 7 (15.22%), 6 (13.04%) and 5 (10.87%) women operated lockers 13 to 24 times, 9 to 12 times, 5 to 8 times and four times in a year respectively. Whereas, in Dungarpur district 1 (2.44%) and 5 (12.20%) women operated lockers 9 to 12 times and 5 to 8 times in a year respectively. On the other side in Udaipur and Dungarpur district 8 (17.39%) and 9 (21.95%) women operated their S.D.L. a/c only once in a year, 5 (10.87%) and 3 (7.32%) twice in a year and 10 (21.74%) and 23 (56.10%) women operated their S.D.L. a/c thrice in a year respectively.

Table 6.90. Whether Respondent Deposit F.D. for Locker Facilities and their Amount

Districts		Did respondent deposit F.D. to getting locker facility			Amount of F.D.				
		Yes	No	Total	Upto 5000	5001 to 20,000	20,001 to 50,000	More than 50,001	Total
Udaipur	N	16	30	46	14	–	2	–	16
	%	34.78	65.22	100	87.5	–	12.5	–	100
Dungarpur	N	2	39	41	1	1	–	–	2
	%	4.88	95.12	100	50	50	–	–	100

As Table 6.90 visualising that out of 46, 16(34.78%) beneficiaries of Udaipur district and out of 41,2 (4.88%) women of Dungarpur district deposited F.D. to get locker facility.

Amount-wise classification showed that 14 (87.5%) and 1 (50%) respondent in Udaipur and Dungarpur district, respectively, deposited F.D. upto Rs. 5,000 to get locker facility. While in Udaipur district 2 (12.5%) women deposited F.D. of Rs. 20 to 50 thousand and in Dungarpur district 1 woman deposited F.D. of Rs. 5 to 20 thousand.

Table 6.91. How much Annual Locker Charges Charged by Banker? And Respondent Opinion about the Rent

Districts		Annual locker charges					Opinion about the rent charge			
		1-250	251-500	501-1000	Do not know	Total	Less	Normal	More	Total
Udaipur	N	12	9	–	25	46	5	28	13	46
	%	26.09	19.56	–	54.35	100	10.87	60.87	28.26	100
Dungarpur	N	5	17	–	19	41	–	21	20	41
	%	12.20	41.46	–	46.34	100	–	51.22	48.78	100

Table 6.91 depicts that 45.65% and 53.66% women of Udaipur and Dungarpur district respectively were paying annual charges of locker upto Rs. 500. While 54.35% and 46.34% women of Udaipur and Dungarpur district, respectively, did not know about the annual charges they were paying for locker. More than fifty per cent women S.D.L. a/c holders of both the districts admitted that locker charges was normal.

Table 6.92. Whether Respondent have S.B. A/c with Bank

Districts		Yes	No	Others	Total
Udaipur	N	36	6	4	46
	%	78.26	13.04	8.70	100
Dungarpur	N	31	10	–	41
	%	75.61	24.39	–	100

*Others : 1. A/c is in the name of Husband.

2. A/c had been but now closed.

In both the district, more than 75% S.D.L. a/c holders also had S.B. a/c with the same bank.

Table 6.93. Experience of Respondents with Bankers

Districts		Very Satisfactory	Satisfactory	Normal	Unsatisfactory	Rude	Total
Udaipur	N	10	13	23	–	–	46
	%	21.74	28.26	50	–	–	100
Dungarpur	N	12	28	–	1	–	41
	%	29.27	68.29	–	2.44	–	100

In the opinion of women S.D.L. a/c holders, male and female employees of banks were very co-operative for them. In the opinion of 10 (21.74%) women of Udaipur district and 12 (29.27%) women of Dungarpur district their overall experience with bank was very satisfactory, while in the opinion of 13 (28.26%) women of Udaipur district and 28 (68.29%) women of Dungarpur district it was satisfactory. Whereas, in Udaipur district 23 (50%) women indicate that their experience with bank was normal.

(E) OPERATION OF LOAN AND ADVANCES ACCOUNT BY WOMEN

Table 6.94. Respondents Having Number of Loan and Advance A/c with Bank

Districts		1	2	Total	Total No. of Loan a/c	Average loan a/c per women
Udaipur	N	32	2	34	36	0.36
	%	94.12	5.88	100		
Dungarpur	N	12	–	12	12	0.12
	%	100	–	100		

The analysis of Table 6.94 showed that the beneficiaries were having number of loan and advances A/c. In Udaipur district 32 (94.12%) women and 12 (100%) women in Dungarpur district had only one loan a/c. In Udaipur district only 2 (5.88%) women had two loan a/c. Every woman had average 0.36, and 0.12 loan a/c in Udaipur and Dungarpur district, respectively.

Bank group-wise analysis of loan a/c (Table 6.95) revealed that in Udaipur district 26 (72.22%) beneficiaries had loan a/c in Public Sector Bank, where as, in Dungarpur district, it was

Table 6.95. Bank Group-wise and Bank-wise distribution of loan and advances A/c

Districts	Bank Group Wise	Public Sector Bank								
	Bank wise	SBBJ	SBI	BOB	Allahabad Bank	PNB	CBI	Vijaya Bank	UBI	Total
Udaipur	N	4	1	6	2	5	4	2	2	26
	%	11.11%	2.78	16.67	5.55	13.89	11.11	5.55	5.55	72.22
Dungarpur	N	–	–	–	*	–	*	*	*	–
	%	–	–	–	*	–	*	*	*	–

Districts	Bank Group wise	Private Sector Bank		Co-operative Bank			Regional Rural Bank		Grand Total
	Bank wise	The Bank of Rajasthan Ltd.	Total	UCCB/ DCCB	MUCB	Total	MAGB/ DBKGB	Total	
Udaipur	N	2	2	5	3	8	–	–	36
	%	5.55	5.55	13.89	8.33	22.22	–	–	100
Dungarpur	N	9	9	3	*	3	–	–	12
	%	75	75	25.00	*	25.00	–	–	100

surprising, that no respondent had loan a/c in this sector. In Private Sector Bank, 2 (5.55%) and 9 (75%) loan a/c belongs to women in Udaipur and Dungarpur district, respectively. In Co-operative Bank, 8 (22.22%) and 3 (25%) loan a/c belongs to women in Udaipur and Dungarpur district, respectively. While in R.R.B. no women of both the districts had loan a/c.

The above analysis clearly indicate that in Udaipur district mostly women had loan a/c with Public Sector Bank while in Dungarpur district, mostly women had loan a/c with Private Sector Bank. In both the district, no women had loan a/c with R.R.B and nearly one-fourth women had loan a/c with Co-operative Bank.

As Table 6.95 showed that in Public Sector Banks women had 26 loan a/c in Udaipur district and women had a/c in SBBJ, SBI, BOB, Allahabad Bank, PNB, CBI, Vijaya Bank, and UBI. 2 and 9 women had loan a/c with The Bank of Rajasthan Ltd. (Private Sector Bank) in Udaipur and Dungarpur district, respectively. In Udaipur district women had 8 loan a/c in Co-operative Bank i.e. 5 in UCCB and 3 in MUCB, where as, in Dungarpur district women had 3 loan a/c in DCCB.

Table 6.96, *(See page 304)* visualise that 10 respondents of Udaipur district and 3 respondents of Dungarpur district opened their loan a/c in particular bank branch because it was near to their working place. 7 and 4 women of Udaipur and Dungarpur district, respectively, opened their loan a/c in particular bank branch because they had good relations with bankers. And 5 respondents of both the district opened their a/c because particular branch was near to their residence. In Udaipur district 10 women opened their loan a/c with particular bank branch on the request of their husband. In Udaipur district, 16 women opened their loan a/c with particular bank branch due to other reasons such as being bank employee, salary deposited and they got easily loan etc.

Total 6.97, *(See page 304)* showed that, one-third and two-third beneficiaries of Udaipur and Dungarpur district, respectively taken loan for Housing. And 5 (13.89%) and 4 (33.33%) respondents of Udaipur and Dungarpur district,

Table 6.96. Reasons for Opening Loan and Advances A/c with Particular Bank Branch

Districts		Near to Residence	Near to Working place	Bank Employee are Friend/ Relative	On Request of Banker	Special Facilities	On Recommendation of DRDA/DIC	On request of Husband/ Father	Others
Udaipur	N	5	10	7	–	–	–	10	6
Dungarpur	N	5	3	4	–	–	–	–	–

Table 6.97. Purpose-wise Distribution of Loan and Advance A/c?

Districts		Vehicle	Housing	Consumer Goods	Education	Business	Self Employment	Agriculture purpose	Under Govt. Scheme	Marriage	Total
Udaipur	N	10	12	5	–	5	2	–	–	2	36
	%	27.78	33.33	13.89	–	13.89	5.56	–	–	5.55	
Dungarpur	N	–	8	4	–	–	–	–	–	–	12
	%	–	66.67	33.33	–	–	–	–	–	–	

Table 6.98. Duration-wise and Amount-wise Distribution of Loan A/c

Districts		Duration-wise						Amount-wise				
		1 year	2 year	upto 3 year	More than 3 year to 5 year	More than 5 year	Total	10,001 to 25,000	25,001 to 1 lac	1 lac to 2 lacs	More than 2 lacs	Total
Udaipur	N	–	1	11	12	12	36	12	15	5	4	36
	%	–	2.78	30.56	33.33	33.33	100	33.33	41.67	13.89	11.11	100
Dungarpur	N	5	–	3	–	4	12	4	1	7	–	12
	%	41.67	–	25.00	–	33.33	100	33.33	8.33	58.33	–	100

Table 6.99. Documents Required by Bank Against Loan

Districts	Caste Certificate	Age Certificate	Educational Certificate	Income Certificate	Ration Card	Training Certificate	Handicapped Certificates	P & L A/c and Balance Sheet	House Document	Vehicle Document
Udaipur	–	1	–	27	9	–	–	5	12	10
Dungarpur	–	–	–	12	–	–	–	–	8	–

respectively taken loan for consumer goods. In Udaipur district respondents also taken loan for vehicle 10 (27.78%), Business 5 (13.89%), Self-employment 2 (5.56%) and for Marriage 2 (5.55%) whereas, in Dungarpur district no respondent taken loan for these purposes. In both districts no women taken loan for Education, Agriculture purpose and under any government scheme.

Duration-wise distribution of loan a/c (Table 6.98) indicate that one-third and two-third respondents of Udaipur and Dungarpur district respectively had taken loan upto the period of three years. In Udaipur district one-third beneficiaries had taken loan in between the period of 4 and 5 years. While in both the district one-third respondent had taken loan for more than 5 years.

Amount–wise distribution of loan a/c showed that, one-third respondents of both the districts had taken loan between Rs. 10 and 25 thousands. 15 (41.67%) and 1 (8.33%) respondents of Udaipur and Dungarpur district respectively had taken loan of Rs. 0.25 lac to Rs. 1 lac amount. And 9 (25.00%) and 7 (58.33%) beneficiaries of Udaipur and Dungarpur district, respectively, had taken loan of Rs. more than 1 lac.

In both the district generally women produce documents related to House and Vehicle, their income certificate, P & L a/c, and Balance sheet, Residential Certificate and Ration Card etc. to bankers against loan. (Table 6.99)

Table 6.100. Marginal Money Arranged by Respondents

Districts						If yes, then amount of marginal money			
		Yes	No	Do not Know	Total	1 to 2000	2001 to 3000	More than 3000	Total
Udaipur	N	12	11	13	36	3	6	3	12
	%	33.33	30.56	36.11	100	25	50	25	100
Dungarpur	N	–	12	–	12	–	–	–	–
	%	–	100	–	100	–	–	–	–

Table 6.100 showed that only one-third beneficiaries of Udaipur district arranged marginal money for loans upto Rs. 3

thousand.

Table 6.101. Time Taken in Sanctioning and Disbursement of Loan

Districts		In sanctioning of loan			in disbursement of loan		
		15 days	16 days to 1 month	Total	15 days	16 days to 1 month	Total
Udaipur	N	31	5	36	32	4	36
	%	86.11	13.89	100	88.89	11.11	100
Dungarpur	N	9	3	12	9	3	12
	%	75	25	100	75	25	100

In the opinion of more than three-fourth beneficiaries they got loan within a month. While rest of the beneficiaries got loan within two months.

Table 6.102. Respondents Opinion about Loan Amount and Source of Arrangement for Insufficient Amount

District		Loan amount was sufficient			If not, than taken from any source		
		Yes	No	Total	Yes	No	Total
Udaipur	N	33	3	36	3	–	3
	%	91.67	8.33	100	100	–	100
Dungarpur	N	12	–	12	–	–	–
	%	100	–	100	–	–	–

The investigation revealed that loan amount was sufficient. Except 3 (8.33%) respondents of Udaipur district, they were requiring more money for their business from Rs. 10 to 30 thousand and they arranged desired amount from their relatives and friends.

Table 6.103 showed that 33.33% and 58.33% women a/c holders of Udaipur and Dungarpur district admitted that the rate of interest charged by bank on loan amount was very high. While 33.33% and 41.67% respondents admitted that it was moderate. In Udaipur district for 16.67% respondents it was low and 16.67% respondents had no idea about the rate of interest they way paying.

Table 6.103. Opinion of Respondent Regarding the Rate of Interest

Districts		Very High	High	Moderate	Low	Very Low	Can't Say	Total
Udaipur	N	5	7	12	5	1	6	36
	%	13.89	19.44	33.33	13.89	2.78	16.67	100
Dungarpur	N	–	7	5	–	–	–	12
	%	–	58.33	41.67	–	–	–	100

Table 6.104 clearly indicate that cent per cent respondents of both the districts utilized the loan for which it has been taken.

Table 6.104. Proper Utilization of Loan Amount

Districts		Yes	No	Total
Udaipur	N	36	–	36
	%	100	–	100
Dungarpur	N	12	–	12
	%	100	–	100

Table 6.105, revealed that 33 (91.67%) and 12 (100%) respondents of Udaipur and Dungarpur district respectively were repaying regular loan instalments. In case of other moratorium period was going on at the time of interview.

All the respondents of Dungarpur district and 26 (78.79%) respondents of Udaipur district were repaying loan through their or their husbands regular income. While the rest 7 (21.21%) in Udaipur district repaying loan through the income generated from their venture.

About 25% respondent of both the districts repaid cent per cent loan amount 8 (24.24%) and 2 (16.67%) respondents of Udaipur and Dungarpur district respectively repaid their loan amount in between 76% and 99%. 15 (45.46%) respondents of Udaipur district repaid their loan from 26% to 75%. While 2 (6.06%) respondents of Udaipur district and 7 (58.33%) respondents of Dungarpur district repaid upto 25% of their loan amount.

7 (21.22%) respondent in Udaipur district and 10 (83.33%) respondent in Dungarpur district were repaying loan instalment

Table 6.105. Repayment of Loan

Districts		Regular payment of loan instalment				Source of repayment					
		Yes	No	Not due	Total	Income generated from venture	Disposal fassets of venture	From claim of insurance co.	Income earned from additional work	Regular income	Total
Udaipur	N	33	–	3	36	7	–	–	–	26	33
	%	91.67	–	8.33	100	21.21	–	–	–	78.79	100
Dungarpur	N	12	–	–	12	–	–	–	–	12	12
	%	100	–	–	100	–	–	–	–	100	100

Districts		Extent of repayment						Reasons for repaying regular instalment					
		Upto 25%	26% to 50%	51% to 75%	76% to 99%	100%	Total	Fear of Legal action	Fear of Social Prestige	Regular follow up by Bank	Moral duty	Deduction from salary	Total
Udaipur	N	2	10	5	8	8	33	6	10	5	7	5	33
	%	6.06	30.30	15.16	24.24	24.24	100	18.18	30.30	15.15	21.22	15.15	100
Dungarpur	N	7	–	–	2	3	12	–	–	2	10	–	12
	%	58.33	–	–	16.67	25.00	100	–	–	16.67	83.33	–	100

simply because any loan that is taken should be repaid that is our moral duty while 5 (15.15%) and 2 (16.67%) in Udaipur and Dungarpur district respectively were repaying loan instalment due to the reminder sent by bank. In Udaipur district rest were repaying loan instalment as they were afraid of legal action 6 (18.18%), due to fear of social prestige 10 (30.30%). In case of 5 (15.15%) respondent loan instalment automatically deduct from their salary.

The Table 6.106, showed that all the respondents of Udaipur district were not faced any problem when they applied for loan and other 3 (8.33%) revealed that application form was complexed.

About 95% and 92% respondents of Udaipur and Dungarpur district respectively not faced any problem when loan sanctioned and disbursed to them. While others faced problem of long duration. In Udaipur district only 2 women found there was low demand of their product after starting of the venture.

Table 6.107 revealed that In Udaipur district, out of 11 women 7 (63.64%) got full employment and 2 (18.18%) women got partial employment by bank loans.

Out of 20 women 5 (25%) women felt that their regular income moderately increase while 7 (35%) felt that their regular income slightly increase by bank loan.

In the opinion of 4 (15.38%) respondent their property highly increase and 13 (50%) respondent felt that their property moderately increase while 6 (23.08%) women felt that their property slightly increase by utilization of bank loan.

Out of 30 women beneficiaries 17 (56.67%) women admitted that their living standard moderately increased while 2 (6.66%) women admitted that their living standard highly increased by utilization of bank loan.

In Dungarpur district 12 (100%) women admitted that their property moderately increased by bank loan. Out of 12 women 5 (41.67%) women admitted that their living standard highly increased while 7 (58.33%) women admitted that their living standard moderately increased by utilization of bank loan.

Table 6.106. Problem Faced by Respondents

Districts		When apply for loan					On the stage of loan sanction and disbursed				
		Problem in getting form	Complexed app. form	Others	No problem	Total	Paid bribe	Apply Jack	Long Duration	No Problem	Total
Udaipur	N	–	3	–	33	36	–	–	2	34	36
	%	8.33	–	–	91.67	100	–	–	5.56	94.44	100
Dungarpur	N	–	–	–	12	12	–	–	1	11	12
	%	–	–	–	100	100	–	–	8.33	91.67	100

Districts		On the stage of Starting venture			
		Lack of Infra structure facilities	No Raw Material	Low Demand of product	Total
Udaipur	N	–	–	2	2
	%	–	–	100	100
Dungarpur	N	–	–	–	–
	%	–	–	–	–

Table 6.107. Impact of Loan

Districts		On Employment generation					On Regular Income					
		Not applicable	Partial	Full	No effect	Total	Not applicable	Highly increase	Moderately increase	Low increase	No effect	Total
Udaipur	N	25	2	7	2	11	16	–	5	7	8	20
	%	–	18.18	63.64	18.18	100	–	–	25	35	40	100
Dungarpur	N	12	–	–	–	–	12	–	–	–	–	–
	%	–	–	–	–	–	–	–	–	–	–	–

Districts		On Increase in Property						On Standard of living					
		Not applicable	Highly increase	Moderately increase	Low increase	No effect	Total	Not applicable	High increase	Moderately increase	Low increase	No effect	Total
Udaipur	N	10	4	13	6	3	26	6	2	17	4	7	30
	%	–	15.38	50.00	23.08	11.54	100	–	6.66	56.67	13.33	23.33	100
Dungarpur	N	–	–	12	–	–	12	–	5	7	–	–	12
	%	–	–	100	–	–	100	–	41.67	58.33	–	–	100

Table 6.108. Experience of Respondents with Banks

Districts		Very Satisfactory	Satisfactory	Normal	Unsatisfactory	Rude	Total
Udaipur	N	11	17	8	-	-	36
	%	30.56	47.22	22.22	-	-	100
Dungarpur	N	5	1	6	-	-	12
	%	41.67	8.33	50	-	-	100

Table 6.108 revealed that, in the opinion of three-fourth women of Udaipur district and fifty per cent women of Dungarpur district the attitude of bankers in the whole process of sanctioning and disbursing loan was quite satisfactory.

7 A Case Study of Women Working in Banking Sector in Udaipur and Dungarpur Districts of Rajasthan

The data for this investigation were collected from the primary sources. For collection of primary data following schedule was constructed and adopted.

THE SCHEDULE FOR WOMEN BANK EMPLOYEES

The schedule was used to collect various information relating to the women working in banking sector. For the purpose, a comprehensive list of 50 women working in Udaipur district was prepared. Out of them 25 women selected on the random basis. Only one woman was working in Dungarpur district. Women bank employee were asked to fill up the schedules containing questions relating to procedure of selection, promotion opportunities, reasons of being in bank service, training, transfer, co-operation of family members, family life, working experience, effects of job on their living standard, Assets, sources of income and family expenditure, confrontation in bank, significant responsibilities and extra remunerative work in bank, working condition in bank, problem faced during working hours, satisfaction with profession and attitude of customers and colleagues towards them etc. along with social, economical and educational status of respondents. Udaipur districts had total 183 bank branches, women were employed in every bank group i.e. public sector bank, private sector bank, co-operative bank and regional rural bank.

Dungarpur district had total 173 bank branches, an amazing feature, that emerged, was only one woman bank employee in the whole district. The only woman was working in DCCB of Dungarpur city. The respondent got employment due to the death of her husband.

The composition of the women bank employee in both the districts is alike i.e. Manager, Accountant officer, Computer operator and clerk.

THE DETAILS OF SCHEDULE OF WOMEN BANK EMPLOYEES

Udaipur District

Table 7.1. Age-wise Distribution of Respondents

District		Age					
		18-25	26-35	36-45	46-50	51-60	Total
Udaipur	N	3	10	11	1	–	25
	%	12	40	44	4	–	100

In Udaipur district (Table 7.1), majority of respondents 21 (84%) falls in between the middle age group of 26 and 45 years of age. On the other hand, 3 (12%) respondents were in the age group of 18 and 25, on the contrary 1 (4%) respondent were belong to the age group of 46-50.

Out of 25 respondents in Udaipur district 20 (80%) were of Hindu, 3 (12%) were of Jain and 2 (8%) were of Muslim caste (Table 7.2). In Udaipur district S.C., S.T., O.B.C., Sikh and Christian women employees were not playing any vital role in banking sector. The above caste pattern also revealed predominance of general major castes.

Table 7.2. Caste-wise Distribution of Respondents

District		Castes								
		Hindu	Muslim	S.C.	S.T.	OBC	Sikh	Jain	Christian	Total
	N	20	2	–	–	–	–	3	–	25
Udaipur	%	80	8	–	–	–	–	12	–	100

Table 7.3 indicates that 11 (44%) women employees were Graduates and 13 (52%) were Post-graduates only 1 (4%) respondents was completed C.A. Inter group.

Table 7.3. Educational Status of Respondents

District		Educational Status							
		Sec./Sr. Hr. Sec.	Graduate	Post-graduate	B.E	M.B.A.	C.A. inter	Ph.D	Total
	N	–	11	13	–	–	1	–	25
Udaipur	%	–	44	52	–	–	4	–	100

Udaipur district (Table 7.4) had 183 bank branches at the end of year 2000. Out of 25 respondents 16 (64%) were working in public sector banks, 4 (16%) were working in co-operative banks, 3 (12%) were working in private sector bank and 2 (8%) were working in regional rural bank.

Table 7.4. Bank-wise and Bank Group-wise Distribution of Respondent

District		Public Sector Bank						
		PNB	SBBJ	BOB	SBI	CBI	Indian Bank	Sub Total
	N	5	3	3	2	2	1	16
Udaipur	%	20	12	12	8	8	4	64

District		Private sector bank		Co-operative banks			Regional rural bank		Grand total
		ICICI	Sub total	UMUCB	UCCB	Sub total	MAGB	Sub total	
	N	3	3	2	2	4	2	2	25
Udaipur	%	12	12	8	8	16	8	8	100

Bank-wise distribution of respondents clearly indicate that most of the women were working in Punjab National Bank, State Bank of Bikaner and Jaipur, Bank of Baroda, State Bank of India, Central Bank of India, ICICI Bank, Udaipur Urban Co-operative Bank, Udaipur Mahila Urban Co-operative Bank and Mewar Aanchlik Gramin Bank.

Table 7.5. Selection Procedure for Recruitment

District		Selection Procedure: On the basis of merit	Direct interview	Competitive exam	Total
Udaipur	N	1	1	23	25
	%	4	4	92	100

Recruitment of respondent (Table 7.5) is one of the most important aspect of service in an organisation like a Bank. Out of 25 (100%) respondents, 23 (92%) were selected through Bank competitive exams and personal interview. One respondent had been selected on the basis of merit in Udaipur Mahila Urban Co-operative Bank and she was Graduate at the time of selection while another respondent had been selected by direct interview in ICICI bank, respondent cleared her C.A. (inter).

Table 7.6. Whether Bank Provided any Training after Selection

District		Yes			No	Total
		Duration of training				
		Upto 2 weeks	2 to 4 weeks	Total		
Udaipur	N	9	4	13	12	25
	%	36	16	52	48	100

Training is the important aspect of service in an organisation like a bank hence it is considered to find out the process and extent of training after recruitment in bank service (Table 7.6). A majority of the respondents in Udaipur district 13 (52%) expressed that they were provided training after joining bank service while 12 (48%) did not get any training. Majority of respondents received training upto two weeks.

Table 7.7 clearly indicates that the main reason accepted by women respondent for being in service was for making career (19), self fulfilment (18), and to supplement family income and to improve family status (14). Another reason were for achieving recognition and respect by 12 respondents, for occupying themselves by 11 and due to low family income by 7 beneficiaries. Whereas very few of them join service for improve marriage prospects (5), to relieve tension arising from family (4) and to earn dowry (2).

Table 7.7. Why Respondents Joined Service

District		Because of low family income	To earn dowry	To improve marriage prospects	To supplement family income and improve family standard	Due to the death or in capacity of main bread winner
Udaipur	N	7	2	5	14	1

District		For occupying themselves	Self fulfil-ment	For achieving recognition and respect	To relieve tension arising from family	For making career
Udaipur	N	11	18	12	4	19

Table 7.8 reveals that 24 (96%) women joined their job as clerk/typist/cashier and 1 (4%) joined service as an accountant. However, 17 (68%) women were remain as clerk/typist/cashier, 2 (8%) were promoted to computer operator, 2 (8%) were promoted to the post of junior officer, 1 (4%) was promoted to manager and 2 (8%) were promoted as special assistant in the same branch. The only respondent who was promoted to manager reveals that transfer and promotion is no where hurdle for her.

Working experience of the respondent is the next important step of investigation and the data in this respect of Udaipur district (Table 7.9) revealed that new appointments were of 7 (28%) females while 9 (36%) respondents had experience of more than fifteen years. Thus, it showed that now females are aware about their career and ready to go to unusual fields. During 1985 to 1995, there were few appointments of females in banking sector.

Table 7.8. Present Status of Respondent and they Begin their Career as

District		Respondent started their career as			Present status of respondents						
		Clerk/Typist Cashier	Accountant	Total	Clerk/Typist Cashier	Computer Operator	Special Assistant	Officer	Accountant	Manager	Total
Udaipur	N	24	1	25	17	2	2	2	1	1	25
	%	96	4	100	68	8	8	8	4	4	100

Table 7.9. Working Experience of Respondents

District		In years					In rural area		
		0-5 years	More than 5 and upto 10	More than 10 upto 15 years	More than 15 years	Total	Yes	No	Total
Udaipur	N	7	4	5	9	25	2	23	25
	%	28	16	20	36	100	8	92	100

Table 7.9 showed that 23 (92%) female had never gone to rural areas and they were not even ready to accept promotion in rural areas because the parents of unmarried respondents would not allow them and married respondents did not want to go there because their family life would get disturbed and education of children, too. However, two respondents worked in rural area but the duration was only three months and one year.

Table 7.10. Whether Respondent will Accept Promotion if Transferred to Another Place

District		Yes	No	Not decided	Total
	N	8	15	2	25
Udaipur	%	32	60	8	100

An important aspect of employment involve promotion or transfer to other district/state. The relevant data in this regard (Table 7.10) revealed that majority of 60% respondents in Udaipur were not ready to accept promotion/transfer while 32% of them were ready to accept it. However, 8% respondents revealed that it depend on the posting place.

Thus, study reveals that respondents who did not want to accept promotion/transfer in other district/state reasons were family life, education of children could get disturbed and some respondents are not accepting promotion due to family responsibilities. Contrary, the rest of respondents who were ready to go other district or state revealed that promotion is no where hurdle for respondent instead it is a matter of happiness and joy.

The study revealed that 18 (72%) females were unmarried and 7 (28%) were married at the time of joining service (Table 7.11). The picture envisages that most of the females were career oriented in their unmarried hood. Whereas, the present marital status of respondent revealed that 80% of them were married. There were no divorcees and widows at the time of joining service and at the time of they interviewed. It also indicated the importance of marriage in Indian society as marriage was considered essential for socio-cultural reason. Which lied in the old tradition of the social structure.

Table 7.11. Marital and Family Status of Respondents and Extent of Co-operation with their Family Members

District		Marital status of respondent at the time of joining service					Present marital status of respondents				
		Unmarried	Married	Divorced	Widow	Total	Unmarried	Married	Divorced	Widow	Total
	N	18	7	–	–	25	5	20	–	–	25
Udaipur	%	72	28	–	–	100	20	80	–	–	100

District		Family status of respondents				Nuclear family						
						Co-operation from husband					Children	
		Alone	Nuclear	Joint	Total	Always	Often	Moderately	Rarely	Never	Total	N.A. due to unmarried
	N	–	16	9	25	8	2	1	2	–	13	3
Udaipur	%	–	64	36	100	61.54	15.38	7.69	15.38	–	100	–

(Contd...)

District		Joint family													
		Co-operation from husband							Co-operation from in-law						
		Always	Often	Moderately	Rarely	Never	Total	N.A.	Always	Often	Moderately	Rarely	Never	Total	N.A.
	N	4	1	–	1	1	7	2	4	1	2	–	–	7	2
Udaipur	%	57.14	14.29	–	14.28	14.29	100	–	57.14	14.29	28.57	–	–	100	–

District		Joint family													
		Co-operation from parents/brother/sister							Co-operation from children						
		Always	Often	Moderately	Rarely	Never	Total	N.A.	Always	Often	Moderately	Rarely	Never	Total	N.A.
	N	8	–	1	–	–	9	–	2	1	–	1	–	4	5
Udaipur	%	88.89	–	11.11	–	–	100	–	50	25	–	25	–	100	–

Family status of respondents showed that majority (64%) belongs to nuclear family. Which indicates that people were migrating to urban areas for employment and living in nuclear family. Respondents were getting maximum co-operation from their husbands were 10 (76.92%) while 2 (15.38%) were rarely getting co-operation from their husbands. In joint family, 5 (71.43%) women were getting full co-operation from their husband and in-laws while 2 (28.57%) were not getting full support from their husband and in-laws 88.89% parents were very supportive to their unmarried/married daughters, brothers and sisters were also very co-operating to their sister and nearly three fourth children were helping to their mothers in day-to-day work.

The investigation revealed that 13 (52%) bank employees were earning Rs. 7 to 10 thousand per month and 6 (24%) bank employees were getting less than Rs. 7 thousand per month while 6 (24%) bank employees were getting more than Rs. 10 thousand per month. This analysis indicate that the economic status of most of the women were quite satisfactory and providing substantial financial support to their families.

Table 7.12 indicate that most of the respondents husband 11 (55%) had income in between Rs. 7001 and 10000 per month and 6 (30%) respondents husband had income more than Rs. 10 thousand per month.

Table 7.12. Income-wise Classification of Respondents and their Husband

District		Respondents income					
		0-5000	5001-7000	7001-10000	10001-15000	More than 15000	Total
	N	2	4	13	5	1	25
Udaipur	%	8	16	52	20	4	100

District		Respondents husband income						
		0-5000	5001-7000	7001-10000	10001-15000	More than 15000	Total	Unmarried
	N	2	1	11	4	2	20	5
Udaipur	%	10	5	55	20	10	100	–

The study revealed that out of the 20 married bank employees, the husband of 8 (40%) married women had not sufficient income for family expenditure while combined income of family was sufficient to meet out the family expenditure (Table 7.13).

Table 7.13. Whether Respondents. Husband and their Income is Sufficient for Family Expenditure

District		Respondents husband income is sufficient for family expenditure				Respondent and their husband income is sufficient for family expenditure		
		Yes	No	Total	N.A.	Yes	No	Total
	N	12	8	20	5	25	–	25
Udaipur	%	60	40	100	–	100	–	100

The respondents were then asked (Table 7.14) if they ever thought of leaving the job if their family income increase and their responses to their query showed that an overwhelming majority 84% of them did not want to leave the job while only 16% of them admitted that they had thought that way.

Table 7.14. Whether Respondents will Leave their Job after Increasing their Family Income

District		Yes	No	Total
	N	4	21	25
Udaipur	%	16	84	100

Main motive behind to join a bank employment is to earn monetary income and later on improvement in living standard and purchase of more assets. Table 7.15 showed that in the opinion of 68% women their living standard improved and 56% women admitted that their family assets increased due to their job while in the opinion of 28% women their living standard improved to the slightest extent and 44% women admitted that their assets slightly increased.

Table 7.15. Effects of Respondents Income

District		On family living standard				
		Highly improved	Improved	Slightly improved	Not improved	Total
Udaipur	N	–	17	7	1	25
	%	–	68	28	4	100

District		Respondents and their husband income is sufficient for family expenditure				
		Highly improved	Improved	Slightly improved	Not improved	Total
Udaipur	N	1	13	11	–	25
	%	4	52	44	–	100

Table 7.16. Whether Respondents have Less Time for their Family Due to their Job?

District		Always	Often	Normally	Rarely	Total
Udaipur	N	5	3	7	10	25
	%	20	12	28	40	100

When women have dual responsibility at home and at bank, that may have not sufficient time for their family members. Table 7.16 shows that 32% bank employees view support this statement, however, 28% women in general felt that somewhere they were lacking in their family duties while 40% of women bank employee had not face this type of problem because their family members were very supportive and co-operative.

Table 7.17. Whether Respondents Job Affected their Kids?

District		Favourably	Unfavourably	Ambifavourably	Total
Udaipur	N	5	3	8	16
	%	31.25	18.75	50	100

Table 7.17 indicate that 50% respondents admitted that their job affected their children in both (negative and positive) ways. 18.75% women respondents were felt that they were not giving appropriate attention towards the studies of their children and to the overall development. While 31.25% women respondent thought that due to increase in income, they are in a position to provide good and higher education to their children.

In last few years bank started using computer, internet and provide facilities like internet banking, digital files in bank, ATM centres at convenient locations and electronic funds transfer service etc. The boom in information technology affected banking sector, so respondents were asked about the effects of information technology on their working 52% bankers felt that they were as busy as earlier because work pressure was same, the nature of job has been changed. Few of them revealed that still their bank was not connected through internet. While 44% of women admitted that they were less busy compare to past (Table 7.18).

Table 7.18. Effect of Computer and Internet on the Working of Respondents

District		Yes	No	Can't say	Total
	N	11	13	1	25
Udaipur	%	44	52	4	100

Next, women bank employees were asked about the privileges of being a female in selection, promotion, transfer and remunerative work (in Table 7.19). Majority of women revealed that they did not have any privilege in selection (88%), promotion (80%), remunerative work (68%) and in transfer (52%).

Table 7.19. Whether Respondents Enjoy Extra Facilities Being a Female Employee?

District		In selection					
		Very often	Often	Normally	Rarely	Never	Total
	N	–	–	1	2	22	25
Udaipur	%	–	–	4	8	88	100

District		In promotion					
		Very often	Often	Normally	Rarely	Never	Total
	N	–	–	5	–	20	25
Udaipur	%	–	–	20	–	80	100

(Contd...)

District		In transfer					
		Very often	Often	Normally	Rarely	Never	Total
Udaipur	N	5	1	6	3	10	25
	%	20	4	24	12	40	100

District		In remunerative work					
		Very often	Often	Normally	Rarely	Never	Total
Udaipur	N	2	1	2	3	17	25
	%	8	4	8	12	68	100

There were no sex discrimination in banking sector in providing significant responsibilities this fact was supported by 92% women respondents in Udaipur district (in table 7.20). Only 8% female has reported that they were rarely provided significant responsibilities by management.

In Udaipur district, 16 (64%) respondents revealed that they had not been given extra remunerative work as provided to the male employees. While 36% women respondents were getting remunerative work such as go to clearing house, officiating, inspection on site etc.

Table 7.20. Frequency of Significant Responsibilities and Extra Remunerative Work

District		Frequency of significant responsibilities in bank					
		Always	Often	Normally	Rarely	Never	Total
Udaipur	N	12	7	4	2	–	25
	%	48	28	16	8	–	100

District		Frequency of extra remunerative work					
		Always	Often	Normally	Rarely	Never	Total
Udaipur	N	4	2	3	2	14	25
	%	16	8	12	8	56	100

The degree of intensity of co-operation towards female banker was same by both male and female colleagues (Table 7.21. In the opinion of 72% respondents attitude of male and female colleagues was co-operative while 28% women admitted that it was normal.

Table 7.21. Cooperation Between Respondents and their Colleagues

District		Cooperation from male colleagues				
		Very co-operative	Co-operative	Normal	Unco-operative	Total
Udaipur	N	4	14	7	–	25
	%	16	56	28	–	100
District		**Cooperation from female colleagues**				
		Very co-operative	Co-operative	Normal	Unco-operative	Total
Udaipur	N	5	13	7	–	25
	%	20	52	28	–	100

Table 7.22 showed that majority (64%) of women banker had professional as well as friendly attitude towards customers. Whereas, 20% women bankers had only professional approach and 16% women bankers had friendly approach toward customers.

Table 7.22. Cooperation Between Respondents and Customers

District		Attitude of female banker towards customer			
		Professional	Friendly	Professional and friendly	Total
	N	5	4	16	25
Udaipur	%	20	16	64	100

District		Attitude of customers towards female banker					
		Very co-operative	Co-operative	Normal	Unco-operative	Rude	Total
	N	6	5	14	–	–	25
Udaipur	%	24	20	56	–	–	100

In the opinion of 44% respondents the attitude of customers toward female banker was very co-operative. While in the opinion of 56% respondents it was normal.

It was not unnatural to face confrontations with bank customers by the respondents in course of their performance of job. The Table 7.23 shows that 72% women expressed that such situation occasionally arises because women are very polite by nature and soft spoken. The main reason behind confrontation was delay in work due to technical problem.

Table 7.23. Frequency and Reason of Confrontation with Bank Customers

District		Frequency of confrontation with bank customers					
		Very often	Often	Normally	Rarely	Never	Total
	N	–	–	3	18	4	25
Udaipur	%	–	–	12	72	16	100

District		Reason of confrontation with customers				
		Delay in work	Technical problem	Customer behaviour	Respondent behaviour	Total
	N	4	16	3	2	25
Udaipur	%	16	64	12	8	100

By this investigation we try to find out satisfaction level of respondent with their political participation, social prestige, economic gains, family life, professionally, free time, and community service (Table 7.24, *See page 330*). Majority of women bank employees (92%) revealed that they had no political participation. Thus, it indicate that women bankers keep themselves away from the dirty politics. Nearly, cent per cent bank employee's were benefitted very positively by social prestige, economic gains and professionally. In the opinion of 84% women bank employee their job was not hurdle in their family life. Community service is one of the most important factor of human life. But only women had sufficient time for community service.

Availability of proper working atmosphere in any organisation increases productivity of workers and investigation about this aspect revealed that 88% respondents were satisfied with working conditions available in the banks. On the contrary, only 4% expressed their dissatisfaction because no drinking

Table 7.24. Opinion of Respondents Regarding Satisfaction with Profession

District		Political participation					Social prestige					Economic gains				
		To great extent	To some extent	To negligible extent	Not at all	Total	To great extent	To some extent	To negligible extent	Not at all	Total	To great extent	To some extent	To negligible extent	Not at all	Total
Udaipur	N	1	1	1	22	25	14	9	2	–	25	10	15	–	–	25
	%	4	4	4	88	100	56	36	8	–	100	40	60	–	–	100

District		Family life					Professionally					Community service				
		To great extent	To some extent	To negligible extent	Not at all	Total	To great extent	To some extent	To negligible extent	Not at all	Total	To great extent	To some extent	To negligible extent	Not at all	Total
Udaipur	N	8	13	2	2	25	8	16	1	–	25	4	9	3	9	25
	%	32	52	8	8	100	32	64	4	–	100	16	36	12	36	100

water, sanitation, dinning and relaxing room facilities were available in the banks (Table 7.25).

Table 7.25. Whether Respondent is Satisfied with Working Conditions in Bank?

District		Highly satisfied	Satisfied	Moderately satisfied	Dissatisfied	Total
Udaipur	N	6	16	2	1	25
	%	24	64	8	4	100

The survey revealed that in banking sector a majority of women bank employee's did not face any problem regarding misconduct by customer (84%), by colleagues (92%), by manager (92%), harassment being a women (92%), Night duty (100%), late working hours (84%), Long working hours (64%), regarding transfers (92%) regarding promotion (80%) and accumulation of task (76%) (Table 7.26).

Table 7.26. Problem Faced by Respondents Regarding their Job?

District		Transfer				
		To great extent	To some extent	To negligible extent	Not at all	Total
Udaipur	N	1	1	–	23	25
	%	4	4	–	92	100

District		Irregular working hours				
		To great extent	To some extent	To negligible extent	Not at all	Total
Udaipur	N	1	3	–	21	25
	%	4	12	–	84	100

District		Night shift duty				
		To great extent	To some extent	To negligible extent	Not at all	Total
Udaipur	N	–	–	–	25	25
	%	–	–	–	100	100

(Contd...)

(Table 7.26 Contd...)

District		Misconduct by colleagues				
		To great extent	To some extent	To negligible extent	Not at all	Total
Udaipur	N	–	–	2	23	25
	%	–	–	8	92	100

District		Misconduct by manager				
		To great extent	To some extent	To negligible extent	Not at all	Total
Udaipur	N	–	2	–	23	25
	%	–	8	–	92	100

District		Long working hours				
		To great extent	To some extent	To negligible extent	Not at all	Total
Udaipur	N	2	4	3	16	25
	%	8	16	12	64	100

District		Misconduct by customer				
		To great extent	To some extent	To negligible extent	Not at all	Total
Udaipur	N	1	2	1	21	25
	%	4	8	4	84	100

District		Promotion delayed				
		To great extent	To some extent	To negligible extent	Not at all	Total
Udaipur	N	2	3	–	20	25
	%	8	12	–	80	100

District		Accumulation of task				
		To great extent	To some extent	To negligible extent	Not at all	Total
Udaipur	N	3	1	2	19	25
	%	12	4	8	76	100

(Contd...)

District		Harassment being women				
		To great extent	To some extent	To negligible extent	Not at all	Total
	N	–	–	2	23	25
Udaipur	%	–	–	8	92	100

The survey revealed that most of the females (36%) never participated in demonstrations with union and 20% females admitted that they rarely participated in demonstrations while 44% women generally participated in bank union demonstrations (Table 7.27%).

Table 7.27. Whether Respondent Participated in Union Activities?

District		Always	Often	Normally	Rarely	Never	Total
	N	6	–	5	5	9	25
Udaipur	%	24	–	20	20	36	100

The study revealed that (Table 7.28) 64% women banker never thought about leaving the job of banker while 36% women bankers admitted that they had thought sometime that way.

Table 7.28. Whether Respondents think about Leaving the Job of Banker

District		Always	Often	Normally	Rarely	Never	Total
	N	–	–	3	6	16	25
Udaipur	%	–	–	12	24	64	100

At last respondents were asked (Table 7.29) if they; had opportunity to choose all over again then what would respondent go for? Majority of working women (72%) in banking sector wanted a full time job with home maker role while 12% of them wanted to remain only housewives. 16% of them wanted to be in another fields like, scientific research, teaching and suitable work with some leisure time to fulfil their hobbies.

Table 7.29. Opinion of Respondent for their Life Wish

District		Full time housewives	Full time employment with home maker role	Other	Total
	N	3	18	4	25
Udaipur	%	12	72	16	100

DUNGARPUR DISTRICT

The only woman bank employee of Dungarpur district was in between the age group of 36 and 45, Hindu by caste and educated upto Senior Hr. Secondary. The respondent took employment as a peon due to the death of her husband. She was working for last three years in rural branch and now promoted as clerk and working in urban branch. The respondent belongs to nuclear family and had full co-operation of her children, but even then, normally she found less time for her family. However, by her job, family income and family standard improved while assets improved upto some extent. Employment affected her children favourably and her income, was sufficient for family expenditure, in case her family income increases, she will not left the job because she relieve her tension arising from family and occupy herself. The respondent treat bank customers professionally and friendly. Behaviour of customers toward beneficiary was normal. Confrontation rarely occur due to delay in work and technical problem. She never participated in trade union activities and she had provided sufficient responsibilities and remunerative work in the bank by Manager. The respondent was ready to take promotion and transfer to any other district/ state and revealed that promotion opportunity in bank was fast. Male colleague were very co-operative toward the respondent. Dungarpur respondent was unable to answer the query about information technology. She was satisfied by the working conditions available in the bank. She had not any problem regarding transfers irregular working hours, long working hours, night duty, promotion delay, misconduct by manager while she had problem to negligible extent regarding accumulation of task, misconduct by customer and harassment being a woman.

8 Conclusion and Suggestions Significance of Women in Indian Society

Human resources being the most significant and active factor of production, become the key to optimize the utilization of all the other material resources. Developing the human resources, upgrading their skill and knowledge would lead to economic and organisational development. In the period of rapidly changing technology and increasing competition, the organisations are becoming highly conscious about the development of its human resources. At the organisational level, H.R.D. may be defined to include the activities and processes undertaken to promote the intellectual moral, psychological, cultural, social and economic development of the individual in an organisation in order to help them to achieve highest human potential as a resource for the community.

The success of any organisation and institution depends on the synergy created by its human resources. An organisation's prime resources consists of men, machine, money and material. Of all the prime resources human resource is accepted as the most vital and valuable. Because other resources depreciate in value with the passage of time and use. The Human resources appreciate in value through increase knowledge experience and efficiency. Human resource is consisted of men and women. To take full advantage of development of men's and women's participation with increased efficiency and skill is very necessary. We cannot isolate women's position as they constitute half of human resource.

Deterioration of women started from 500 B.C. and continued till the end of British period. With the advent of Manusmriti women's equality prohibited with man, women's education ceased lower down the marriageable age for girls, remarriage, widow marriage, inter-caste marriage and even remain unmarried was disapproved by Manu. The custom of Sati became popular in pre-Mugal period by the ruling classes. Women's right regarding marriage were brutality; demolished. The women's life became insecure and worse with the muslim invasion in the country. In this environment new evils formed i.e. seclusion, Infanticide, Dowry system, Devadasi system, Illiteracy, and Shaven head of widow etc., polygyny, Humiliating widowhood, early marriage, unequal marriages. On the eve of British rule, Indian woman not only lost her independence but she was not able to think on her own. She was drastically tied in the evil customs and their condition reached to the maximum degree of deterioration. The attitude of British government not to interfere with the religious sentiments of local people stopped all social reforms for a century. 19th century, marked a "Social Reform Movement" Raja Ram Mohan Roy was the first Indian who initiated Social Reform Movement. He worked very hard to ban Sati custom. Ishwar Chandra Vidyasagar was a great social reformer he attacked on early marriage, polygamy, Illiteracy among the females, B.M. Malabari, a Parsi social reformer who was against early marriage and widowhood. The notable social reform made by P.C. Banerjee, M.G. Ranade, Mahatma Phulay, Lokhitwadi, Durgaram and others from all part of our country raised their voice against the unjust practices.

20th century is the independence of our country as well as of women. Government enacted following legislation before and after independence to improve the condition of women and provide better opportunities for the development.

- Indian Penal Code, 1860.
- Indian Evidence Act, 1872.
- Guardians and Wards Act, 1890.

- Indian Succession Act, 1925.
- Child Marriage Restraint Act, 1929.
- Representation of the People Act, 1951.
- Hindu Marriage Act, 1955.
- Immoral Traffic (Prevention) Act, 1956.
- Dowry Prohibition Act, 1961.
- Foreign Marriage Act. 1969.
- Medical Termination of Pregnancy Act, 1971.
- Criminal Procedure Code, 1973.
- Family Courts Act, 1984.
- Indecent Representation of Women (Prohibition) Act, 1986.
- Commission of Sati (Prevention) Act, 1987.
- The National Commission for Women Act, 1990.

The important role of women in national development was specially recognised through the declaration of the UN Decade for women 1976-85, world wide, the approach to women's role has undergone a significant change. In India too, the special initiatives towards women has been primarily one of promoting primary health and child welfare initiatives till the 4th Five Year Plan. The Fifth Plan laid emphasis on the need to extend training to women in vocational trades and also the need to provide working women's hostels to mitigate the problem of working women, in large cities. In Sixth Five Year Plan, special reservations were made for women in the target for receiving benefits, under the TRYSEM and IRDP. Further, a special programme for Development of Women and Children in Rural Areas (DWCRA) was also formulated. The Seventh Plan emphasised the need to integrate inputs covering health, educational and capacity building inputs and also ensuring their participation through the specific reservations for women in development initiatives, to make any realistic impact on the overall improvement of women in the society. Setting up of the National Commission on Self Employed Women and women in the Informal Sector, preparation of a National Perspective Plan for women's development, setting up of Women's Development Corporations in various states are some other initiatives which have together institutionalized the issue of Women's development as an inherent part of the working of the governments rather than treating the same as a subsidiary activity. The special programmes in the English and Ninth Five Year Plans have addressed the requirements of women in its totality towards empowering them to participate in the economic development of the Country, through comprehensive programmes for access to health and educational facilities, access to credit, access to promotional inputs for self help initiatives including setting up of micro-enterprises etc. The Swarna Jayanti Sahari Rojgar Yojana (SJSRY)- 'The Golden Jubilee Urban Employment Programme has a special component for Development of Women and Children in Urban Areas (DWCUA). As part of the scheme special incentive is extended to the urban poor women who decide to set up self employment ventures in a group as opposed to individual effort. Groups of urban poor women are encouraged to take up any economic activity suited to their skill, training, aptitude and local conditions. Besides generation of income, this group strategy strives to empower the urban poor women by making them independent as also providing a facilitating atmosphere for self-employment.

The National Commission for Women (NCW) was set up as a statutory body in January 1992, under the National Commission for Women Act, 1990, to review the constitutional and legal safe-guards for women, recommended remedial legislative measures, facilitate redress grievances and advice the government on all policy matter affecting women. The state commission for women have been set up in many state. UNESCO announced on 8th March, 2000 (International Women's Day) to make March 8 Women's Day all over the world.

Women represent half of the talent and potential qualifications on the planet, and their low representation in key positions is a loss for society. No country can advance while large segment of its population lags behind. The women are expected to look after the home and health, be it father's home before marriage, husband home later. Inspite of so many hurdles and limitations the participation of women in entrepreneurial and professional activities are steadily increasing. A high proportion of working women in India is employed in the unorganised sector, so their work still remains invisible and under estimated. All of those who believe in this myth that female participation in work is relatively low becomes false when we consider the overall profile of rural women. To uplift women, money needs to be injected into the education sector, particularly for girls because this is education which make us aware about our rights, duties, morals and courage to do something and to attain some goal in life. If the women would be educated it would more surely be passed on to the next generations. Ever since the freedom movement of the country the role that women can play in every dimension of developmental activity has been recognised.

Now, women are also entered in unusual fields like science research, space technology, politics, etc. However, their percentage are comparatively low. 311 (7.3%) women I.A.S. officers in 1985 which increased upto 512 (10.3%) in 1997. Women I.P.S. Officers were 18 (0.8%) in 1985 increased upto 108 (3.5%) in 1999. Women I.F.S. officers were 50 (9.3%) in 1985 and increased upto 67 (11.4%) in 1998.

In Politics, the number of women members of Rajya Sabha were 15 (6.9%) in 1952 which has been reached upto 18 (7.3%) in 1998. The number of women members of Lok Sabha were 14 (2.8%) in 1952 which has been increased upto 49 (9.02%) in 1999. The number of women members in Rajasthan State Assembly were 9 in 1957 while in 1999, 14 (7%) women members were elected in 200 Member State Assembly. To increase women's participation in politics, Government of India reserved 33% seats for women in local government institutions.

A considerable progress has been made by women, in India, but even then in rural areas a typical Indian woman neither read nor write. She rarely moves out of her home. She receives lower wages than men do for her toils when she works outside, and despite having an income has no control over the way the money she earns in spent. Apart from working for wages, she is responsible for the care of her household and children. In poor households her domestic tasks are almost always labour intensive requiring tremendous effort. Maximum child birth takes place largely within the unhygienic precincts of her small home assisted by local often untrained, dai. Many of her children die in the first year of their life, chances of survival getting slimmer for girls receiving less health care in comparison to boys. Confined girls role of procreating and child rearing, she will eat last and left over food after the husband, children and other family. Her health will be the last to receive attention. She will be completely unaware that constitutionally she is guaranteed equal rights along with men.

Women's issues need to be focussed upon since they have been neglected for centuries. What ever our country has achieved in whatever way it has progressed in past 50 years. We could have probably done it 10 times better if women had been given equal status in society.

DEMOGRAPHIC PROFILE OF WOMEN

According to the 1991 census, the total population of women were 4070.72 lacs, 209.62 lacs 14.19 lacs and 4.36 lacs in the country, state of Rajasthan, Udaipur and Dungarpur districts respectively.

During 1961 to 1991, the decadal female variation rate in Dungarpur district was remarkably high in comparison to the Country, State of Rajasthan of Udaipur district. During the same span of period, sex-ratio in Dungarpur and Udaipur district was very high in comparison to the country and the state of Rajasthan. Sex-ratio of urban and rural female was remarkably high in Dungarpur district in comparison to the Udaipur district.

1. Area-wise Distribution of Population

Percentage of rural females was remarkably high in Udaipur and Dungarpur districts in comparison to the country and the State of Rajasthan. During 1961 to 1991, census ratio in Udaipur district of rural female was decreased 89.56 to 83.50% while in Dungarpur district ratio of rural female was decreased from 95.05% to 93.12%.

During last thirty years (1961-1991), growth of female population was high in Udaipur (100.14%) and Dungarpur district (115.84%) compared to the country (91.16%) while lower compared to the state of Rajasthan.

Growth of rural female was higher in Dungarpur district (111.46%), Udaipur district (86.77%) and in the State of Rajasthan (101.81%) compared to the country (72.16%). Growth of Urban female was also higher in Udaipur district (214.86%). Dungarpur district (200%) and state of Rajasthan (206.24%) compared to the country (184.12%).

2. Caste-wise Distribution of Population

According to 1991 census, caste-wise distribution of females shows that percentage of Hindu and Jain females were more in Dungarpur and Udaipur district compare to the State of Rajasthan and the Country. While the percentage of Muslims, Sikhs, Christians and Buddhist were lower in both the districts compare to the Country and the State of Rajasthan. During last forty years (1961-1991) growth of S.C. female population was very low in Udaipur district (88.71%) as compare to the Rajasthan State (122.33%), Dungarpur district (122.22%) and the country (110.46%). While the growth of S.T. female population was quite high in Udaipur district (142.13%) Dungarpur district (138.01%) and the state of Rajasthan (137.66%) compare to the country (125.02%).

3. Educational Distribution of Population

During last thirty years (1961 to 1991), the percentage of female literacy was low in Dungarpur district in compare to the Country, the State of Rajasthan and Udaipur district. In Udaipur and Dungarpur district female literacy was very low in rural areas compare to urban areas. Rural females of Udaipur and Dungarpur district were more illiterate compare to the country and the state of Rajasthan percentage of literacy in urban areas was more in Udaipur and Dungarpur district compare to the State of Rajasthan but low compare to the country.

4. Occupational Distribution of Population

The 1991 census indicate that, the percentage of female main workers were low in Dungarpur and Udaipur district in comparison; to the country and the state of Rajasthan. While the percentage of female marginal workers were quite high in Dungarpur district in comparison to the Country, State of Rajasthan and Udaipur district. Percentage of female non-workers were reducing during census year 1971 to 1991.

BANKING DEVELOPMENT IN UDAIPUR AND DUNGARPUR DISTRICTS

A. COMMERCIAL BANK'S

1. Branch Expansion

(i) Network of Branches

In Udaipur and Dungarpur district total number of branches in 1969 were 25 and 7 which increased to 119 (376%) and 41 (48.6%) at the end of March 2000, respectively.

(ii) Rural and Semi-urban Branches

In Udaipur district, share of rural and semi-urban branches decreased from 68% to 55.46% in the period of December 1969 to March 2000. In Dungarpur district all the branches were working in rural and semi-urban areas.

(iii) Public Sector and Private Sector Branches

In both the districts, Public Sector Banks accounted for most of the bank branches. At the end of March 2000, the public sector Bank branches accounted for 77.31% and 90.24% branches in Udaipur and Dungarpur district, respectively.

2. Deposit Mobilisation and Credit Deployment

The aggregate deposit of Udaipur and Dungarpur district rose from Rs. 532 lacs to Rs. 127503 lacs and Rs. 39 lacs to 32545 lacs, over the span of the period in between the nationalisation of the banks in 1969 and March 1999. During this period advances increased to Rs. 52367 lacs from Rs. 186 lacs in Udaipur district and in Dungarpur district Rs. 6495 lacs from Rs. 6 lacs. In the year of 1969 credit deposit ratio in Udaipur and Dungarpur district was 34.9% and 15.38% respectively while in 1999 CDR was 41% and 20%.

B. CO-OPERATIVE BANKS

1. District Central Co-operative Bank

At the end of March 2000, 9 branches of each UCCB and DCCB were working in Udaipur and Dungarpur district. Advances of UCCB increased by Rs. 74.33 lacs in June 1971 to Rs. 3154.17 lacs in March 2000. And the volume of deposit increased from Rs. 32.57 lacs in June 1971 to Rs. 5681.45 lacs in March 2000. While the advances of DCCB reduced from Rs. 111.89 lacs is 1978-79 to Rs. 57.40 lacs in 1995.

2. Primary Land Development Bank

There were 3 and 2 branches of PLDB functioning in Udaipur and Dungarpur districts respectively. During the period of June 1974 to March 2000 PLDB's advances increased from Rs. 39.52 lacs to Rs. 2846.68 lacs in Udaipur district. While in Dungarpur district it increased from Rs. 68.69 lacs to Rs. 88.80 lacs in the period of 1978 to 1995.

3. The Urban Co-operative Bank

The Urban Co-operative Bank was functioning with 7 branches in Udaipur district at the end of March 2000. While in Dungarpur district no Urban Co-operative Bank has been established so far. From June 77 to March 2000 deposit and advances of Udaipur Urban Co-operative Bank increased from Rs. 4.49 lacs to Rs. 7063.22 lacs and from Rs. 4.82 lacs to Rs. 4150.48 lacs respectively.

4. The Udaipur Mahila Urban Co-operative Bank and the Mahila Samridhi Urban Co-operative Bank

The UMUCB and the MSUCB were came into existence in the year of 1994 and one branch of each bank is functioning in Udaipur city. The management of these banks are vested in the hands of women and all the shareholders of these banks are also women. In Dungarpur district yet no MUCB and MSUCB has been established.

C. REGIONAL RURAL BANKS

The Mewar Anchalik Gramin Bank (MAGB) started its operation in the year of 1983 with 10 branches in Udaipur district and at the end of March 2000 there were 41 branches of MAGB working in the district. Dungarpur Banswara Kshetriya Gramin Bank (DBKGB) started its operation in 1984. At the end of March 2000, functioning with 21 branches in Dungarpur district. During the period of Dec. 83 to March 2000, deposit and advances of MAGB increased from 35.09 lacs to 8379.29 lacs and 11.43 lacs to 2270.73 lacs respectively. While the advances disbursed by DBKBG was Rs. 19.64 lacs, Rs. 41.29 lacs in the year of 1985, 1995, respectively.

ECONOMIC DEVELOPMENT OF WOMEN UNDER DEVELOPMENT PROGRAMMES

The government started various development programmes to bring out social and economic changes in the country. As the problem of poverty and unemployment was turning explosive in the late 70's and there after, various self-employment scheme and poverty removal programmes were launched to eradicate the problem. TRYSEM, PMRY, SJSRY, SGSY and IRDP are such important schemes. The Commercial Banks, RRB's, Co-operative Banks and non Banking financial institutions like state financial Corporation, Khadi and Village Industries board etc. were closely associated and involved in preparing these project report so as to avoid delays in sanctioning of loans and to ensure adequacy of financing.

DEVELOPMENT PROGRAMMES

1. Integrated Rural Development Programme (IRDP)

During the period of 1992-93 to 1998-99 performance of women benefitted under IRDP scheme was better in Dungarpur district 2771 (26.07%) in comparison to Udaipur district 3748 (19.42%) but females of Dungarpur district benefitted by less amount in comparison to Udaipur district females.

2. Training of Rural Youth for Self-Employment (TRYSEM)

Under TRYSEM scheme, rural youth living below poverty line are imparted training in various trades and are assisted in getting settled under, that particular trade. In both the districts

(62.01%) females were benefitted in Dungarpur and Udaipur district respectively during the period of 1993-94 to 1998-99.

3. Swarnajayanti Gram Swarozgar Yojana (SGSY)

SGSY aims at establishing a large number of micro enterprises in the rural areas. During 1999-2000, coverage of females under this Yojana was quite poor in both the districts. Against the target of 40%, female beneficiaries were 55 (14.40%) and 274 (11.52%) in Dungarpur and Udaipur district respectively.

4. The Swarna Jayanti Shahari Rozgar Yojana (SJSRY)

The SJSRY provide gainful employment to the urban unemployed poor through encouraging the setting up of self-employment ventures. Dungarpur district has showed very good performance regarding coverage of females under NRY/SJSRY scheme. During the span of period 1992-93 to 1999-2000 against the target of 30%, female beneficiaries were 276 (39.96%) and 540 (20.38%) in Dungarpur and Udaipur district respectively.

5. Prime Minister's Rozgar Yojana (PMRY)

Under PMRY educated youths are assisted in starting self-employment venture through a package of financial help. During the period of 1993-94 to 1999-2000, female beneficiaries in Udaipur district was 194 (5.45%) benefitted by Rs. 126.27 lacs (5.48%) of loan amount, where as in Dungarpur district 62 (4.78%) females were benefitted by Rs. 20.77 lacs (3.92%) of total loan amount.

TESTING OF HYPOTHESIS

1. The results of this investigation clearly approves the hypothesis that "Women of big cities have more banking habits compare to the women of small cities."

This conclusion has been based on following findings:

(a) In Udaipur district every woman had average 1.56 S.B. A/c, 0.81 F.D. A/c, 0.46 S.D.L. A/c, 0.36 Loan A/c and 0.05 current A/c while in Dungarpur district every woman had only 1.09 S.B. A/c, 0.48 F.D. A/c, 0.41 S.D.L. A/c, 0.12 loan A/c and 0.02 current A/c.

(b) Frequency of Udaipur district female was more in comparison to Dungarpur district females, At least 60% women of Udaipur district and 48% women of Dungarpur district visited their bank once in a month.

(c) Credit card facility availed by 5% women respondent of Udaipur district while in Dungarpur district only 3% women had credit card. Travellers cheque availed by 19% women of Udaipur district and only 3% respondents of Dungarpur district. Gift cheque facility used by 22% respondents of Udaipur district whereas, in Dungarpur district 12% beneficiaries availed this facility. MT/TT/DD and safe deposit locker facility availed by 13% and 46% respondents of Udaipur district respectively while in Dungarpur district 15% and 39% respondents availed the above mentioned facility, respectively. ATM (14%), Quantum deposit (6%), Demate (5%) and stock investment facility (6%) were availed by Udaipur district respondents while in Dungarpur district no one was availing these facilities.

(d) In Udaipur district, nearly 50% S.B. A/c, Current A/c, S.D.L. A/c and NRI A/c were operated by women themselves while in Dungarpur district these A/c were operated by less than 25% women.

2. The results of this investigation clearly disapproves our hypothesis "Women bank employees has been given more weightage in banking sector comparatively to the male employees."

This conclusion has been arrived at on the basis of following findings:

In Udaipur district majority of women bank employees revealed that they did not had any privilege in selection (96%), promotion (80%) and in transfer (52%) being a female. In Dungarpur district women bank employee also had very similar opinion.

3. The results of this investigation partially disapproves our hypothesis: "Well educated women are well known and availed credit card, traveller's cheque and gift cheque facilities provided by bank."

This conclusion has been arrived at on the basis of the following findings:

(a) More than 70% educated women (U.G./P.G.) of Udaipur and Dungarpur district knew about credit card-facilities and nearly 6% educated women of both the districts availed this facilities.

(b) 62% and 46% educated women of Udaipur and Dungarpur district, respectively knew about traveller's cheque and only 18% and 6% educated women of Udaipur and Dungarpur districts respectively availed this facilities.

(c) Nearly 69% educated women of both the districts knew about gift cheque facilities and nearly 17.5% women availed this facilities.

4. An evaluation of I.R.D.P., SGSY, SJSRY/NRY, TRYSEM and PMRY, in Udaipur and Dungarpur districts of Rajasthan clearly approves the hypothesis that "Women were not given proper weightage in government sponsored schemes" in Udaipur and Dungarpur district except TRYSEM and SJSRY/NRY of Dungarpur district.

The result of this investigation arrived on the following basis:

(a) In last 7 years, only 20.07% and 26.07% females of Udaipur and Dungarpur districts, respectively were benefitted under I.R.D.P. scheme.

(b) Under SGSY scheme too, in last year, target of 40% female beneficiaries were not achieved in Udaipur and Dungarpur districts. It was only 11.52% in Udaipur district and 14.40% in Dungarpur district.

(c) Under SJSRY/NRY scheme too, in last 7 years, target of 30% female beneficiaries were not achieved, in Udaipur districts 20.38% were benefitted while in Dungarpur district, the percentage was 37.96%.

(d) Under PMRY scheme no reservation was fixed for females. In last 7 years only 5.44% and 4.78% females were benefitted under PMRY scheme in Udaipur and Dungarpur districts respectively.

(e) In last 7 years against the target of 40%, 61.70% and 92.32% women were benefitted under TRYSEM scheme in Udaipur and Dungarpur districts, respectively.

5. The results of this investigation clearly approves the hypothesis that "Banking institution plays a vital role in economic development of women.

The important conclusion has been arrived at on the basis of an analysis of the women A/c holders and women bank employees.

(a) Impact of current A/c on females indicate that, one third beneficiaries of Udaipur district and half of Dungarpur district admitted that their income level sufficiently increased. In the opinion of 40% respondents of Udaipur district and cent per cent beneficiaries of Dungarpur district their property increase upto sufficient level. 60% women current A/c holder of Udaipur district admitted that their living standard sufficiently improved by operation of current A/c while in Dungarpur district cent per cent women admitted that their living standard slightly improved by operation of current A/c.

(b) Impact of loan A/c on female in Udaipur district indicate that 63.64% women got full employment and 18.18%, got partial employment, 35% women and 50% women felt that their regular income slightly increased and their property moderately increased, respectively by utilization of bank loan amount. While 50.67% women admitted that their living standard moderately increased. In Dungarpur district 100% women admitted that their property moderately increased by bank loan and 41.67% women admitted that their living standard highly increased while rest 58.33% women admitted that their living standard moderately increased by bank loan.

(c) In the opinion of 68% and 28% women bank employees of Udaipur district their living standard increased and slightly increased by their job respectively. In the opinion of 56% and 44% women their family assets improved and slightly improved respectively. While in the opinion of Dungarpur district women bank employee by her job family income 'increased' and family living standard and assets also improved upto sufficient extent.

ANALYSIS OF FIELD WORK

The data for this investigation were collected from the primary source. For the collection of primary data following two schedules were constructed and used.

1. The scheduled for women bank account holders.
2. The schedule for women bank employees.

The first schedule has been prepared to collect information relating to women account holders of various bank branches. The schedule shared views and opinion of the selected women on S.B. A/c, Current A/c, R.D. A/c, F.D. A/c, N.R.I. A/c, S.D.L. A/c, and Loan A/c. The second, schedule was used to collect information relating to the women working in banking sector. The schedule used to obtain information about reasons for joining of job, selection procedure, satisfaction from bank job, promotion opportunity, extent of co-operation from family members and staff, family life, problems faced during bank job and effect of women bank employees job on their income assets, living standard and on their children education's development etc.

For the first schedule 100 women bank A/c holders were selected at random from Udaipur and Dungarpur district, so in all 200 women were selected for this study. While for second schedule we selected 25 women bank employees from Udaipur district at random while in Dungarpur district only one woman was working in banking sector so we selected only one woman bank employee.

THE MAIN FINDINGS OF THE FIELD STUDY ARE AS UNDER

1. 55% and 61% women A/c holders selected for this study were from Udaipur and Dungarpur districts respectively, were belong to middle age group of 31 to 50 years while 31% and 35% respectively belong to younger age group 19 to 30 years. And 14% and 4% respondents respectively belong to old age group of 51 to 70 years.

   In Udaipur district by caste 54% women A/c holders were Hindu, 28% Jain while in Dungarpur district, by caste, 44% were S.C./S.T. and 40% Hindu. There were no Christian and Muslim women A/c holder in Dungarpur district.

2. In Udaipur district 83% women were Graduate and Post-graduate and technical qualified, whereas in Dungarpur district only 43% women were Graduate and Post-graduate. In Udaipur district, 17% women were educated upto Senior Hr. Secondary, whereas, in Dungarpur district 50% women were studied upto Senior Hr. Secondary. There were no illiterate A/c holders in Udaipur district while 7% women A/c holder were illiterate in Dungarpur district.

   In Udaipur district respondent constitute most of the urban population (73%) on the contrary, Dungarpur district constitute most of the rural (49%) and semi-urban (40%) population. In both the districts, occupation-wise distribution showed that more than half respondents were working class. In Udaipur district, majority of working respondents engaged in teaching (35%) and service (11%) while in Dungarpur district majority of women engaged in teaching (24%) and as Agricultural labour (11%).

3. In Udaipur district, 21 (84%) women bank employees selected for this study were belong to middle age group of 26 to 45 years while 3 (12%) women bank employees were belongs to age group of 18 to 25 years and by caste, 80% respondents were Hindu, 3 (12%) were Jain and rest 2 (8%) were Muslims. Educationally (96%) bank employees were graduates and post graduates while in Dungarpur district bank employees belong to the age group of 36 to 45 years, Hindu by caste and educated upto Senior Secondary.

   The study revealed that in Udaipur district, 18 (72%) females were unmarried and 7 (28%) were married at the time of joining bank service. At present 80% respondents were married. Family status of respondents showed that 16 (64%) belong to Nuclear family and 9 (36%) belong to Joint family and nearly 75% women were getting full support from their family members in nuclear as well as joint family. The respondent of Dungarpur district belongs to nuclear family and had full support of her children.

4. In both the districts, S.B. A/c was most popular A/c among the females and nearly cent per cent females had S.B. A/c with banks. In Udaipur district one half women had F.D. and S.D.L. A/c with bank while in Dungarpur district only one third women had these A/c. Another popular A/c in women was Loan A/c one-third and one-eight women had loan A/c in Udaipur and Dungarpur district, respectively. In both the district, Current A/c, NRI A/c and Recurring Deposit A/c was not very popular among the females.

   In Udaipur district S.B. A/c, F.D. A/c, S.D.L A/c, and Loan A/c were more popular among the women compare to Dungarpur district. In Udaipur district, every woman had average 1.56 S.B. A/c, 0.81 FD A/c, 0.46 S.D.L. A/c and 0.36 Loan A/c. While in Dungarpur district, every woman had only 1.09 S.B. A/c, 0.48 F.D. A/c, 0.41 S.D.L. A/c, and 0.12 loan A/c. In Dungarpur district R.D. A/c and N.R.I. A/c were popular upto some extent compare to Udaipur district.

5. In both the districts, cent per cent women had N.R.I. and current A/c with public sector banks. In Udaipur district more than two-third women had different types of accounts with public sector banks while in Dungarpur district only one half of the women had various A/c with public sector banks except Loan A/c. After public sector banking most of the women had A/c's with private sector banks. Co-operative banks were more popular among the women of R.D. and F.D. A/c holders of Dungarpur district compare to Udaipur district, Women had very few A/c with RRB's. In both the district, no women had current A/c, NRI A/c, R.D. A/c and Loan A/c with RRB's. In Udaipur district very few women had S.B. and F.D. A/c with RRB's while in Dungarpur district upto some extent women had S.B. A/c Loan A/c with RRB's.

6. In Udaipur district out of 25 women bank employees 16 (64%) were working in public sector banks, 4 (16%) were working in co-operative banks 3 (12%) were working in private sector bank and 2 (8%) were working in RRB. In Dungarpur district respondents was working in co-operative Bank.

   In Udaipur district 23 (92%) women bank employees were selected through bank competitive exams and personal interview while 2 women were selected on the basis of merit and direct interview. 52% women had opportunity to receive training after selection and majority of respondents received training upto two weeks. While in Dungarpur district respondent got employment as a peon due to the death of her husband.

7. In both the districts women prefer S.B. A/c with bank mainly because of safety of money, more liquidity and to earn interest on their savings, while current A/c holders prefer A/c due to overdraft facility provided by banks. F.D. A/c holders had A/c because of more interest and safety of money S.D.L. A/c holders like to keep valuable like jewellery and important documents. R.D. A/c holders prefer R.D. A/c because it was the

best mode of regular saving, to earn interest and to get lump-sum amount after maturity.

8. Main reason of opening of different types of A/c with particular bank branch was due to bank branch was near to residence, on the request of husband, bank employee was friend/relative of respondents and the other reason of opening A/c was due to salary deposited, being employee in the same bank for getting ATM, quantum deposit, demate facilities, over draft facility and near to the working place.

9. In both the districts, nearly cent per cent R.D., N.R.I., and S.D.L. A/c holders, three fourth F.D. A/c holders and more than 50% S.B. A/c holders had joint A/c with their husband or family members. Most of the Current A/c holders had individual A/c with bank.

   In both the districts, more than two-third R.D. and F.D. A/c were operated by women themselves. In Udaipur district, nearly 50% S.B. C.A., S.D.L. and N.R.I. A/c were operated by women themselves while in Dungarpur district these A/c were operated by less than one fourth women.

10. Most of the beneficiaries were well aware about Fixed Deposit scheme (95% in Udaipur district and 72% in Dungarpur district) and Recurring Deposit Scheme (64% in Udaipur district and 53% in Dungarpur district). Monthly pension scheme, cash certificate scheme and insurance linked deposit scheme were known by 42%, 31% and 22% respondents of Udaipur district, respectively, while in Dungarpur district only 20%, 11% and 15% respondents, respectively knew about the scheme. Very few respondents knew about the scheme of annuity deposit, deposit under permanent income plan, reinvestment deposit and scheme for N.R.I. in both the districts.

11. The study indicate that, sufficient number of women had knowledge about safe deposit locker (81% in Udaipur and 40% in Dungarpur), credit card (68% in Udaipur and 45% in Dungarpur), Travellers cheque

(55% in Udaipur and 36% in Dungarpur) and Gift cheque scheme (63% in Udaipur and 44% in Dungarpur). In both the districts many, women also had knowledge about MT/TT/DD, ATM standing instruction to bank and stock investment scheme. Women of Udaipur district had more knowledge about different bank services comparison to Dungarpur district. In Udaipur district few respondents also had knowledge of technical cell, quantum deposit and demate facilities. In Udaipur district ICICI, IDBI, The Bank of Rajasthan Ltd. and PNB were providing such type of facilities, while in Dungarpur district, no bank was providing such type of facilities to public.

Maximum number of women 46% in Udaipur and 39% in Dungarpur district were availing the facilities of safe deposit locker. Another facilities availing by the women A/c holders were gift cheque (22% in Udaipur, 12% in Dungarpur), MT/TT/DD (13% in Udaipur and 15% in Dungarpur). Very few beneficiaries enjoy the facilities of travellers cheque, credit card and standing instructions to bank for regular payment, in both the districts. The respondents of Udaipur also enjoy the facilities of ATM, Demate, quantum deposit and stock investment upto some extent.

12. The research showed that, two-third females were aware about PMRY scheme, in both the districts. Nearly, one third women A/c holder had knowledge about N.R.Y., S.G.S.Y, SJSRY and IRDP scheme, in both the districts, very few beneficiaries were aware about TRYSEM, National rural employment programme, credit to minority communities, differential rate of interest scheme, lead bank scheme, priority sector lending scheme, and credit authorisation scheme. There were 8 respondents of Udaipur district and 11 of Dungarpur district who did not aware about any single scheme. Udaipur district women A/c holders had more knowledge in comparison to Dungarpur district A/c holders in the following scheme; N.R.Y., TRYSEM, National rural employment programme, credit to

minority communities, differential interest rate scheme, priority sector lending, credit authorization scheme. On the contrary, Dungarpur district respondents had more knowledge about lead bank scheme, and twenty point programme in compare to Udaipur district respondents.

13. The study clearly indicate that, 73% and 64% women of Udaipur district and 56% and 57% women of Dungarpur district generally visit bank for withdrawal of money and deposit of savings, respectively. Nearly one-third women of Udaipur district visited bank to operate safe lockers issue of cheque book and completion of passbook while in Dungarpur district only 29%, 15% and 8% women visited bank for the above reasons, respectively. Another reason to visit bank branch for loan by 22% respondents of Udaipur district and 7% of Dungarpur district. In Udaipur district respondents also visit for issue of draft (11%), to get technical advice (4%), to seek information on bank scheme (7%) and repay loan (6%) while in Dungarpur district no respondent visited bank for these purpose.

    This investigation clearly indicate that in both the districts women S.B. A/c holders were generally not visit their bank branch for deposit of money (62% in Udaipur and 71% in Dungarpur district), deposit of cheque (70% in Udaipur and 93% in Dungarpur district), withdrawal of money (62% in Udaipur and 59% in Dungarpur district), completion of pass book (62% in Udaipur; and 81% in Dungarpur district) issue of cheque book (65% in Udaipur and 85% in Dungarpur district), and issue of draft (92% in Udaipur and 77% in Dungarpur districts). etc. women generally depend on their male family members for operation of their S.B. A/c.

    Frequency of Udaipur district female was more in comparison to Dungarpur district females. At least 60% women of Udaipur district and 48% women of Dungarpur district visited their bank once in a month.

The study clearly indicate that women of Udaipur district operate their S.B. A/c, Current A/c and Safe Deposit A/c frequently compare to the women of Dungarpur district. While frequency or R.D. A/c and NRI A/c was nearly same in both the districts.

14. In the opinion of two-third women S.B. and Current A/c holders of both the districts, they deposit and withdraw of money within 15 minutes from bank. While they got new cheque book from bank within 16 to 30 minutes. 93% and 66% S.B. A/c holders of Udaipur and Dungarpur district respectively were availing cheque-book facility.

15. In both the districts cent per cent women S.B. and Current A/c holders maintain minimum balance in their A/c and nearly cent per cent women N.R.I. A/c holders and three fourth S.B. A/c holders had knowledge about the balance in their A/c. On the other side current A/c holders of Udaipur district were aware about their balance while in Dungarpur district vice-versa.

16. In both the districts nearly one-half women S.B. A/c holders, and one-third women F.D A/c holders, and cent per cent women R.D. A/c holders of Dungarpur district were not knew that how much interest they were getting on their deposits.

    After liberalisation R.B.I. continuously decreases in bank rate so depositors are getting less rate of interest on their deposits. So depositors were not satisfied with the rate of interest, this views were presented by cent per cent women NRI A/c holders, two-third S.B. and F.D. women A/c holders of both the districts and two-third R.D. A/c holders of Dungarpur district also had the same opinion.

    On the other hand, in the opinion of nearly two-third and one-third women Loan account holders of Udaipur and Dungarpur district respectively bank charged very high rate of interest on loans.

    In both the districts nearly 50% women did not know about the annual charges they were paying for lockers and rest were paying locker charges upto Rs. 500 per annum. In the opinion of 28.26% and 48.78% women locker holders of Udaipur and Dungarpur districts banks were charging high rent for lockers.

17. About two-third, S.B. A/c holders in both the districts and nearly two-third Current A/c holders of Udaipur district checked their passbook/statement after its completion while in Dungarpur district no women current A/c holder checked their statement after completion.

18. The investigation showed that near about two-third women A/c holders were aware about bank lending scheme of Housing and vehicle in both the districts. About half of the beneficiaries had awareness about bank lending scheme of consumer durable, SSI, loan against deposit and for agricultural activities in both the districts. Respondents also had knowledge about following bank lending scheme; Loan for allied activities, children's education, Export finance, overdraft against approved securities, marriage, on gold ornaments and for artisans in both the districts. Women of Udaipur district had more knowledge about following schemes, loan for housing, vehicle, consumer durable, small scale industries, loan against deposits, children's education, export, finance, over draft against approved securities, marriage, on gold ornaments, and loan for artisans in comparison to Dungarpur district. While women A/c holders of Dungarpur district had more knowledge about bank lending scheme of finance to agricultural activities, allied agricultural activities in comparison to Udaipur district.

19. The study showed that cent per cent bank A/c holders of both the districts had first choice to invest their savings in bank due to more liquidity and safety of money. Second choice of investment of money was post office (50% in Udaipur and 45% in Dungarpur district) L.I.C. is also one of the favourite mode of investment revealed by respondents (35% in Udaipur and 24% in

life. 31% and 22% respondents of Udaipur and Dungarpur district, respectively keep some money in the form of cash for transaction and for precautionary motive. Less than one-fourth of respondents invest their money in gold, property, share and debentures while some keep it with friends and relatives. In Udaipur district, respondent also like to invest their saving in UTI (18%) and co-operatives (11%). In both the districts, no respondents like to invest money with chit funds because much better mode of investment of money already available for them.

The study revealed that 18% women of Udaipur district and 49% women of Dungarpur district did not like to invest their savings other than banks. The respondents who prefer other institutions than bank mainly because of simple procedure, more interest on savings, less interest on loan and tax incentives by 22, 27, 18 and 16 respondents of Udaipur district and by 25, 20, 11 and 16 respondents of Dungarpur district respectively. Another reason of preference to other institutions was more liquidity, desired service and faster loan etc.

20. About one-third and two-third beneficiaries of Udaipur and Dungarpur district, respectively taken loan for housing. And 14% and 33% respondents of Udaipur and Dungarpur district respectively taken loan for consumer goods from banks. In Udaipur district many women also taken loan for vehicle, business, marriage and for self-employment. In both the districts no women taken loan for education, agriculture purpose and under any government scheme.

    The survey revealed that in both the districts all women R.D. A/c holders and more then three-fourth women F.D. A/c holders were not taken any loan against their A/c.

21. The survey revealed that about 57% beneficiaries in Udaipur district and 31% in Dungarpur district respectively were approached for their loan requirement to banks and 18 and 24% beneficiaries were approached

for their loan requirement to their friends/neighbour/relative in Udaipur and Dungarpur district respectively. While very few respondents approach to money lenders for their requirement in both the district.

22. Nearly three-fourth females revealed that they got loan within a month while rest of the female got loan with in two months.

23. The investigation showed that loan amount was sufficient for 91.67% and cent per cent loan A/c holders of Udaipur and Dungarpur districts respectively. 8.33% respondents of Udaipur district arranged loan from their relation and friends and cent per respondents of both the districts utilized the loan for which it has been taken.

24. Cent per cent women R.D. A/c holders of Udaipur and Dungarpur districts had R.D. A/c duration of 2 to 3 and 5 years, respectively. All women were depositing monthly instalment very regularly. About 62% respondents depositing monthly instalment of more than Rs. 1000 in both the districts. Rest of the respondents were depositing monthly instalment in between Rs. 300 and Rs. 1000.

In both the districts, one-third women had invested their money in short term F.D. for 6 months to 1 year while nearly two-third women had invested their money in F.D. for 3 years. The study clearly indicate that 50% women of Udaipur district and 75% women of Dungarpur district had F.D. upto Rs. 20 thousand while rest of the women had F.D. of Rs. 0.5 to 1 lac, amount.

The study regarding loan A/c revealed that one-third and two-third women of Udaipur and Dungarpur districts respectively had taken loan upto the period of three years. In Udaipur district one-third women had taken loan in between the period of 3 and 5 years. While in both the district, rest one-third women had taken loan for more than 5 years. One-third women of both the districts had taken loan between Rs. 10 and 25 thousand on the other hand 25% and 58% women of Udaipur and Dungarpur districts respectively, had taken loan of more than Rs. 1 lac.

25. Nearly cent per cent women loan A/c holders of both the districts were repaying regular loan instalment from their or their husband's regular income. Maximum respondents of Udaipur district were repaying regular instalment due to the fear of losing social prestige, legal action taken by bank, and due to moral duty while in Dungarpur districts respondents were repaying loan instalment simply due to moral duty.

26. In both the districts cent per cent current A/c holders were availing cash credit and overdraft facilities but many women were not knowing about their limit because their A/c was operated by their husband. No incidental charge was charged by bank from current A/c holders.

27. Generally bankers emphasise on applicant of S.D.L A/c they must first open S.B. A/c with that bank branch so they may deduct annual rent of locker from S.B. A/c whenever required. The survey revealed that in both the districts more than 75% SDL A/c holders also had S.B. A/c with the same bank branch.

    Generally bank demands F.D. for opening of S.D.L. A/c but the survey clearly indicate that in Udaipur district only 35% and in Dungarpur district only 5% women deposited F.D. for getting locker facility and in most of the cases women deposited of Rs. 5000 only.

    Nearly 75% women F.D. A/c holders in Udaipur and Dungarpur districts renew their F.D. after its maturity.

28. Main reason accepted by women bank employees of Udaipur district, being in service was, for making career, (19), self fulfilment (18), to supplement family income and improve family status (14), to get recognition and respect (12), occupying themselves (11), low family income, (7%), improve marriage prospects (5), to release tension and earn for dowry (2).

29. The survey revealed that in Udaipur district 24 (96%) women joined bank service as clerk/typist/cashier and 17 (68%) women were still work as clerk/typist/cashier and rest 7 (28%) were promoted on different post. 9 (36%) respondents had experience of more than fifteen years, 9 (36%) respondents had experience five to fifteen years. While 7 (28%) women had experience of less than five years but 23 (92%) women bank employees never serve to rural area branch and they; were not ready to accept promotion in rural area. 60% women were not ready to accept promotion or transfer while 32% of them were ready to accept it and 8% respondents revealed that it depends on the posting place. In Dungarpur district, women bank employees were working in rural area from last three years and now promoted clerk and working in Urban branch. The respondent was ready to take promotion or transfer at any place.

30. The investigation revealed that in Udaipur district 13 (52%) bank employees were getting salary of Rs. 7 to 10 thousand per month and 6 (24%) bank employees were getting more than Rs. 10 thousand per month. While 6 (24%) bank employees were getting less than Rs. 7 thousand. Out of 20 married bank employees, the husband of 8 (40%) respondents had not sufficient income while their combined income was sufficient to meet out their family expenditure. In case of family income increase still 84% beneficiaries did not want to leave their bank job.

    Respondent of Dungarpur district revealed that in case of her family income increase still she will not leave the job because she releases her tension arising from family and occupy herself.

31. In the opinion of 83% and 92% women A/c holders of Udaipur and Dungarpur district respectively, generally bankers were available on their seats. In general behaviour of bankers were very satisfactory 85% and 89% women A/c holders of Udaipur and Dungarpur district respectively admitted this fact.

In the opinion of 72% respondents of Udaipur district attitude of male and female colleagues was co-operative while 28% women bank employee admitted it was normal. Majority (64%) of women bankers had professionally as well as friendly attitude towards customer. Whereas, 20% women bankers had only professional approach and 16% women bankers had friendly approach towards customer. In the opinion of 44% and 56% respondents attitude of customers towards female banker was very co-operative and normal respectively. 72% women bank employees of Udaipur district expressed that confrontation occasionally arises with customer because women are very polite by nature and soft spoken. The main reason behind confrontation was delay in work due to technical problem. The respondents of Dungarpur district treat their customers professionally and friendly, she felt behaviour of customers towards female banks employee was normal, confrontation rarely occur with customer. She also revealed that male colleague were very co-operative.

32. There were no sex discrimination in banking sector in providing significant responsibilities that fact was supported by 92% women respondents, majority of women revealed that they did not had any privilege in selection (96%), in promotion (80%), in remunerative work (80%) and in transfer (52%), being a female. 64% respondents revealed that they had not been given remunerative work as provided to male employees. Respondent of Dungarpur district had provided sufficient responsibilities and remunerative work by the bank manager.

33. By uses of modern technology like computer and inter net etc. Only 44% women of Udaipur district admitted that they are less busy compare to the past.

34. The study revealed that in Udaipur district, 32% women bank employees had not sufficient time for their family members, 28% women felt that some where they were lacking in their family duties while 40% of women bank

employees had not face this type of problem because their family members were very supportive and co-operative. 50% respondents admitted that their job affected their children in both ways (positive and negative). 18.75% women respondent felt that they were not giving appropriate attention towards the studies of their kids and to the overall development while 31.25% women respondents thought that due to increase income, they are in a position to provide good and higher education to their children. Bank employee of Dungarpur district felt that she has not sufficient time for her family but she felt that her job affected her children favourably.

35. The study revealed that in Udaipur district (92%) women bank employees had no political participation and 56% women bank employees admitted that generally they never participated in demonstrations with union. Nearly, cent per cent bank employees were benefitted very positively by social prestige, economic gains and professionally. In the opinion of 84% women bank employees their job was not hurdle in their family life. 48% women had no time for community service. Respondent of Dungarpur district also had same opinion.

36. Impact of current A/c on female showed that, one third beneficiaries of Udaipur district and half of Dungarpur district admitted that their income level sufficiently increased. In the opinion of 40% respondents of Udaipur district and cent per cent beneficiaries of Dungarpur district their property increase upto sufficient level. 60% women current A/c holders of Udaipur district admitted that their living standard sufficiently improved by operation of current A/c while in Dungarpur district cent per cent women admitted that their living standard slightly improved by operation of current A/c.

Impact of loan A/c on female indicate that in Udaipur district 63.64% women got full employment and 18.18% women got partial employment, 35% women and 50%

women felt their regular income slightly increased and their property moderately increased respectively, by utilization of bank loan amount. While 56.57% women admitted that their living standard moderately increased. In Dungarpur district 100% women admitted that their property moderately increased by bank loan. And 41.67% women admitted that their living standard highly increased while rest 58.33 women admitted that their living standard moderately increased by utilization of bank loan.

In the opinion of 17 (68%) and 7 (28%) women bank employees their living standard 'increased' and 'slightly increased' by their job respectively. In the opinion of 14 (56%) and 11 (44%) women their family assets 'improved' and 'slightly improved' respectively. Dungarpur district woman admitted that by her job family income increased and family living standard and assets also improved upto sufficient extent.

37. 30% and 16% bank A/c holders of Udaipur and Dungarpur districts felt that more time taken by bankers in providing different services. More paper work in banks this view is presented by 32% and 45% women A/c holder of Udaipur and Dungarpur districts, respectively. Women bank A/c holders of Udaipur was less satisfied with bank services compare to women A/c holder of Dungarpur district.

Nearly 92% female Loan A/c holder of Udaipur and Dungarpur districts had not faced any problem when apply for loan and during sanctioning and disbursement of loan. Very few respondents faced the problem of complexed application form and long duration in sanctioning and disbursement of loan.

The study revealed that in banking sector women bank employee faced the problem of long working hours (36%), accumulation of task (24%), regarding promotion (20%), late working hours (16%), misconduct by customer (16%), misconduct by colleague (8%), misconduct by manager (8%) regarding transfer (8%)

and (4%) women expressed their dissatisfaction about drinking water, sanitation, dining and rest room facilities. The women bank employees of Dungarpur district had problem to negligible extent regarding accumulation of task, misconduct by customer and harassment being a women.

38. The customer service centre scheme were known by 56% and 37% women A/c holders of Udaipur and Dungarpur district, and nearly one-third women bank A/c holders of both the districts know that higher authority meet them about their grievances.

39. The study revealed that 64% women banker never thought about leaving the job of banker. In the opinion of 72% women banker, they will again choose a fulltime job of banks with home maker role while 12% of them wanted to remain only housewives and rest 16% wanted to be in another fields.

SUGGESTIONS

1. In Udaipur district very few women had N.R.I. A/c (2%), R.D. A/c (3%) and Current A/c (5%) while in Dungarpur district only 2%, 4% and 12% women had current A/c, N.R.I. A/c and Loan A/c respectively. In Dungarpur district only one-third women had F.D. and S.D.L. A/c. Hence it is suggested that the bank should publicise more and more utility and advantages of R.D. A/c, Current A/c and Loan A/c among the women so that operate more R.D. A/c Current A/c and loan A/c.

2. In Udaipur and Dungarpur districts women had very few A/c with R.R.B's, no women had Current A/c, N.R.I/A/c, R.D. A/c and Loan A/c with R.R.B/s. In Udaipur district very few women had S.B. and F.D. A/c with RRB's while in Dungarpur district upto some extent women had S.D. and Loan A/c with RRB's and only 8% women were employed in R.R.B's in Udaipur district while no women were employed in Dungarpur district. So it is suggested that RRB's must made special efforts to open women A/c's and RRB's management also employed more women in their staff. In Udaipur

district women had very few F.D. and R.D. A/c with co-operative bank's so it is also suggested that Co-operative Bank must made some special efforts so women also open F.D. and R.D. A/c's with co-operative Banks.

3. In Udaipur district only 11%, 12%, 12% and 14% women had knowledge about Annuity deposit, deposit under permanent income plan, reinvestment deposit and scheme for N.R.I. respectively. However, in Dungarpur district too, only 8%, 7%, 7% and 5% women respectively aware about the above mentioned bank deposit schemes. So it is suggested that bankers should make more efforts to popular these deposit schemes, in that way, more and ore women would aware about these schemes and benefitted by these deposit schemes.
4. About half of the women were not aware about bank lending scheme of SSI, loan against deposit and for agricultural activities in both the districts. More than half respondents were not aware about following bank lending scheme loan for allied agriculture activities, loan for children's education. Export finance, overdraft against approved securities, loan for marriage, loan against gold ornaments and loan for artisans in both the districts. Hence, bank should do more effort to make people aware about bank lending scheme and encourage them to take loan for economic development of nation.
5. One-third and two-third beneficiaries of Udaipur and Dungarpur district, respectively taken loan for Housing. And 5 (13.89%) and 4 (33.33%) respondents of Udaipur and Dungarpur district respectively, taken loan for consumer goods. In Udaipur district respondent also taken loan for vehicle 10 (27.78%), Business 5 (13.89%), self employment 2 (5.56%) and for marriage 2 (5.5%) whereas, in Dungarpur district no women taken loan for these purposes. In both the district no women taken loan for Education, Agriculture purpose and under any government scheme. Hence, women A/c holders suggested to take advantage of loan facility provided

by Banks, in Dungarpur district only 3% and 12% respondents were using the above mentioned facility, respectively. In Udaipur and Dungarpur district about 15% respondents availed MT/TT/DD facility. 14% Udaipur district respondent availed ATM facility while none in Dungarpur district. In Udaipur district, about 5% respondents were using credit card, Quantum deposit, Demate and Stock investment facility while in Dungarpur district only 3% respondents were using credit card and 'standing instruction for regular payment facility' and no respondent were availing ATM, Quantum deposit Demate and stock investment facility. Hence, it is suggested that bank should use appropriate channel of advertisement to make popular bank services and their benefits.

6. In Udaipur district more than 80% respondents were not aware about Technical Cell, Quantum deposit and Demate facilities while more than half respondents were not aware about MT/TT/DD, standing instructions to make regular payment, ATM, and stock investment facilities. In Dungarpur district cent per cent respondents were not aware about Technical Cell, Demate facilities and Quantum deposit while nearly 90% women were not aware about standing instruction to make regular payment, ATM facilities and stock investment. And nearly 60% respondents were not aware about Credit card, Travellers cheque, Gift cheque, MT/TT/DD and S.D.L.

   Maximum number of women 46% in Udaipur district and 39% in Dungarpur district were availing the facility of S.D.L. provided by banks. In Udaipur district, 19% and 22% respondents were using Travellers cheque and Gift cheque facility, respectively.

7. Nearly 70% women A/c holders had no knowledge about NRY, SGSY, SJSRY and I.R.D.P. Scheme, in both the districts. About 80% beneficiaries were not aware about TRYSEM, National rural employment programme, Credit to minority communities, Differential rate of interest scheme, Lead bank scheme,

priority sector lending scheme and credit authorisation scheme. If women were not aware and take advantage of these self employment scheme then there is no use of these schemes. Hence, government should do more effort to make people aware about all government sponsored schemes.

8. Under SGSY and SJSRY/NRY, there were 40% and 30% reservation for female beneficiaries both schemes was failed to fulfil the target. There were no reservation for women under IRDP and PMRY scheme. The percentage of female was drastically low. Hence, it is suggested that government should do efforts to make these schemes more popular among the women for an effective achievement of the objectives.

9. Nearly 65% women of Udaipur district never visited bank to operate safe lockers, issue of cheque book and to completion of passbook while in Dungarpur district 71, 85 and 92 women not visited bank for above reasons respectively. In Udaipur district 78% respondents were not visited for loan purpose while in Dungarpur district there were 93% respondents. In Udaipur district about 93% respondent yet not visited for issuing draft, to get technical advice, to seek information on bank scheme and to repay loan while in Dungarpur district no respondent yet visited for these purpose.

   This investigation clearly indicate that in both the districts women S.B. A/c holders were generally not visited their bank branch for deposit of money (62% in Udaipur and 71% in Dungarpur district), Deposit of cheque (70% in Udaipur and 93% in Dungarpur district), withdrawal of money (62% in Udaipur and 59% in Dungarpur district), completion of passbook (62% Udaipur and 81% in Dungarpur district) issue of cheque book (65% in Udaipur, and 85% in Dungarpur district) and issue of draft (92% in Udaipur and 77% in Dungarpur district) etc. Hence, women must keep themselves ready to be in touch of day to day functioning of bank and take massive part in operation of their all A/c's. Then in real sense banking habits among the women increases.

10. In Udaipur district 50% women were not operating their S.B, A/c, Current A/c, S.D.L. A/c and N.R.I. A/c while in Dungarpur district these A/c were not operated by nearly 75% women. These A/c were operated by respondent's husband and by other family members. Hence, women should not to be very dependent on their male counterparts. They must operate their A/c by themselves and also keep knowledge of their A/c.
11. In Udaipur and Dungarpur district cent per cent current A/c holders were availing cash credit and overdraft facilities but most of the women were not knowing about their limit because their A/c is operated in all respect by their husband hence it is suggested that when women is having an account they must keep full knowledge of their A/c and play active role.
12. In both the district, nearly one half women S.B. A/c holders and one-third women F.D A/c holders and cent per cent women R.D. A/c holders were not knew that how much interest they were getting on their deposits. Hence, it is suggested that women should aware about their A/c's detailed information.
13. Nearly 30% S.B. A/c holders in both the districts and nearly 30% Current A/c holders of Udaipur district and cent per cent women A/c holder of Dungarpur district did not check their pass book/statement after completion. Hence, women having an account must knowing about the balance in their A/c and should confirm the authenticity of balance by checking pass book/statement.
14. Many S.B. A/c holders suggested that all the bank should have reduced bank charges for DD/MT/TT at least to S.B. A/c holders.
15. Many A/c holders suggested that like ICICI Bank and IDBI Bank other banks also provide facilities of Quantum Deposit i.e. S.B. A/c should be linked with F.D. A/c.

16. Most of the bankers do not renew F.D. at the same day they mostly call customers next day. Banking institution is for the facility of customers so, they are suggested, at the time of renewal of F.D. they should send reminder and renew F.D. at the same day.
17. The study shows that 82% women of Udaipur district and 51% women of Dungarpur district also like to invest their saving's other than bank because of simple procedure, more interest on savings, less interest on loan and tax incentives, faster loan and better services. If bank improve their services and provide more interest on deposit, charges less interest on loan and adopt simple procedure then they can attract more customer.
18. In Udaipur 36%, 36% and 28% women bank employees had experience of more than 15 years, 5 to 15 years and less than 5 years. 70% bank employees joined their service as clerk/typist/cashier and still they are working on the same post. The main reason is they were not ready to accept promotion on transfer. It is surprising that in Udaipur district 23 (92%) women bank employees were never serve in rural area branch. 60% women were not ready to accept promotion on transfer. Hence it is suggested that like bank officer, it must be essential for clerical staff to serve few years in rural areas and on promotion they must go to rural branches.
19. In Udaipur district, 64% women working in banking sector revealed that they had not been given remunerative work as provided to male employees. Hence, it is suggested to bank officials that there should not be sex discrimination in the working environment because women are not less capable than men.
20. In Udaipur district, 56% women bank employees admitted that they generally never participated in union activities. Hence, it is suggested to women bank employees to take part in the union activities if the demand of the union are genuine. They should not keep quite when their rights are infringed.

21. 32% and 45% women A/c holders of Udaipur and Dungarpur district, respectively revealed that they faced more paper work problem in banks.

    Women working in banking sector of Udaipur district faced the problem of long working hours (36%), accumulation of task (24%), regarding promotion (20%), late working hours (16%), misconduct by customer (16%), misconduct by colleague (8%), misconduct by manager (8%), regarding transfer (8%) and 4% women expressed their dissatisfaction regarding drinking water, sanitation, dining and rest room facility. Hence it is suggested that bank should simplify their proforma, and formalities etc. Bank should increase their efficiency in providing better and friendly services to their customer and bank should provide healthy and encouraging environment for women bank employees.

22. The customer service centre scheme were not known by 44% and 63% women A/c holders of Udaipur and Dungarpur district respectively and about two-third women bank A/c holders of both the districts did not know that higher authority meet them about their grievances. These schemes are for solving the grievances and the problem of customer so it is suggested that women must take more and more advantage of these type of facility.

23. To increase women's participation in politics proposal of 33% seats reservation for women in State Assembly and Central Parliament is still under consideration. It has been presented by the government in parliament but refused by the same opposition party. Hence, it is suggested to politicians provide reservation to women as early as possible so women will be able to take active part in the best decision making process. Instead of thinking about their selfish ends politicians must think broadly about nation development through uplift women in Indian politics.

24. During 1961 to 1991, the decadal female variation rate of Dungarpur district was remarkably high in

comparison to the country, state of Rajasthan and Udaipur district and during last thirty years (1961-1991), growth of female population was high in Dungarpur district (115.84%) and Udaipur district (100.14%) compared to the country (91.16%). Health deptt. of Dungarpur district should immediately take contraceptive methods to control population.

25. During last forty years percentage of literate females is low in comparison to literate males in Udaipur and Dungarpur districts. A nation's welfare depends upon its educational system. It is the educated nations that are the civilised nations and it is the civilised nations that rule the world. There can not be any educated people without educated women. If general education had to be limited to men and women, that opportunity should be given to women, for them it would more surely be passed on to the next generations. Hence money must be injected in to the education sector and government should start special programmes for girls education specially in rural areas.

26. There are 3 and 2 branches of the PLDB functioning in Udaipur and Dungarpur district respectively. The number of PLDB is very meagre looking to the requirements. It is suggested that the bank should have at-least one branch in each of the blocks of the districts.

27. The UMUCB and the MSUCB were came into existence in the year of 1994, and one branch of each bank is functioning in Udaipur city. The management of these banks are vested in the hands of women and all the share holders of these banks are also women. The UMSUCB provides loan only to women. In Dungarpur district yet no MUCB and MSUCB has been established. It is suggested that few branches of UMUCB and UMSUCB must be opened in Udaipur district for an effective achievement of the objective and in Dungarpur district MUCB and MSUCB should consider the establishment of at least one branch.

28. The Udaipur urban co-operative bank Ltd. UUCB has— branches, all are functioning in the city properly. The bank has been hither to catering to needs of retail traders, artisans and the SSI in the city of Udaipur. In the district of Dungarpur no urban co-operative Bank has been established so far. It is suggested that urban co-operative Bank should be established in Dungarpur districts as early as possible.

29. At the end of March 2000, RRB of Dungarpur district was functioning with 21 branches. The number or RRB's branches are very small looking to the requirement of the district. Hence it is suggested that the bank should open few more branches in the district.

30. Credit deposit ratio is yet another indicator of the progress made by the banking sector in serving the needy areas. Since the nationalisation of commercial banks, CDR in the districts have undergone considerable changes. In the year of 1999 the CDR in Dungarpur district was only 20%. The Lead Bank of Dungarpur district must try to stop the out flow of funds and pay more attention to the local utilisation of funds.

Bibliography

Acharya, Sarthi; *Employment of Women in India; A Historical Review* 1901-1951, Vol. 22, No. 3, October, 1979.

Adarkar, B.N.: *"Commercial Banks in India after Nationalization"* A.D. Shraff Memorial Lecture 30 March, 1971.

Agarwal R.C. (1980): *"Women Power—The Neglected Factor in Development Manpower Journal,* Vol. XVI, No. 3, October-December.

Agarwal Sushila: *Status of Women,* Printwell Publishers, Jaipur, 1988.

Agarwal, Bina (1985): *"Work Participation of Rural Women in Third World, Some Data and Conceptual Biases"*, Economic and Political Weekly.

Agarwal, Bina 1980: *"Rural Women, Poverty, and National Resources"*, Economic and Political Weekly.

Agarwal, H.N.: *A Portrait of Nationalised Banks,* Inter India Publications Delhi, 1979.

Agarwal, B.P. (1982): *Commercial Banking in India after Nationalization: A study of their Policies and Progress* (New Delhi Classical Publishing Co.).

Agarwal, Bina, *"Reports on the Current Status and Needed Priorities of Women's Studies in Asia and the Pacific"*, APDC, Kuala Lumpur, 1983.

Agarwal, J.C., *The Progress of Education in Free India,* Arya Book Depot, New Delhi, 1984, pp. 395-396.

Ahmed K.: *Women's Higher Education: Recruitment and Relevance,* Vikas Publishing House, New Delhi, 1977.

Ahuja K. (1979): *"Women Workers in Rural Rajasthan"*. The HCM State Institute of Public Administration Jaipur.

Ahuja P. et al (1984): *"Time Utilization Pattern of Rural Households in Relation to Size of Family and Socio-Economic Status"*, PAV Journal of Research, Vol. 21, No. 3, pp. 436-441.

Alfred Desouza(ed) (1975): *"Women in Contemporary India"*, Manohar Book Service, Delhi.

Altekar, A.S.: *Position of Women in Hindu Civilization, from Pre-historic Times to the Present Day*. New Delhi: Motilal, Banarsidas, 1973.

Alterkar, A.S.: *The Position of Women in Hindu Civilization,* Motilal Banarsidas, New Delhi, 1956.

Anker, R. Khan, M.E. Gupta, R.B. (1988): *"Women's Participation in the Labour Force. A Methods Test in India for Improving it's Measurement,* International Labour Office, Geneva.

Anker, Richard (1983): *"Female Labour Force Participation in Developing Countries: A Critique of Current Data Collection. Techniques," Mimeographed World Employment Programme* Research Working Paper; ILO; Geneva.

Atmanand (1990): *"Women Labour Force: Trend• and Pattern of Employment,"* Khadi Gramodyog, Vol. XXXVI, No. 6, Mar, p. 247-54.

Awasthi, Indra (1982): *Rural Women of India A Socio Economic Profile of Jammu Women,* B.R. Publicity Corporation, Delhi.

Baker, Berheide, Grecpel (1980) Gugin, Lipety, Segal: *"Women Today"* Brooks/Code Publishing Co. California.

Banerjee, Nirmala (1989): *Trend's in Women Employment 1971-81* "Economic and Political Weekly, Apr. 29, p. 20-21.

Bardhan Kalpana (1985): *"Women's Work, Welfare and Status: Force of Tradition and Changes in India"* Economic and Political Weekly, Vol. XX, No. 5, Dec. 14, p. 207.

Bhagwati, Jagdish; (1973): *"Education, Class Structure and Income Equality"*, World Development, Vol. 1, No. 5, May, 1973.

Bhandari, R.L. (1982): *Educational Development of Women in India*, Ministry of Education and Culture, New Delhi, p. 36.

Bhatia V.K. (1986): *"Some Emerging Dimensions of Women Work Force"*, Man-Power Journal Vol. XXII, No. 2, July-Sept, p. 31-44.

Bhatt, Ela (1991): *"Strategies for Women's Employment"*, The Economic Times, New Delhi, Monday, 6th May.

Buhler, G. (1964): *"The Laws of Manu:* Sacred Books of the East, Trans, Vol. 25, Motilal Banarsidass, New Delhi.

Burraq Andrea and Burra Neera (1993): *Women and Wasteland Development in India,* Sage Publications.

Census of India (1981): *Series 18, Rajasthan Primary Census Abstract*, Udaipur, p. VIII-IX.

Census of India (1981): *Series-18 Rajasthan, Part 11 B, Primary; Census Abstract*.

Census of India (1981): *Series-18, Part II-A, General Population Tables.*

Census of India 1991, *Rajasthan, Series-21, Provisional Population Total*, p. 33.

Census of India, 1961, 1971 and 1981 *Relating to A Primary Census Abstract for Rajasthan and India.*

Census of India, 1971, *Series-18, Rajasthan*, Part II B (1), Economic Tables (Tables B-1 Part A and B-II), p. 2-30.

Census of India, 1981 *Series-18, General Population Statement, No. 8 Sex Ratio, 1901-1981*, p. XXDIII.

Census of India, 1981, Series 1, India and Rajasthan Part 11. Chatterjee, Ruchira (1984): *"Marginalisation and the Induction of Women in Wage Labour. The Case of Indian Agriculture"*, World Employment Programme, ILO, Geneva.

Census of India, 1981, *Series 18, Rajasthan Part 11-B*, p. 6.

Census of India, 1981, *Series-1, India Part II-B(1)* XXIII.

Census of India, 1981, *Series-18, Rajasthan, Part II a and B, Vol. 1(1) General Economic Tables,* pp. 202-339.

Chakravarty S. (1975): *"Farm Women Labour "Waste and Exploitation"*, Social Change, Vol. 5, No. 1-2, pp. 9-16.

Chattopadhya, Kamaladevi, (1975): *The Women's Movement Then and Now, in Indian Women,* (ed) Devaki Jain Publication Division Ministry of Information and Broadcasting Govt. of India.

Chaudhary, T.P.S. and Sharma, B.M. (1961): *"Female Labour of Farm Family in Agriculture"* Agricultural Situation in India, Vol 16, No. 5.

Chauhan Poonam S.: *Lengthening Shadow C(1) Status of Women in India,* Monak Publications (P) Ltd., New Delhi, 1996.

Chitnis, Suman (1983): *"Women and Development Not by Constitutional Guarantees or Legal Provisions Alone,"* The Indian Journal of Social Work, XLIII, No. 4, January.

Chopra, Kusum (1978-79): *Role of Female Participations in the Developed and Relatively Backward Regions of India,* Centre for the Study of Regional Development, Jawahar Lal Nehru University, New Delhi.

Committee on Status of Women in India, Ministry of Social Welfare, Govt. of India, New Delhi, 1974.

Cormack, Margaret (1961): *The Hindu Women,* Asia Publishing House, Bombay.

D., Mello, Flavia (1984): *"Domestic Violence"* Women's Centre Publication, Bombay.

Dang, A.K.: *Bank Credit in India.*

Das Lal, D.K.: *Sex Discrimination Against Female Workers in Unorganised Sector.*

Das, Veena, (1976): *Indian Women, Work, Power and Status in Indian Women,* (Ed.) B.R. Nanda, Vikas Publishing House.

Davic, C: *Rural Credit in India.*

Desai Neera (1974): *Women in Modern India,* Vora and Company, Bombay.

Desai Vasant (1979): *Indian Banking: Nature and Problems,* Himalaya Publishing House, Bombay.

Desai, A.R. (1985): *"Women's Movement in India,: An Assessment"*, Economic and Political Weekly, June 8, pp. 992-93.

Desai, Neera, Maithreyi, Krishnaraj (1987): *"Women and Society in India"*, Ajanta Publication, New Delhi, New Delhi, 1987, p. 84, 121-123.

Desai, S.S.M: *Rural Banking in India,* Himalaya Publishing House, Bombay.

Deshpande Sudha (1992): *Structural Adjustment and Feminization Vol. 35 (4) Feminisation Vol. 35 (4)* B.R. Publishing Corporation.

Devaki Jain and Malini Chand (1980): *"Importance of Age and Sex Specific Data Collection in Household Surveys,* EXCAP Bangkok, Sept. (Minimeo).

Devaki, Jain and Nirmal Banerjee (ed): *Women and Poverty—the Tyranny of the Household,* Vikas, New Delhi, 1985.

Devancy, Barlarapee (1977): *"The Labour Supply of Married Women: An Analysis of the Allocation of Time to Market and Non-Market Activities,"* D.A., May 1978. Vol 38, No. 11, pp. 6828 A.

Devasia Leelamma, Devaisa V.V: (1994): *"Empowering Women for Sustainable Development"*.

Devendra Kiran (1990): *"Status and Position of Women in India"* Vikas Pub. Pvt. Ltd.

Dholaka, Ravindra, H. (1985): *"On Estimating Women's Contributions to National Product"*, Manpower-Journal, Vol. XXI, No. 3, Oct.-Dec.

District Census Hand Book Udaipur and Dungarpur, Series-18, Rajasthan, Village and Town Directory, Primary Census, Abstract, Parts XIII A B, 1981.

Dixan, Ruth B. (1982): *"Mobilizing Women for Rural Employment in South Asia: Issues of Caste, Class and Patronage"*, Economic Development and Cultural Change, Vol. 30, No. 2, Chicago, pp. 373-390.

Dube Leena (1997): *Women and Kingship,* Sage Publications.

Dube, Leela (1980): *"Review of Studies of Women in South East Asia"*, UNESCO, Bangkok.

Everett, Jana, (1979): *Knowledge and Social Change in India,* New York: St. Martins Press, 1979.

F.A.O.: *Report of the Work Shop on Integration of Women in Agricultural and Rural Development,* held at NIRD, Hyderabad, India, Nov. 17-22, 1980.

Fairchild, Johnson E.: *Women, Society and Sex,* New York: Sheridan House, 1952.

FAO (1975): *"The Role of Women in Development"* (E/CONF 66/ BP/11), United Nations. N.Y., Paper Conference of the International Women's Year, Mexico City, 19 June-2 July.

Ferber A.A. and B.G. Birnbaun and C.A. Green (1983): *House Work Vs. Market-Work: Some Evidence. How the Decision is made",* Review of Income and Wealth, Series 31, pp. 147-159.

Ferber A.A. and B.G. Birnbaun (1980): *House Work Priceless or Valueless?":* Review of Income and Wealth:, Series 28, No. 4, December, pp. 387-400.

Gadgil, D.R. (1965): *"Women in the Working Force in India,* Asia Publishing House, Delhi.

Gandhi, M.K. (10 April, 1938): *To the G-1 Women of India,* Young India.

Gangrade K.N. and Gattia J. (ed.): *"Women and Child Workers in the Unorganised Sector",* Concept Publishing Company, New Delhi, 1983.

Gannicott, Kenneth (1986): *"Women, Wages and Discrimination: Some Evidence* from Taiwan", Economic Development and Cultural Change, Vol. 34, No. 4, July, pp. 721-730.

George Tobias (1971): *Human Resources in India,* Meenakshi Prakshan.

Gold Schmidt–Clement, Luisella (1982): *"Udaipur Work in the Household; A Review of Economic Evaluation Methods",* Women, Work and Development Series No. 1, ILO, Geneva.

Ghadially, Rehana (1988): *Women in Indian Society, South; Aisa.*

Ghosh, D.N.: *Banking Policy in India—An Evaluation,* Allied Publishers, New Delhi.

Government of India: *Report of the Commissioner for Scheduled Castes and Scheduled Tribes, (XVIIth Report), Part-1,* 1979-81, New Delhi.

Government of Rajasthan: *Scheduled Tribes of Rajasthan:* A statistical Analysis (1979-80), M.L.V. Tribal Research and Training Institute. T.A.D. Dept. Rajasthan, Udaipur.

Govt. of Rajasthan: *Tribal Women and Development: Agenda-Paper,* Written for the National Conference on Tribal Women and Development, (12th-30th July 1988), Udaipur.

Gulati, L. (1975): *Female Work Participation A Study of Inter State Differences",* Economic and Political Weekly, Vol. X, Jan-11.

Gulati, L. (1979): *"Female Labour in Unorganised Sector,"* Economic and Political weekly, Vol. XIV Ap. 21, 1979, p. 17.

Gulati, L. (1984): *Profiles in Female Poverty—a Study of Five Poor Working Women in Kerala,* Hindustan Publishing Corporation, New Delhi.

Gupta, Amit K.: (1986): *"Women and Society"* Print India Publishers.

Gupta, Padmini S.: *The Study of Women of India,* New Delhi: India Book House, 1974.

Hate, C.A (1969): *"Changing Status of Women in Post Independence India"* Allied Publications Pvt. Ltd. Bombay.

Hirway; I. (1991): *Counting Gain,* The Economic Times; Monday, March 18.

Hirway; Indra (1979): *Female Employment in Rural Gujarat: Some Issues",* The Indian Journal of Labour Economics, Vol. XXII, No. 3, Oct.

Hukku, V.N.: *Bank Deposit in India.* Jodhpur University Co-operative Ltd., Jodhpur.

Indian Council of Social Science Research, (ICSSR): *"Status of Women in India".* A Synopsis of the Report of the National Committee, 1971-74.

Indian Institute of Bankers (1978): "*Commercial Banking*, Vora & Co. Bombay.

Isely Barbara, J. (1992): "*Women's Roles: Perceptions and Practice in A South Indian Village*, Journal of Rural Development, Vol. 11, No. 5, pp. 521-536.

Jacobson, J. and Wadley, Susan (1977): "*Women in India: "Two Perspectives*, South Asia Books, Columbia.

Jain Devaki (1980): *Women's Quest for Power*, Vikas Publications, New Delhi.

Jain Shashi (1988): *Status and Role Perception of Middle Class Women*, Puja Publishers.

Jain Suman (1991): *National Commission For Women Economic Implications"*, Yojana, April 15, p- 24.

Jatey Surinder (1981): *Impact of Planned Social Change and Modernization of Rural Woman*—A Pilot study in Western U.P., ICSSR Research Abstract, 10 (1-2).

Jayaswal, Suvira (1981): "*Position of Women in Early India a Histographical, Reappraisal Paper"*, Presented at the First Conference of Women's Studies, pp. 2-3.

Jethani Urmila (1994): *'Single Woman'* Rawat Publications.

Jha, K.K. (1979): "*Rethinking in Marriage Institution*, Chintamani Prakashan, Patna.

Joshi, Rama, (1973): "*Status of Women: Agricultural Workers"*, ICSSR (Unpublished Mimeo).

K. Saradamoni and Joan Mencher (1982): *Muddy Face, Dirty Hands—Rice Production and Female Agricultural Labour"*, Economic and Political Weekly, Review of Agriculture, Vol. 17, No. 52, Dec. 25.

K. Schidkrant (1982): "*Dependence and Autonomy: The Economic Activities of Scheduled Hansa Women in Kano Nigeria*. In Bay, E.G. (ED.), *Women and Work in Africa*, pp. 55-82, Colorado: Boulder West View Press.

Kakkar, Sudhir (1980): *The Inner World*, Oxford University Press.

Kala, Rani: Role Conflict in Working Women, Chetna Publishers, New Delhi, 1979.

Kapoor Usha (1995): *Women and Welfare: A Study of voluntary;* Agencies Indus.

Kapur Promilla (1974): *The Changing Status of the Working Women in India.* Vikas Publishing House Pvt. Ltd.

Karakal, Gopal (1977): *Prospective in Indian Banking,* Popular Prakashan, Bombay.

Kaur S. (1987): *Women in Rural Development,* Mittal Publications, Delhi.

Kaur Satnam R.K. Punia (1988): *"Work Participation of Women in Rural Households: An Empirical Study"* Guru Nanak Journal of Sociology, Vol. 9, No. 2, Oct. 1988, pp. 51-75.

Kaur, Satnam (1987): *Women in Rural Development,* Mittal Publications, Delhi.

Kenny Mary (1978): *Woman X Two, How to Cope with a Double Life,* Sidgwick and Jackson Ltd., London.

Khan Qamaruddin: *Status of Women in Islam,* Sterling Publishers Pvt. Ltd. 1990.

Khan, M.A. and Aysha Noor (1982): *"Status of Rural Women in India",* Uppal Pub. House.

Khandker, Shahidur, R. (1988): *"Determinants of Women's Time Allocation in Rural Bangladesh",* Economic Development and Cultural Change, Vol. 37, No. 1, Oct. pp. 111-126.

Khanna, Girija and Varghese, M.A. (1978): *"Indian Women Today",* Vikas Publishing House Pvt. Ltd., Delhi.

Kidwai, Shaikh M.H. (1976): *Women Under Different Social and Religious Laws,* Seema Publications.

King V. (1975): *Women and Religion: The Status and Image of Women in Major Religious Traditions,"* In Women in Contemporary India, Manohar, New Delhi.

Krishna Murty, J. (1984): *"Changes in Indian Work Force",* Economic and Political Weekly, Vol. XIX, No. 50, Dec. 15, pp. 2121-2125.

Krishna Kumari, N.S. (1987): *Status of Single Women in India (A Study of Spinsters, Widows and Divorcees):* Joint Women's Programme Publication, New Delhi, Uppal Publishing House.

Kumar and Singh (1983): *"Role of Women in Rural Economy"*, Kurukshetra Jan.

Kumar Shashi (1995): *"Rural Women"* Har-Anand Publishers.

Kumari, Jyotsna (1988): *"Female Rural Working Force Needs a Better Deal"*, Yojana, May 1-15, p 18-19.

Lal, A.K.: *Status of Women in Urban Setting Analysis of Role Differentiation in the Family.*

Lebra Joyce, Paulson Joy, Everett Jane, (1984): *"Women and Work in India"* Promilla and Co. New Delhi.

Leonard Nadler 1980, *Corporate Human Resources Development.*

Llewellyn, J.E.: *"The Legacy of Women's Uplift in India"* Sage Publications.

M.E. Khan, R. Anker, S.K. Ghosh D. and B.C. Patel (1992): *"Methodological Issues in Collecting Time Use Data for Female Labour Force"*, Indian Journal of Labour Economics, Vol. 35, No. 1.

Mahadevan, K. (1989): *"Women and Population Dynamics Perspectives from Asian Countries,* Sage Publications.

Mahajan V.S. (1989): *"Women's Contribution to India's Economic and Social Development"*. Deep and Deep Publication.

Mahapatra P.C. and Pattanik (1988): *"How Can We Improve Socio-economic Condition of Women,* "Yojana, Vol. 32, No. 9, May 16-31.

Malathy, R. (1988): *"The Value of Household Services of Women in India"*, Artha-Vijnana, Vol. 30, No. 1, March.

Malathy; R (1989): *"The Demand for Non Market Time: The Case of Married Women in An Urban Setting"*, Anvesak, June-Dec. Vol. 19, No. I, II, pp. 135-149.

Malathy; R. (1990): *"The Demand for Non-Market Time: The Case of Married Women in Urban Setting"* Indian Journal of Labour. Economic Vol. 33, No. 2.

Manohar, K.M. (ed) (1983): *Socio-Economic Status of Indian Women,"* Seema Publications, New Delhi.

Mathur, Deepa (1992): *Women Family and Work,* Rawat Publication, Jaipur.

Mathur, R.S. (1978): *"Female Work Participation Rate,"* Indian Journal of Labour Economics, Vol. XX, No. 4, January.

Mazumdar, Vina (1975): *"Status of Women in India"*, Demography India, Vol. IV, No. 2.

Mazumdar, Vina and Kumud Sharma (1979): *Women's Studies: Need Perception and the Change"*, Economic and Political Weekly, Vol. 14, Jan. 30.

Mehta B.C. (1991): *"Fertility Decisions in Small Communities* (Project Report) Mimeo Unpublished, p. 4. Sukhadia University, Udaipur.

Mehta Basant (1989): *The Organisation and Working of Lead Bank Scheme in India,* Vohra Publishers and Distributors, Allahabad.

Mehta Basant (1992): *"Lead Bank Scheme–A New Horizon for Development"* Discovery Publishing House, New Delhi.

Mehta Basant (1994): *Dimensions of Socio-Economic Development (ED.)* Discovery Publishing House, New Delhi.

Mehta Basant (1994): *Role of Commercial Bank in Removal of Poverty and Unemployment,* Shiva Publishers and Distributors, Udaipur.

Mehta Basant (1997): *"Perspective of Tribal Economy"*. Intellectual Book Corner Pvt. Ltd., New Delhi.

Mehta Basant (1997): *"Perspective of Tribal Economy"*. Intellectual Book Corner Pvt. Ltd. New Delhi.

Mehta N.C. and V.A. Pal: *Rural Banking* National Institute of Bank.

Mehta, Sushila (1982): *"Revolution and the Status of Women in India"*, Metropolitan Book Company (P) Ltd., New Delhi.

Meis, Maria: *"Indian Women and Patriarchy"*, Concept Publishing Company, New Delhi, 1980, p. 130.

Mencher, John P. Saradamon. K. Panicker, Janaki (1979): *"Women in Rice Cultivation: Some Research Tools"* in Sondra Zeidenstein (ed.) *Learning About Rural Women,* Special Issue of Studies in Family Planning. The Population Council, New York, Vol. 10, Nos. 11/12, pp. 408-412.

Miller, Barbara D. (1982): *"Female Labour Participation and Female Seclusion in Rural India: A Regional view"*, Economic Development and Cultural Change, Vol. 30, No. 4, July, pp. 777-792.

Mincer, J. (1962): *Labour Force Participation of Married Women* in H.G. Leais (ed.), Aspects of Labour Economics, Princeton University Press, Princeton, New Jersey, pp. 63-97.

Mincer, Jacole and Soloman, Polacher (1974): *Family Investment in Human Capital: Earnings of Women"*, Journal of Political Economy, 82-212.

Mishra T.K. (1988): *"Make Them Equal Partners in Development"*, Yojana, Vol. 32, No. 9, May 16-31.

Mitra Ashok, Srimany Adhir K. and Pathak Lalit P. (1979): *"The Status of Women", "Household and Non-household Economic Activity"*, Allied Publications Pvt. Ltd. ICSSR, Delhi.

Mitra, Ashok (1979): *"The Status of Women", Literacy and Employment,* Allied Publications Pvt. Ltd., ICSSR, Delhi.

Mitra, Ashok, P. Lalit and M. Shekhar (1920): *"The Status of Women: Shifts in Occupational Participation 1961-1971"*, An ICSSR Study.

Mudler, Ruth Dixan (1985): *"Women's Work in Third World Agriculture"*, International Labour Office, Geneva.

Mukherji, Anindita and Verma Neelam (1987): *"Socio Economic Backwardness in Women"* Ashish Publication House.

Mukherji, M. (1987): *"Contribution to and Use of Social Product by Women"*, in Jain D. and Banerjee M. (ed.). *Women in Poverty: Tyranny of the Household Investigative Essays on Women's Work,* New Delhi, India, Shakti Books _ A Division of Vikas Publishing House Pvt. Ltd.

Mukherji, Vatsala (1989): *"Status of Women: Economic Policy for LDC's"* Economic Times, Jan. 18, Saturday, p. 7.

Mutalik, Desai V.R.: *Banking Development in India,* Manakatalas.

N.J. Usha Rao (1983): *"Women in Developing Society"*, Ashish Publishing House, New Delhi.

Nagar Savita (1998): *Working Women in India, Society;* Classic Publications, Jaipur.

Naidu, L.L. (1985): *Bank Finance and Rural Development*, Chugh Publications, Allahabad.

Nair, G. Ravomdram (1988): *"Women Workers: The Lingering Paradoxes"*, Social Welfare, Vol. XXXV, No. 2, May.

Nair, Kamal (1970): *"Female Work Participation and Economic Development, A Regional Analysis"*, Economic and Political Weekly, Vol. V, No. 12, May-23.

Narang Sandhya (1994): *Dilemma of Married Women Teachers in India*, Himanshu Publications.

National Institute of Bank Management (1975): *"A Frame Work for Banking Development Programmes for a State"*.

National Institute of Bank Management (1982): *"Banking Structure and Performance"*.

Nayer, Rohini (1987): *"Female Participation Rates"*, Economic and Political Weekly Vol. XXII, No. 51, Dec. 19.

Nirmala V., Bhat, K.S. Mohsin MD. and Kamalah B. (1992): *"Work Participation of Married Women with. Living Households Case of Rural and Urban Pondicherry"*. Artha Vijnana, Sep. Vol. 34, No. 3, pp. 315-355.

Oakley. Ann (1974). *"Housewife"*, Allenhane London.

Padhy, R.C. (1980): *Commercial Banks and Rural Development*, Publication Services, New Delhi.

Panandikar, S.G. and Mithani, D.M. (1975). Purushothaman, Sangeeta (1988): *"The Empowerment of Women in India"*, Indian Review of Books.

Papanek Hanna: *"Men, Women and Work: Reflections on the Two-person Career;* American Journal of Sociology, Vol. 78, No. 4.

Parikh Indira J. and Garg K. Pulin (1989): *"Indian Women"* Sage Publications.

Pawar M. (1989): *"The State of Women in Rajasthan: A Situational Review:* Prashasnika, Vol. 18, No. 1-4, Jan-Dec., pp. 69-76.

Peggy Sandy (1973): *"Towards a Theory of the Status of Women"*, American Anthropologist, Vol. 75, No. 5, p. 1695.

Phadnis, Urmila and Malani Indira (ED.): *"Women of the World"*, Vikas Publishing House Pvt. Ltd., New Delhi, p. 13-14.

Puri, Shashi (1974): *Role of Farm Women in Animal Husbandry Programme*, Kurukshetra, Vol. 22, No. 33.

Ram Krishan Sharma, K. (1986): *Financial Institutions and Regional Development in India*, Chug Publications, Allahabad.

Ramanamma A., Bambawale V. (1987): *"Women in Indian Industry"*. Mittal Publications, Delhi.

Ramkrishna, V. (1983): *"Social Reform in Andhra"* Vikas Publishing House Pvt. Ltd., New Delhi.

Ramu, G.N. (1989): *Women, Work and Marriage in Urban India*, Sage Publications.

Rangarajan, C. (1982): *Innovation in Banking on Foird*, IBH Publishing Co., New Delhi.

Rani, Kala (1976) *Role Conflict in Working Women*, New Delhi: Chetan Publications.

Ranjan Kumud. *Women and Modern Occupation in India.*

Rao Ramchandra B. (1982): *Current Trends in India Banking*, Deep and Deep Publications, New Delhi.

Rao, S.V. Ramani, Ghosh Sharmila, Joshi Geeta and Acharya Sudha (1994): *"Women at Work in India*, Vol. 2 Sage Publications.

Reddy, D.N. (1979): *"Female Work Participation – A Study of Inter State Differences – A Comment*, Economic and Political Weekly, 10 (23), June–7.

Reddy, D.N. (1979): *"Female Work Participation in India: Facts, Problems and Politics"*, Indian Journal of Industrial Relations; Vol. 15, No. 2, Oct. p. 198.

Reddy, D. N. (1979): Female Work Participation in India", Indian Journal of Industrial Relations, Vol. 15, No. 2, p. 198.

Registrar General and Census Commissioner India, *Census of India, 1981*, India—A Hand Book of Population Statistics, 1988.

Rehman, M.M. and Biswal Kamala Kanta (1993): *Education Work and Women*, Common Wealth Publications.

Report of the Committee of Experts on Unemployment, New Delhi, 1981.

Rosen, H.S. (1974): *"The Monetary Value of a House Wife: A Replacement Cost Approach"*, American Journal of Economics and Sociology Vol. 33, pp. 65-73.

Roy, Anubha (1988): *"Women Agricultural Labour in Bihar: A District-wise Analysis of Census Data*, Indian Journal of Labour Economics, Vol. 31, No. 4.

Sakia, P.D. Gogai, K. and Lekhra Anjali (1986): *"Indian Rural Women"* Mittal Publications, Delhi.

Sandhu, H.K. and Dhesi, T.K. (1974): *"The Economic Contribution of Women to Agricultural Development"*, PAV Journal of Research, Vol. 14, No. 1, pp. 96-102.

Satnam Kaur and R.K. Punia: *"Work Participation of Women in Rural Household"*, An Empirical Study, Guru Nanak Journal of Sociology, Vol. 9, No. 2, Oct.

Sen Gupta, P. (1974). *The Story of Women of India*, Indian Book Co. New Delhi.

Sen, G and C. Sen (1985): *"Women's Domestic Work and Economic Activity Results from National Sample Survey"*, Economic and Political Weekly, Vol. XX, No. 17.

Sethi Nishi and Malaviya Achla (1996): *Rural Women Development Through Medin*, Classical Publishing Co.

Sharma Alakh, N., and Singh S. (1993): *"Women and Work Changing Scenario in India"*, Indian Society of Labour Economics, Patna. B.R. Publishing Corporation.

Sharma B.M. (1994): *Women and Education*, Commonwealth Publishers, New Delhi.

Sharma R.K. (1981): *Nationalism, Social Reform and Indian Women*, Janaki Prakashan.

Sharma Shakti (1987): *"Report of the National Commission on Self Employed Women and Women in Informational Sector*, Self Employed Women Association, Ahmedabad.

Sharma, B.P. (1974): *The Role of Commercial Banks In India's Developing Economic*, S. Chand and Co. Delhi.

Sharma, R.N. and Sengupta C. (1984): *Women Employment at SEEPZ Bombay*, Unit for Urban Studies Tata Institute for Social Science, Bombay.

Shashi S.S. (1978): *The Tribal Women in India*, Sandeep Prakashan, Delhi, 1978 Publication.

Shobha (1987): *"Rural Women Participation Rates in Rural India"*, Economic and Political Weekly Vol. XXII, No. 51, Dec. 19, p. 2207-2215.

Shrinivas, M.N. (1978): *The Changing Position of Indian Women*, Oxford University Press, Bombay.

Shrivastava, V. (1972) *"Employment of Educated Married Women, Its Causes and Consequences with Reference to Chandigarh"*, Ph.D. Thesis in Sociology, Chandigarh, Punjab University.

Shrivastava, Vinita (1978): *"Employment of Educated Married Women", India (It's Causes and Consequences)*; National Publishing House, New Delhi.

Siddiqui, Mujibul Hasan (1993): *"Women Education"*, Ashish Publication House.

Singal, S. and Shrinivasan, K. (1991): *"Rural Women's Participation in Paid Work, Their Satisfaction and Felt Needs"*, Khadi Gramodyog, Vol. XXXVII, No. 9, June pp. 344-351.

Singh, M. (1989): *"Women and Development Process in India"*, Khadi Gramodyog, Vol. XXXV, No. 4, pp. 195-205.

Singh, M.K. (1987): *"Participation of Women in Economic Development Trends and Issues"*, Vol. 23, No. 1, pp. 93-95, Industrial Journal of Industrial Relations.

Singh, T.R. (1968): *Participation of Rural Women in Decision Making Process Related to the Farm Business in NES Block Jabalpur*, Unpublished M.Sc. Thesis, JNKVV, Jabalpur.

Singh; J.P., Vyas, N.N. and Mann R.S (1985): *"Tribal Women and Development"*, Rawat Publications Through L.V. Tribal Research and Training Institute, Udaipur.

Singha, L.R.: *Regional Planning and Rural Development*.

Sinha J.N. (1981): *"Economic Census Data a Note"*, Economics and Political Weekly, Vol. 17, Feb 6, 1985.

Sinha S.D. (1980): *Impact of Technological Development in Agriculture on Women in Rural Areas, a Two Village Profile*, ICSSR, New Delhi.

Sinha, Pushpa (1987) *Role Conflict Among the Working Women*: Janki Prakashan, New Delhi.

Sinopoulos, P.A. (1990): *"Working Women in Greece: Their Social Penalty and How it can be Quantified"*. The Journal of Sociological Studies, Vol. 9 Jan, p. 1-13.

Smith, Stanley K. (1981): *"Determinants of Female Labour Force Participation and Family Size in Mexico City"*, Economic Development and Cultural Change, Vol. 30, No. 1 October.

Souza Alfred de (1975): *"Women in Contemporary India"*, Indian Social Institute, New Delhi.

Standing, Hillary (1985): *"Women's Employment and Household: Some findings from Calcutta"*, Economic and Political Weekly, Vol. XX, No. 17, April 27.

State of the World's Women Report, 1985 Economic Times, July; 14, Sunday, pp. 5.

Stone Philip J. (1979): *"One Being Up Against the Wall Women's Time Pattern in Eleven Countries"*, *in Public Policy in Temporal Perspective (ed.)*. The Hauge, Mounten.

Subramaniam, C.V.: *Human Resource Management*, S. Chand. Co. Ltd.

Subramanyam (1982): *Modern Banking in India*, Deep and Deep Publications, New Delhi.

Subramanyam: *Trends and Progress of Banking in India.*

Sundaram, K. (1988): *Inter State Variations in Labour Force Participation Rates of Women in India*, Working Paper, ILO-ARTEP, New Delhi.

Szalai, Alexander(ed.) (1972): *The Use of Time: Daily Activities of Urban and Sub-Urban Population in Twelve Countries*, The Hague, Moriton.

Thakur, B.T.: *Organisation of Indian Banking.*

Tokhi, M.R. (1975): *Rural Banking in India* Sharma D.P. United Nations (1980), *"Sex Based Stereotypes, Sex Biases and National Data Systems*, New York, doc ST/ESA/STAT/99, New York.
Usha Rao N.J. (1985): *"Women in Developing Society"*, Ashish Publishing House, New Delhi, II Edition p. 99.

"Towards Equality"–Report of the Committee on Status of women in India, Ministry of Social Welfare Govt. of India, 1974 and 1975.

Tripathy, S.N. and Das S (1991): *"Informal Women Labour in India"*, Discovery Publishing House, New Delhi.

Varghese, N.V. (1991): *Women and Work Force; An Examination of the Female Marginalization Thesis in the Indian Context*. Indian Journal of Labour Economic, Vol. 34, No. 3, p. 62.

Vaswani, T.A. (1974): *Indian Banking System,* Lalvani Publishing House, Bombay.

Vishwanathan K.V. (1983) *Reserve Bank of India, Functions and Working,* Reserve Bank of India, Bombay.

Vyas, Anju and Singh Sunita (1993): *Women's Studies in India,* Sage Publications.

Whyte, R.O and Whyte, P. (1982): *The Women of Rural Asia,* West View Press, Colorado.

Wignaraja, Ponna (1990): *Women, Poverty and Resources,* Sage Publications.

Wong, R. and Levine, R.E. (1992): *"The Effect of Household Structure on Women's Economic Activity and Fertility Evidence from Recent Moters in Urban Mexico"*, Economic Development and Cultural Change, Vol. 41, No. 1, October, p. 89-102.

Zarina Batty; (1980): *"Economic Role and Status of Women, a Case Study of Women in the Beedi Industry in Allahabad,* World Employment Programme, Working Paper.

JOURNAL AND MAGAZINES

1. Banker
2. Capital
3. Commerce
4. Eastern Economics
5. Economic Trends
6. Journal of Banking & Finance

7. Journal of Banking Studies
8. Journal of Rural Development
9. Khadi Gramodyog
10. Kurukshetra
11. National Bank Review (Nabard)
12. Pigmy Economic Review
13. Pragyan
14. Productivity
15. Rural India
16. Southern Economists
17. The Indian Economic Journal
18. The Indian Institute of Bankers
19. Udyog Beakar Patrika
20. Urban Credit
21. Yojana

RESERVE BANK PUBLICATIONS

1. Annual Reports on Currency and Finance
2. Annual Reports of Reserve Bank of India
3. Annual Report of Trends and Progress of Banking in India
4. Reserve Bank of India, Monthly Bulletins
5. Statistical Tables relating to Banks in India, RBI.

BANK'S PUBLICATIONS

1. Annual Action Plan of Udaipur, Rajsamand and Dungarpur Districts
2. Bank of Baroda—News Letters
3. District Credit Plan of Udaipur, Rajsamand and Dungarpur Districts
4. Pigmy Economic Review

5. Proceeding of District Level Review Meeting of Udaipur Rajsamand and Dungarpur Districts

6. State Bank of India, Monthly Review

7. UCO Bank Review

8. UCO Tower

GOVERNMENT OF INDIA PUBLICATIONS

1. District Census Hand Book

PUBLICATIONS OF THE GOVERNMENT OF RAJASTHAN

1. Basic Statistics of Rajasthan Directorate of Economics and Statistics Rajasthan, Jaipur

2. Census of India

3. Statistical Abstract, Rajasthan, Directorate of Economics and Statistics Rajasthan, Jaipur

ANNUAL PUBLICATIONS

1. India

2. Times of India Annual Directory and Year Books

3. Economic Times Annual

NEWS PAPERS

1. Economic Times

2. Financial Express.

Index